SEAN McLOUGHLIN
Ireland's Forgotten Revolutionary

SEAN McLOUGHLIN

IRELAND'S FORGOTTEN REVOLUTIONARY

Charlie McGuire

MERLIN PRESS

© Charlie McGuire, 2011

Published in the UK in 2011
by The Merlin Press Ltd.
99b Wallis Road
London
E9 5LN

www.merlinpress.co.uk

Reprinted 2016

ISBN. 978-0-85036-705-8

British Library Cataloguing in Publication Data
is available from the British Library

All rights reserved. No part of this publication may be reproduced, stored in a retrieval system, or transmitted, in any form or by any means, electronic, mechanical, photocopying, recording or otherwise, without the prior permission of the publisher.

Printed in the UK by Lightning Source

Contents

Acknowledgements	7
Introduction	9
Chapter 1: The Making of a Revolutionary, 1895-1916	12
Chapter 2: Sean McLoughlin and the Easter Rising, 1916	23
Chapter 3: The Emergence of a Socialist Republican, 1917-1921	41
Chapter 4: The Triumph of Reaction, 1921-1923	76
Chapter 5: One Last Push for the Workers' Republic, 1923-1960	114
Conclusion	140
Appendix	162
Bibliography	172
Index	183

Acknowledgements

I would like to thank Gerry Kavanagh, librarian at the National Library of Ireland, for his enthusiastic assistance in the research for this book. Gerry's help over the several years that this research was conducted was invaluable and without it some of the vital details of Sean McLoughlin's life would have remained undiscovered. Others who deserve thanks are: Dr Tony Varley, my former PhD supervisor at the National University of Ireland, Galway, and Dr Brian Hanley, of Queens University Belfast, both of whom read through and commented helpfully on draft versions of this work; Jack McLoughlin and June Whitehead nee McLoughlin, both of whom were always willing to share their memories and recollections of their father; Margaret Shiel, nee McLoughlin, the daughter of Sean's brother Danny, and her son Brendan and daughter Stella, all of whom provided much valuable information on Sean's early life; sadly, Margaret died in July 2009. Raymond Challinor and Mike Milotte, both of whom kindly provided copies of tape recordings; Ross Connolly, the son of Sean's former associate Roddy, who sadly died in August 2010; and Ken Loach. I also wish to thank the staff of the following for their assistance and courtesy during my research visits: the National Library; the National Archives; the Irish Labour History Archives; the Military Archives; University College Dublin Archives; The Public Records Office, Belfast; the Manchester University Labour History Archives; the British Library of Political and Economic Science; the British National Archives, Kew; Teesside Archives; the Mitchell Library, Glasgow; the General Records Office, Edinburgh and the Russian State Social and Political Archives, Moscow. I'd like to say a personal thank you to my parents, my brother Frank and sister Louise, nieces Sarah-Marie, Eilish and Stephanie, and nephew Garry. I also wish to thank Kam, Gary and Havana for their support. Finally, I would like to show my appreciation to my partner Shani and daughter Xanthe, for all the love they have given. This book is dedicated to Shani and Xanthe.

Introduction

Sean McLoughlin was an important, if little remembered, figure during the Irish revolution, 1916-23. He began these years as a nationalist and republican activist in the Gaelic League, Fianna Eireann and the Irish Volunteers, and ended it as a leading figure within the Irish communist movement. In between, he was also Commandant-General of the army of the Irish Republic, as the events of Easter Week 1916 reached a climax, a Volunteer organiser in Tipperary and Limerick during the 1917-1919 period, a commandant of an IRA flying column during the Civil War and a mass orator of exceptional ability within the socialist movement in Britain.

McLoughlin's contribution to the Irish revolutionary struggle was both practical and theoretical. During the Rising, his leadership qualities, principally his ability to think rationally and act decisively in the most difficult of circumstances, catapulted him to the head of military command. This was at a point in the fighting when the fortunes of the revolutionaries were at their lowest ebb. Similarly, as a Volunteer recruitment officer and Civil War commandant, it was his ability to organise effectively and inspire those around him which lay behind his success in those fields. But whilst McLoughlin was a committed and talented activist with clear leadership qualities, he was also a thinker; one who was influenced by and tried to apply to Irish conditions the newest and most modern revolutionary socialist theories, which swept through Europe in the post-1917 era. Many of his speeches and writings were studded with this thinking, and as a result the prescriptions he offered for the Irish revolution were often innovative and original.

McLoughlin's significance has not yet been recognised. True, some of his activities have received attention. In the main these focus on the Easter Rising and McLoughlin's promotion to the head of military command by James Connolly.[1] These rare mentions, based on an account McLoughlin penned in 1948 are, however, largely scant and fleeting; they tell us little of McLoughlin and nothing of his politics. In truth, McLoughlin has long been a figure ignored by most Irish historians. Contemporary works on the Easter Rising have done little to redress this situation. Barton and Foy's account of 1916, a book which was praised by a prominent Irish historian as 'the best overview' of that event, omitted McLoughlin's name altogether.[2] Charles Townshend's more recent work – a significant book, and one that was based on exhaustive archival research – was little better in this respect. In this account, McLoughlin makes only a solitary appearance, in connection with his initial posting to the Mendicity Institute, before promptly disappearing from sight.[3] McLoughlin's socialist activities have received even less coverage. Despite being a leading figure in various Irish and British socialist organisations, McLoughlin's socialist involvements have been touched upon only by Mike Milotte, Raymond Challinor and Emmet O'Connor in their studies of these movements.[4]

So obscure has Sean McLoughlin become, that at the outset of this research none of the few Irish historians who had heard of him could state with any degree of confidence the year, or even century, in which he was born or the decade in which he died. The fact that the death of the Commandant General of Easter Week could pass by unnoticed in Ireland, not only by Irish historians but also by those in control of the Irish state, as well as the media, highlights just how far he has been consigned to oblivion. It also says much about the nature of the state that emerged in Ireland in the decades following 1922; a state that upheld and promoted class interests very much at odds with the socialism of McLoughlin; a state, perhaps, that needed to ensure that its history reflected these interests.

To date, there has been no attempt to analyse McLoughlin's importance to, or even chronicle his involvement in, the events which made the Irish Revolution. The purpose of this book, therefore, is to examine Sean McLoughlin's life, evaluate his contribution to the Irish Revolution and, by doing so, not only begin to rescue from obscurity one of modern Irish history's significant figures, but also throw new light on the tumultuous events of 1916-23 that did so much to shape the character of modern Ireland.

Notes

1   See for example, Max Caulfield, *The Easter Rebellion*, (Dublin: 1963), Peter de Rosa, *Rebels*, (London: 1991), Thomas Coffey, *Agony at Easter*, (London : 1970), Conor Kostick/ Lorcan Collins, *The Easter Rising*, (Dublin: 2000)
2   Barton/Foy *The Easter Rising* (Stroud: 1999, 2004). The historian was Roy Foster (on front cover of 2004 edition).
3   Charles Townshend, *The Easter Rebellion*, (London: 2005) p. 171-2.
4   Mike Milotte, *Communism in Modern Ireland: The Pursuit of the*

Workers Republic Since 1916 (Dublin: 1984), Raymond Challinor, *The Origins of British Bolshevism* (London: 1977), Emmet O'Connor, *Reds and the Green, Ireland, Russia and the Communist International 1919-43* (Dublin: 2004). Of the three, O'Connor offers most detail on McLoughlin's activities during the years 1916-24.

1

The Making of a Revolutionary, 1895-1916

Introduction

Sean McLoughlin was born on 2 June 1895, the son of 35-year-old Dublin coal labourer Patrick McLoughlin and his wife Christina, nee Shea.[1] Recalled as a committed labour and 'union man',[2] Patrick McLoughlin had been a founder member of the Irish Transport and General Workers' Union (ITGWU), and had both worked and organised workers on the railways as well as the docks. He and Christina – who was remembered by her family as an 'extreme nationalist'[3] – had been married twelve years, but Sean was only the second of what would eventually be six children. The others were Daniel, Sean's senior by two years, and Patrick, Mary, Christina and Christopher, his juniors by two, five, eight and ten years respectively.[4] The family resided in North King Street, a busy mixture of tenement flats and small shops on the north side of the Liffey. It was here, first at number 5, later number 4, that McLoughlin spent the first twenty years of his life.

Not much is known about McLoughlin's formative years. He attended schools at North Brunswick Street,[5] and North Richmond Street,[6] before leaving in his early teens. McLoughlin appears to have been close to both his father – who was nicknamed Ruggie, (apparently as a result of his rugged appearance) and was remembered as a big-hearted person – and his older brother Danny. Both boys took on various odd jobs together including, on occasion, herding cattle to the docks, and it would seem that it was Danny who later got Sean his job in O'Dea's mattress making factory. Sean was also keen in learning foreign languages. With the money he earned from his odd jobs, he would often go to the docks and pay sailors to teach him some of the languages they had learned. This would be an interest he would maintain for many years afterwards. Indeed, one of McLoughlin's most treasured possessions was a French language book, originally owned and given to him by Sean Heuston. He kept it for the rest of his life. Danny, on the other hand, as a budding musician who had already mastered the clarinet, would use any spare money he had for music lessons.

The first signs of McLoughlin's ability as a writer were also evident during these early years. Danny, a talented athlete, played for a local football team. It is not clear if Sean was part of the team, but he did produce a team newsletter complete with match 'reports' which he would read out and which were said to be hilarious.[7] Penmanship was a skill that McLoughlin would retain and display throughout his years of political activity, when the subject matter was a great deal more serious than football.

Early Political Involvements

During McLoughlin's early life, there was a surge in the development of Irish nationalist politics. This led to the strengthening of bodies like the Gaelic League and Irish Republican Brotherhood (IRB), and the creation of new organisations such as Fianna Eireann, the Republican scout organisation founded by Constance Markievicz in 1909, and Sinn Fein, launched by dual-monarchist Arthur Griffith in 1905.

McLoughlin soon became involved in this movement. When he was around fifteen years of age, he joined the Colmcille branch of the Gaelic League, which met at 5 Blackhall Street.[8] The treasurer of this branch was Michael Staines,[9] who would later be both a TD in the revolutionary Dail, and the first commissioner of An Garda Siochana. Staines's brother, Liam, who died as a result of wounds sustained during the Rising, was another activist in this branch.

In the summer of 1913, McLoughlin joined Na Fianna Eireann. He was enrolled by Patrick Ryan and was a member of An Cead Sluagh, which drilled in Camden St.[10] Other members of this sluagh included Eamon Martin, who was a founding member of the Fianna.[11] Garry and Patrick Holohan were also involved, as were the Mellows brothers Liam, Frederick and Barney. Of those three, however, only Barney was active in the sluagh during the time McLoughlin was a member. Liam was touring the country as a national organiser, whilst Frederick was already suffering from the TB which would claim his life in August the following year.[12] Another prominent figure associated with this sluagh was Con Colbert, who gave drilling instructions,[13] the weapons for which were bought by the members, who paid 1/- per week for a Martin rifle, and 2/6 per week for the higher quality Lee Enfield.[14]

The Lockout

1913 also saw McLoughlin influenced in a socialist direction by the events of the Dublin Lockout. This attempt by the Dublin employers to break the young transport union and all that it stood for, turned into a six-month-long class war, the most bitterly fought dispute in Irish labour history. Led by Jim Larkin and James Connolly, who were themselves jailed during the

Lockout, the workers faced considerable repression and violence from the police, with two of their members, James Byrne and James Nolan, clubbed to death in the first week. The eventual result of the strike left the ITGWU in a badly weakened condition, but still alive; the instigator of the dispute, William Martin Murphy, owner of the *Irish Independent*, President of the Dublin Chamber of Commerce, boss of the Dublin United Tramways Company, and veritable 'Paladin of the Dublin employers',[15] had failed in his prime objective.

The Dublin Lockout was an epic industrial, social and political event. With Larkin leaving for the USA shortly afterwards, it saw Marxist Connolly emerge as the leading figure within the Irish labour movement and head of both the ITGWU and the new Irish Citizen Army (ICA). Organised initially as a strike defence force, the ICA under Connolly would soon be transformed into an armed detachment of the Irish working class, ready for offensive action. The Lockout also had a radicalising effect on the most advanced sections of Irish nationalism. The IRB journal *Irish Freedom* devoted much of its column space to attacks on the Dublin bosses.[16] Veteran Fenian Tom Clarke wrote in outrage about the 'downright inhuman savagery' of the Dublin police, whilst Padraig Pearse condemned the horrendous poverty endured by the workers, contrasting it sharply with the loafing of the elite.[17] In fact, for one historian Pearse was so affected by the events of 1913 and the levels of working-class misery that it revealed, that he was now inclined politically towards a 'cautious socialism'.[18] Although perhaps not visible at the time, these developments within both the working class and advanced nationalists would prove to be significant in the period ahead.

This radicalising process also reached into the Fianna. Most Dublin Fianna boys were from working-lass backgrounds and many were caught up in the events of the Lockout. Garry Holohan, for example, recalled the spread of the dispute to the docks, where he had been working as an electrician, and how support and solidarity action was offered to the strikers.[19] With Dublin Castle giving 'full support to the employers' and the DMP and RIC patrolling the quays, Holohan felt that the strike 'took on a national outlook' and considered the stance of the workers to be 'heroic'.[20]

As an activist within the ITGWU, McLoughlin's father was heavily involved in the Lockout. This in itself may well be the source of McLoughlin's later socialist involvements and opens the possibility that he held such views from a young age. In relation to the Lockout, McLoughlin later said that it was the 'ruthless war made upon the working class of Dublin which sowed the seed of revolt harvested three years later'.[21] This suggests that it was an event that had a considerable impact on him. McLoughlin also had contact with Jim Larkin during this period. Aware that the family were struggling and had little to eat, like many other families during the Lockout, Larkin visited the McLoughlin household at Christmas and brought with him some herrings. Larkin's kind act meant that Christmas 1913 was remembered by the McLoughlin family as the 'Christmas of the herrings'.[22] It was an act that may have stimulated in McLoughlin an interest in Larkinism and, again, leaves open the possibility that he was already a socialist at this early stage of his life. Certainly, this was the view of his close colleague in both the Republican and communist movements, Paddy Stephenson, who later recalled that McLoughlin had clearly 'identified' with Larkin during the events of 1913.[23]

There were other significant developments during this period. The Ulster industrialists, apparently fearful that their economic interests would perish in an Ireland detached from the empire by a wall of tariffs,[24] opposed government legislation to grant Irish home rule and threatened force to prevent it from becoming operable. Large parades of the newly formed Ulster Volunteer Force were held, and key sections of the British ruling class declared a willingness to go to any lengths in their support.[25] The grim prospect of partition was raised soon after. This provoked an inevitable response from nationalist Ireland, and in November 1913 a new nationalist organisation, the Volunteers, was founded. McLoughlin became involved in the new body immediately upon its creation, and helped form a company which met initially at Father Matthew Hall, Church St. Eventually moving to North Brunswick St, behind McLoughlin's old school, this was D Company of the First Dublin Battalion, and was captained by JJ Keane, at that time also a leading GAA activist.[26]

War and revolution

In August 1914, the First World War broke out. This changed completely the conditions in which all nationalist bodies were operating and provoked convulsions within their ranks. On the one hand opportunities for revolution beckoned, whilst on the other the internal weaknesses and divisions within these organisations, not always evident, became exposed and were severely exacerbated; the more revolutionary sections of the middle class would soon be in conflict with the socially conservative elements that dominated the leadership of nationalist Ireland. From two separate directions an impetus towards revolt began; The IRB, who, with German aid, wished to turn England's difficulty into Ireland's opportunity, and James Connolly, who saw in an Irish working-class revolt the torch that could set alight 'a European conflagration that will not burn out until the last throne and the last capitalist bond and debenture will be shrivelled on the funeral pyre of the last war lord'. [27]

The impact of war was soon felt in the Volunteers. In September 1914, the organisation split following leader John Redmond's Woodenbridge speech 'at which he told the young men of the Volunteers that their duty lay in France fighting for England'.[28] The overwhelming majority of the 180,000 strong organisation swayed by Redmond's argument that this would actually help Ireland gain post-war self-government, stayed loyal to him, with many joining the British army as a result. But a small minority, perhaps 12,000 at most, regarded Redmond's stance as that of treachery and repudiated his leadership, forming afterwards the Irish Volunteers (IV).

The war was to have a significant impact on McLoughlin, both personally and politically. His older brother, Danny, had decided to join the British army, hoping that involvement and training in the army music bands might pave the way for a future career in that field. The outbreak of war, however, saw him soon transferred to the frontline in Flanders. Although disagreeing vehemently with the decision that his brother had made, Sean did not burn his bridges with him, and even benefited from the firearms training that Danny provided him during his time on leave. Politically, McLoughlin adopted a militant stance and was amongst those who broke from Redmond. Giving an early indication of his leadership qualities, it was McLoughlin who headed the anti-Redmond faction within D Company.[29] As a result, he was able to sway a majority of the company against Redmond; these then fused with G Company of the new Irish Volunteers. McLoughlin became a Lieutenant in this company, which was captained by Sean Heuston.[30] The two would have a close association throughout the next eighteen months or so.

In 1915, Tom Clarke initiated McLoughlin into the IRB.[31] The brotherhood had a strong grip on both the Fianna and that revolutionary section of the Volunteers that had broken from Redmondite nationalism. It was also by now well into the planning process for a Rising. Despite this, though, it still lagged behind the pace set by Connolly, who was clearly the most dynamic figure in the anti-War agitation in Ireland, the most concerned about the threat of conscription, which hung like a spectre over Irish workers, and the most insistent of the need for an immediate proletarian strike against British imperialism. McLoughlin, however, was not greatly active in the IRB, and seems to have devoted most of his energies towards the Fianna and Irish Volunteers.

In August 1915, McLoughlin was a marshal at one of the biggest national events in living memory, the funeral of Jeremiah O'Donovan Rossa.

O'Donovan Rossa, a former editor of the Fenian journal, *The Irish People*, had spent five years in English prisons in the 1860s, a period when penal conditions for Irish revolutionaries were particularly brutal. During his incarceration he had been returned as MP for Tipperary, underlining the high regard in which he was held throughout Ireland. After his death in the USA, his body was returned to Ireland, where it lay in state for two days. The funeral procession to Glasnevin cemetery involved tens of thousands, and was organised by the Volunteers and the Fianna. One participant, Sean Hynes, recalled McLoughlin marshalling the parade, recounting 'well do I remember the clatter of his hob-nailed army boots on the sets of the silent, crowded streets'.[32]

It was also in 1915, that McLoughlin had his first inkling that plans might be afoot for a Rising. In the course of a discussion with Sean MacDiarmada, Sean Heuston, and a number of Volunteers, McLoughlin raised the question of whether there should be any resistance offered, in the event of police attempts to disarm Volunteers. McDiarmada replied to the effect that any violent attacks now might ruin prospects for a rising. 'It looks as if we mean business', commented McLoughlin to Heuston later. 'Yes', came the reply, 'and before long you will know more about it.'[33]

At the beginning of 1916, Heuston took over command of D Company, and was followed there by McLoughlin, who retained his position as Lieutenant.[34] The other officer in the company was Liam Murnane. Paddy Stephenson was Quartermaster, whilst Dick Balfe was a section commander. It was the smallest company in the First Battalion, Dublin Brigade, and did not parade more than thirty or forty men at any one time. McLoughlin soon became prominent. On St Patrick's Day, 1916, The Irish Volunteers organised military reviews in all principal towns. This was the first occasion that McLoughlin was placed on his own to operate, without orders, under a general directive. He was placed in charge of a unit of six, and tasked with the shadowing of those detectives from the G division, Dublin Metropolitan Police, who would be on duty at the Dublin parade. In the event of any attempt to arrest Padraig Pearse, or any other leader, McLoughlin's unit, armed and operating in plain clothes, was to 'bump off ' the offending officers.[35] McLoughlin and his men tailed a well-known Dublin detective, Henry Bruton, and eventually scared him off. But their paths would cross again on more than one occasion in the years ahead.

Planning for the Rising
The early part of 1916 also saw James Connolly finally decide to ally his ICA with the IRB for a joint strike against British rule in Ireland.[36] Connolly's

perspective of a European wide proletarian revolt against the ongoing slaughter of the First World War had been dashed by the actions of those European socialist leaders who decided to support the war aims of their respective governments. Forced to change his strategy, he was compelled to join his forces with those of the revolutionary nationalists, sections of which had supported him during the Lockout. With the IRB wielding crucial influence over the Fianna and Irish Volunteers, Connolly's small ICA would have a much greater chance of success through alliance. It was not the revolt he had envisaged.[37] But at the same time, Connolly had placed a small section of the Irish working class at the head of the struggle against British imperialism, instructing it that the struggle must go on, beyond the aims of its temporary allies, and towards the socialist republic.[38] Easter 1916 was set as the date for the Rising.

In early April, McLoughlin was informed that 'there was a likelihood of action' at Easter.[39] There was no mention, however, that a Rising was being organised, and McLoughlin believed the comment referred to the planned landing of a consignment of arms from Germany and its distribution. He was told that any attempts by the British to obstruct the dispersal of the arms might lead to a revolt, but there was no suggestion made to him that a Rising was the actual intention.[40] The beginning of the week preceding Easter saw McLoughlin comply with an instruction to take time off his work, which was in O'Dea's mattress making factory. He spent the first day or two shifting boxes of bombs into safe houses, close to Chancery Place at the Four Courts. McLoughlin then spent time collecting in arms for D Company which, although small was, he considered, fast becoming the best-armed unit in the First Battalion.[41]

On the Wednesday before Easter, McLoughlin was instructed by Heuston to take his Fianna sluagh to the Three Rock Mountain in Co. Dublin. This was a favoured spot for Fianna drilling and close to the country cottage of Constance Markievicz. The purpose of this particular instruction, though, was more serious than mere drilling. McLoughlin was told to take all the arms available to his Fianna sluagh to the Three Rock. In the event of any attempt by the British to interfere with the expected arms shipment, he was to move his unit down to overlook DunLaoighre, where it would be joined by other detachments and would seek to prevent the movement of British troops in from England.[42] McLoughlin left his home in North King St on Thursday, laden down with two Lee Enfields, six revolvers and about a half-dozen Mills bombs. The sluagh stayed at their Three Rock camp until the early hours of Saturday morning, before receiving an order from Heuston to return to Dublin. Unknown to McLoughlin, the arms shipment, aboard the *Aud* in Kerry, had not been landed and was eventually intercepted by the British.[43] All plans relating to its dispersal were therefore off. After cycling back to Dublin, with a bagful of rifles, revolvers, and bombs on his back, McLoughlin was told of the situation and instructed to proceed to the Gaelic League hall in Blackhall St later that evening.

At a meeting held in the hall on the Saturday evening, McLoughlin was told by Heuston that the Rising would begin the next day. On Sunday morning, however, Eoin MacNeill, IV Chief of Staff, countermanded the order for parades and manoeuvres, which were to be the signal for the commencement of the Rising. MacNeill, who along with IV Secretary Bulmer Hobson was not trusted by or part of the secret military council that planned the Rising, had only reluctantly agreed to the insurrection, after learning about it on the Thursday before Easter. Initially of the view that any planned Rising should be called off, MacNeill had changed his mind when he was visited by Sean MacDiarmada and informed that a huge arms shipment was about to be landed in Kerry. The sinking of the *Aud*, though, led to a second change of mind on his part, and the issuing of the countermanding order.[44] This threw the plans of the insurrectionaries into turmoil, but at a meeting of the Military Council on Sunday a decision was taken to rise the following day. Efforts were made to spread this new order as widely as possible, but in the event only a tiny minority of the available forces would hear the news in time, and be in a position to take part in the fighting. McLoughlin was amongst them. D Company had been due to mobilise at four o'clock on Sunday afternoon, but eventually met late in the evening, again at the Gaelic League hall. Here, they were told that MacNeill's order was to be ignored, and that the Rising was on. Many of the men spent the night at Blackhall St, sleeping on the floor after discussing into the small hours of the morning that which lay ahead. McLoughlin awoke at five o'clock. Despite having had only a few hours 'fitful' rest,[45] he was far from weary, but energised and ready to play his part in the events of a week that would change both his life and the entire course of modern Irish history.

Notes

1   Birth Certificate of Sean McLoughlin.
2   Brendan Shiel (great-grandson of Patrick McLoughlin) quoted in *Irish Echo*, 19/25-4-2006.
3   Ibid.
4   National Archives, (NA) 1911 Census returns, reel 46/84/85.
5   Sean McLoughlin, 'Memories of the Easter Rising', in *Camillian Post*,

Spring 1948, p. 9.
6   University College Dublin Archives, (UCDA) 'Notes on Communism in Saorstat Eireann' Sean McEntee papers, P67/523.
7   I am obliged to the Shiel family for this background information on Sean and Danny McLoughlin.
8   NA, Sean McLoughlin, Statement to Bureau of Military History, WS290, p. 1.
9   NA, Michael Staines, Statement to Bureau of Military History, WS 284 p. 1.
10 NA, Sean McLoughlin, WS290 p. 1.
11 NA, Eamon Martin, Statement to the Bureau of Military History, WS591 p. 4.
12 CD Greaves, *Liam Mellows and the Irish Revolution*, (London, 1971), p. 68.
13 NA, Eamon Martin, p. 4.
14 NA, Michael Staines, p. 1.
15 FSL Lyons, *Ireland since the Famine*, (London 1973), p. 282.
16 Padraig Yeates, *Lock-Out: Dublin 1913*,(Dublin: 2000) p. 220.
17 Ibid., pp. 219-220. Pearse's articles were later published in the collection *From a Hermitage* (1915) and drew praise from James Connolly (*Workers' Republic*, 3-7-1915).
18 Charles Townshend, *The Easter Rebellion*, (London: 2005) p. 112.
19 NA, Garry Holohan, Statement to the Bureau of Military History, WS 328 pp. 17-20.
20 Ibid. Holohan also recalls how electricians on the docks tied live wires to the drinking cans of strike-breakers.
21 Sean McLoughlin, 'Heritage of Easter Week' in *Irish Worker*, 19-4-1924.
22 I am obliged to the Shiel family for this and information on Patrick McLoughlin's involvements in the ITGWU.
23 *The Socialist*, 10-6-1920.
24 See: Emil Strauss, *Irish Nationalism and British Democracy*, (London: 1951) pp. 231-2. The subsequent economic programme of Cumann na nGaedheal would suggest, however, that these fears were misplaced and that Home Rule would have been compatible with the interests of the Irish bourgeoisie, north and south.
25 See, for example, RJQ Adams, *Bonar Law*, (Stanford: 1999) p. 109.
26 NA, Sean McLoughlin p. 1.
27 *Irish Worker*, 8-8-1914.
28 NA, Eamon Martin, pp. 15-16.

29 *The Socialist*, 10-6-1920.
30 NA, Sean McLoughlin, p. 2.
31 NA, Sean McLoughlin, p. 2.
32 *Evening Herald*, 24-5-1966.
33 NA, Sean McLoughlin, p. 2.
34 Ibid., p. 3.
35 NA, Sean McLoughlin, pp. 2-3.
36 CD Greaves, *Life and Times of James Connolly*, (London: 1986), pp. 387-93.
37 Connolly's political life-work had been devoted to the establishment of a socialist republic, the struggle for which would be led by the working class. Two factors pushed Connolly to organise a rising in 1916, in which his small workers' army would become allied with the much larger forces of the advanced petty-bourgeoisie. Firstly, Connolly believed that the increased militarization of the British state in Ireland, its growing 'heavy-handedness' and the threat of conscription, was driving Ireland to the point of a revolt that had, as he made clear in letters to Arthur McManus in November 1915 and January 1916 (*The Socialist*, 17-4-1919), social revolutionary possibilities. Secondly, Connolly's analysis of the war itself, and his post-war perspective. He clearly believed that the war was a result of the crisis of a decaying British capitalism and imperialism, as opposed to a general crisis of world capitalism and imperialism. (*Irish Worker* 29-8-1914, *Workers' Republic*, 20-11-1915). He saw the British Empire as a brake on the economic, political and cultural progress of colonial nations throughout the world and Ireland in particular. (*Workers' Republic* 9-10-1915). For this reason Connolly, now aware that a European proletarian revolt was not going to materialise, took the position that the next best outcome was the destruction of the British Empire. But Connolly also feared that if the British won, they would be able to offset their declining power for another generation. This would allow them to carry through the partition of Ireland, a step that Connolly felt would both destroy any prospect of catholic-protestant working-class unity and usher in a 'carnival of reaction' (*Irish Worker, 14-3-1914)*. In addition, Connolly looked at the disappearing liberties of the working class in both Ireland and Britain, and felt that these might be permanently lost in the post-war period (See for example, *Workers' Republic* (8-4-1916). Because he did not see the war as a general crisis of capitalism, just its British variant, Connolly did not foresee the post-war convulsions that would rock European capitalism in the 1917-1919 period. He did not hold

to the perspective of a maturing European working-class revolt, but felt that the Irish working class's only chance of avoiding the terrible fate he saw awaiting it lay in an immediate strike at the British before the limited window of opportunity afforded by the war was closed off for another generation. Isolation and the smallness of his own ICA compelled Connolly to join forces with the larger advanced nationalist bodies. But although the Rising cannot be seen as an insurrection led by the Irish working class, Connolly's motivations for taking part in it as well as his aims for it were based on socialist considerations.

38 At no point in his life did James Connolly argue that the interests of the Irish working class were compatible with those of the Irish bourgeoisie. His comments to the ICA to 'hold onto their rifles', as their aims differed from those of the nationalists, have been well covered. See, for example, Levenson, *James Connolly: a Political Biography*, (London: 1977) p. 292. For corroboration that Connolly did hold to such a viewpoint and did issue this instruction, see the comments of Joe Metcalfe, an ITWGU organiser who met Connolly at Liberty Hall shortly before the Rising, *The Wicklow People*, 5-6-1937 and also the comments of ICA Easter Rising participant, Seamus McGowan at the Republican Congress conference in September 1934, *Irish Workers' Voice*, 13-10-1934.
39 NA, Sean McLoughlin, p. 3.
40 Ibid.
41 Ibid., p. 4.
42 Ibid., pp. 4-5.
43 Dorothy McArdle, *The Irish Republic*, (London: 1968) p. 149.
44 Townshend, *Easter Rebellion*, pp. 134-37.
45 Sean McLoughlin 'Memories of the Easter Rising', *Camillian Post*, Spring 1948, p. 3.

2

Sean McLoughlin and the Easter Rising, 1916

Introduction

The Easter Rising has been described by some as a rebellion that was planned with no real chance of military success but which through a gallant, if token, stand and certain defeat would achieve its real aim – that of the re-awakening and redemption of an Irish nationalist spirit almost snuffed out by the war.[1] The evidence normally cited for this view is based largely on a few extracts from the writings of Padraig Pearse, which are said to be overly pre-occupied with notions of sacrifice and death.[2] But when looking at the degree of preparation and the nature of the engagement envisaged, as well as the Bureau of Military History accounts of those who took part in the Rising, it is clear that this position is not tenable and that the Rising was planned in the belief that victory was possible. Although lacking heavy artillery, the Irish Volunteers outnumbered the British army in Ireland by two to one and could more than match them in Dublin.[3] They had also tried, successfully they believed, to secure German aid. Added to this was the knowledge that the British state was toiling badly in its European war. All of this combined to create a degree of optimism amongst republicans that victory could be secured.

The choice of tactics decided upon by the Republicans also highlighted their determination to succeed. Rather than attack British garrisons openly, which would have been the perfect way of effecting the blood sacrifice, it was decided to seize key buildings in Dublin and fortify them as defences. These were to be used to prevent or retard the movement of British troops from their garrisons towards the city centre, where the provisional government was to be established. With Risings also planned for several provincial towns, it was hoped that the longer the centre could be held, the greater were the chances of sparking revolt throughout the country. As has been pointed out by military historians, the planning was technically sound, in that it forced the British to confront the most difficult task any army can face, that of fighting its way through a defended city.[4]

The scuttling of the *Aud* and the countermanding order, however, hamstrung the Republican effort and drastically reduced its chances of success. The advance of the British in Dublin would now be swifter, with prospects of a general rising outside the city much weaker. But by sticking as closely as possible to their original plans, albeit with much depleted forces, the Republicans still clung to the perspective that Dublin could be held, and a more widespread rising fomented. Victory was still the objective. This did not happen and the Rising was eventually isolated and crushed. Rather than marking the end of the Revolution, however, the events of Easter Week 1916[5] were only the start of a challenge which would eventually undermine British rule in Ireland to it foundations.

The Rising was an event of critical importance to the life of Sean McLoughlin. He began Easter Week as a Lieutenant, but ended it as Commandant-General of the army of the Irish Republic. During the Rising, he would display leadership qualities unusual in one so young, as well as courage in what became extremely hostile and difficult conditions. It was as a result of his Easter Week role, and the way in which he performed it, that McLoughlin became a prominent figure in the Irish revolutionary movement, as well as a figure of genuine historic importance.

The Easter Rising

At six o'clock on Easter Monday morning, McLoughlin and Heuston left for Liberty Hall. En route, they visited various safe houses in Bridgefoot Street and dumped boxes of ammunition and bombs that would be used later in the day.[6] Shortly after arriving at Liberty Hall, McLoughlin met with James Connolly, who sent him to deliver orders to Volunteers stationed in Kimmage. After this, McLoughlin travelled to George's Church at Hardwicke St, which was the mobilization point for D Company. Out of a possible thirty-six only fourteen of the company had shown up, displaying clearly the negative effect of MacNeill's countermanding order.[7] The men then marched to Beresford Place, where several hundred Volunteers had assembled awaiting instructions. Finally, around mid-day, D Company set off on its mission. The company was instructed to seize the Mendicity Institution on the quays.

The Mendicity was adjacent to the Royal Barracks and the purpose in taking it was to keep in check the British troops stationed there, in order to allow the larger garrisons in the GPO and Four Courts time to establish their positions. That Connolly attached great strategic importance to this post can be evidenced from the recollections of Beaslai, who noted how Connolly spoke of nothing else during a meeting he had with him on that first day.⁸ The takeover was conducted without a hitch and McLoughlin helped to barricade the position by placing a number of carts at the nearby Queen St Bridge. Shortly afterwards, the position was subjected to its first attack, by a column of between 200-250 British troops. However, the Republicans – with Dick Balfe recalling that 'it was a case of shoot and one could not miss' – broke this up, shooting dead in the process the British Commanding Officer.⁹ The scene was thus set for one of Easter Week's most bitterly-fought engagements.

A serious problem facing D Company was the lack of food within the Mendicity. In consequence, McLoughlin volunteered to fetch some supplies, as well as the bombs and ammunition which had been dumped earlier that morning. The assignment was tricky but no one else appeared willing to undertake it. McLoughlin managed to complete it successfully and even did so without having to spend any money. In the pub, which he visited to buy some provisions, a fellow-member of D Company, who should have been 'out' himself, served him. McLoughlin later commented that he had never seen service so quick in Ireland or with so little neglect for the money!¹⁰ After returning to the Mendicity, McLoughlin travelled to Heuston's home to pick up more arms and supplies, and then made his way to the GPO to brief Connolly on the situation. Here, McLoughlin was told that the mobilization had been a success and that, under the leadership of eight commandants, the Republicans held large parts of the city. He then left for the Mendicity, noticing for the first time the Irish tri-colours fluttering above the many buildings which had now been taken over by the Republican forces.

Back at the Mendicity, the Republicans had broken up a second British attack. Concerns, however, were growing amongst the Volunteers about the general situation; had the Rising been a success? What was happening in the city? And what about the rest of the country: had there been Risings elsewhere? The sight of a tram trundling past the Mendicity towards the city centre, suggesting things were normal in the town, coupled with the growing concern that McLoughlin seemed to have been gone a long time, intensified these worries, and led Heuston to consider that the Rising must have failed. As a result, he told the men to clean themselves up, and get ready to leave for home. Some of them were complying with this order when McLoughlin suddenly returned. The impact of his return was striking. Informing the Volunteers that 'the British had been beaten off everywhere they had attacked', and (wrongly) of how 'the Germans were trying to land troops in Limerick', McLoughlin was able to raise morale to the point where the Mendicity men now began to think in terms of when, rather than if, the Irish Republic would be established. 'He would have made a great propaganda minister', commented Paddy Stephenson many years later, reflecting on the galvanizing effect the report had on the Volunteers that first evening in the Mendicity.[11]

McLoughlin stood guard during the first night but enjoyed a quiet time as the British decided against further attacks for the time being. The following morning he left for the GPO to collect more arms and supplies, taking care to climb over the walls east of the Mendicity, in order to avoid the attentions of the British troops who as yet were unable to surround the building. The journey to the GPO was becoming more dangerous, especially as McLoughlin had to cross a bridge in order to reach the north side of the Liffey. But in exposing himself to the attentions of British snipers, McLoughlin was learning exactly where the enemy was situated and the course of its movements. It was knowledge that would become vital later in the week.

McLoughlin met briefly with Ned Daly at the Four Courts before reaching the GPO. There, both Connolly and Pearse expressed surprise that the Mendicity was still holding out – they had expected it to hold out for three or four hours at most – and readily agreed to McLoughlin's request for reinforcements. McLoughlin felt that from a military perspective it was better to push outposts to the limit and Connolly concurred with this view.[12] Ten or so Volunteers from Swords were dispatched, and followed a route mapped out for them by McLoughlin. Again, this acted as a morale-booster for the small garrison at the Mendicity, and raised their numbers to around twenty-five.

The Fall of the Mendicity

The decision to send reinforcements to the Mendicity was prescient, because Tuesday turned into a day of fierce fighting at the institution. British troops took up position in the houses opposite to the Mendicity and strafed it with gunfire. Attempts, though, to mount a bayonet charge were broken up again by the Republicans, who used the same 'rear, then head' method of attack which had been deployed to such good effect the previous day.[13] By evening, the situation was calm and, as on Monday, the night passed relatively quietly.

The lull of Tuesday night, however, was merely the prelude to an all-out assault from the British on Wednesday morning. Occupants of houses on each side of the institution were ordered to leave. British troops stationed themselves in Thomas Street, Bonham Street, Watling Street and Bridgefoot Street, and soon had the Mendicity surrounded. The fighting became fierce, and in some instances at very close quarters; JJ Brennan, for example, later recalled firing at a British soldier only twenty feet away.[14] By noon, however, the position of the Volunteers was hopeless. The British were now throwing hand grenades in through the windows of the building and outnumbered the Republicans by over ten to one. With ammunition and supplies exhausted, the Volunteers had little option but to surrender. After shooting dead one of the Republicans, Peter Wilson, the British accepted this surrender and packed the remaining twenty-three or so off to the Royal Barracks.

McLoughlin was not amongst this grouping. As the Mendicity had not been expected to hold out for so long, lack of supplies had been an ever-present concern. Early on Wednesday morning, McLoughlin and Paddy Stephenson slipped through the British lines and journeyed to the GPO. This was by now a hazardous journey, and the pair had to dodge a hail of bullets from British troops stationed in Watling Street, to the west of the institution.[15] After a long and roundabout route, via Usher Street, Church Street Bridge, the Four Courts, North Brunswick Street, North King Street, Capel Street, Great Britain Street, (Parnell Street) Denmark Street, and Henry Street, they made it to HQ. Here they briefed Connolly on the latest developments and picked up more supplies and ammunition. Connolly 'unusually animated and excited' by the news was so impressed by the resolve of the Mendicity garrison, that he had a special message of praise and encouragement typed up for the men.[16] He also considered that their success in holding off the British signalled perhaps that there were fewer British troops in Ireland than he had previously thought, raising his hopes that success might be possible.

McLoughlin and Stephenson set off once more for the Mendicity, but by the time they neared the institute the final British assault was well underway. It was then that disaster almost struck:

> When we reached the end of Church St, we heard very loud and intense firing going on in the direction of Queen St, and we realized this action must be taking place around the Mendicity…terrific firing was going on and a large crowd had assembled to watch the movement of the troops. I moved into the crowd with the idea that it might have been possible to rush across the Queen St bridge. When the troops moved further across the bridge some women standing in a group looked at us and recognizing me as a Volunteer said, "There is one of them". The troops in their immediate vicinity made a rush, but were blocked by the crowd, and we ran towards Smithfield as all the arms I was carrying was a small automatic pistol which was useless in such a position, but

we were not pursued.[17]

After the fall of the Mendicity, McLoughlin went to the Four Courts garrison, and was asked by Ned Daly to take command at the Chancery Place end. During the night, there was heavy firing all along the quays. Some of this firing was directed at McLoughlin's position from houses opposite, but was returned by his unit, and appeared to pass by quickly. The following morning, McLoughlin decided to join up with the GPO garrison, but before doing so, paid a visit to Richmond hospital in North Brunswick Street. His fellow Fianna member Eamon Martin had been shot during an attack on Broadstone station and was lying in a critical condition in the hospital. McLoughlin was initially prevented from entering the building, but after a heated argument with hospital staff, managed eventually to get in. After seeing Martin, who was unconscious but would later make a full recovery, McLoughlin was beckoned into the office of the house surgeon. He thought the surgeon wished to complain about the manner in which he had forced his way into the hospital, but was pleasantly surprised when the man handed him two pouches of ammunition, containing nearly one hundred rounds, commenting on how he might need them.[18] Leaving North Brunswick Street, McLoughlin crossed into North King Street, where he had a chance meeting with his mother. McLoughlin recalled that his mother expressed no objections to his involvement in the Rising, 'never for a moment during that brief conversation did she show that she disapproved of my action', but was unhappy that his fifteen-year-old sister, Mary, had taken part. Mary McLoughlin was a member of Clan na Gael and had been working as a courier throughout Easter Week, travelling between the GPO, College Green and the Jacobs factory garrison headed by Thomas MacDonagh.[19] Her mother, however, felt she was 'too young for that sort of thing' and asked McLoughlin to send her home. McLoughlin, unaware that his young sibling had taken part, did send her home upon reaching the GPO. After returning, Mary was locked in her room by her relieved mother, and told that she would be staying at home until the Rising was over. But this was not the end of Mary McLoughlin's Easter Week story. She had found a revolver on her travels, and wished to hand it over to the Volunteer leaders. With her mother busy in the kitchen, cooking her a meal, she 'escaped' from her room through the window and made it back to the GPO, where, unknown to Sean McLoughlin, she again worked as a courier until the latter part of the week.[20]

The Boy Commandant

It was in the GPO on the Thursday of Easter Week that McLoughlin's rise to prominence began. By then the HQ was under heavy fire. British reinforcements had arrived in large numbers, and there were now around 12,000 British troops in Dublin.[21] Fortified positions had been built at Brunswick St, College Green and Findlater's Place, and were maintaining a continuous barrage on three sides of the GPO.[22] In addition, the heavy artillery bombardment that had began the previous day had intensified and was destroying buildings throughout Sackville St. Morale within the GPO was not good and fears were growing that the end might be close at hand. James Connolly, aware that the GPO was being surrounded and concerned that the British might be crossing from the quays up through Liffey Street, sectioned off thirty men and placed them under McLoughlin's command. His orders were to take over the offices of the *Irish Independent* and from that vantage point stem any movement of British troops from the south side of the Liffey.[23]

McLoughlin's unit had problems in getting into the offices, but these were solved when he smashed through the windows of a nearby furniture store and from there gained access to a yard which led to the backdoor of the *Independent*. There, McLoughlin cleared out a number of caretakers, who had locked the main doors causing the initial delay. The offices were then occupied and a watch posted throughout the night. During that night, McLoughlin clambered onto the roof of the *Independent* and was awestruck at the spectacle that filled his eyes. The whole Sackville St area, it seemed, was a raging inferno. The Dublin Bread Company building, Reis stores, the Waverley hotel, Hoytes' oil works, Clery's and the Imperial hotel and many other buildings were being swallowed whole by the blaze. In fact, the fire was so fierce that the windows of the GPO, separated from it by the width of Sackville Street, were scorched and smouldering.[24] McLoughlin feared that Republican hopes of victory were similarly being consumed:

> In front was a roaring sea of flame leaping to the sky, with the crackle of musketry and cannon pealing the accompaniment. Behind was another terrific blaze from the Linen Hall barracks, which had also gone up. It was apparent now that we were doomed. No stories of landing Germans would be believed. It was a handful of daring men against the wrath of a mighty Empire, with the odds on the Empire.[25]

At around six o'clock the following morning, McLoughlin received a message from Pearse to return with his unit to the GPO. After reaching HQ, he was informed by Desmond Fitzgerald of Connolly's injuries. These had occurred the previous day when, stepping out into a laneway to observe McLoughlin's unit take the *Independent,* ricocheting shrapnel shattered Connolly's leg and ankle.[26] McLoughlin himself recalled that he and others of his unit had to pick shrapnel out of their boots and clothing after reaching the *Independent,* so thick had the air been with it, and that on his way back to the GPO that morning one of his men had been hit with it.[27]

The injuries to Connolly were a severe blow to the Republicans. He was confined to a stretcher, in obvious agony, and as such unable to direct events or respond to the rapidly changing situation. Things soon got worse. At mid-day, the British shelling recommenced and this time direct hits were scored on the GPO. Despite the best efforts of the occupants, the building was soon ablaze. One immediate danger here was from the stockpiles of gelignite bombs that had been placed in the basement; they were close to a lift-shaft down which showers of sparks were now cascading. In response, McLoughlin took some of his unit down to the basement and began the process of moving them to safety. This was a dangerous task, as the bombs were homemade and unstable. The hair-raising nature of the assignment was made worse for McLoughlin when, carrying an armful of the devices, he was knocked flat on his back by a jet of water from the O'Rahilly, who was trying to control the blaze.[28] Fortunately none exploded and McLoughlin completed the work 'very hurriedly and rather recklessly'.[29]

By now, the fire in the GPO was out of control and an evacuation was deemed necessary. Some of the wounded had been moved to the Coliseum theatre, a vast pillarless construction, viewed by its architects as the last word on theatre construction, but wrongly believed also to be fireproof. McLoughlin discussed the situation with Pearse and Sean MacDiarmada. Both were of the opinion that a general retreat should be made down Moore Street, towards the Williams and Woods factory on Great Britain Street, where a new HQ could be established. For McLoughlin, however, this plan was 'mad'.[30] En route to the GPO the previous day, he had learned that the whole of that street, including Williams and Woods, was now occupied by the British, rendering any attempt to approach it as one which would lead to 'certain death'.[31] McLoughlin proposed instead that a retreat be conducted down Henry Street, towards the Four Courts, where contact could be made with Ned Daly's garrison and a regroupment of forces carried out. As he was pointing this out, however, McLoughlin was informed that the O'Rahilly had already left the GPO with a party of men, and was heading towards the Williams and Woods factory. On hearing this, McLoughlin dashed out of the GPO and ran up Henry Place in order to stop him. He was too late. By the time McLoughlin reached the opening to Moore Lane, the Sherwood

Foresters had cut down the O'Rahilly and twenty-one of his unit.

It was here in this deteriorating situation that McLoughlin took control. Turning back towards the GPO, he could only look on as the HQ garrison finally began to evacuate, with most running in his direction. The scene was chaotic:

> I turned back towards the Post Office and saw the whole garrison coming towards me at the run. There was terrible confusion – almost panic. No one seemed to have any idea what to do. Somebody shouted that we were being fired upon from the roof of a mineral water factory. I detailed a number of men to break the door down. Another party entered from the opposite door and they opened fire on each other- one man was killed and several wounded. I was incensed with rage calling "have you all gone mad-what the hell is wrong!" and I drove them towards the wall threatening them.[32]

Order was disappearing fast. Many volunteers ran from the GPO straight to Moore St, where they were cut to pieces by the heavy machine gun fire of the British troops stationed at the corner of that street and Great Britain St. McLoughlin diverted the fleeing masses up Henry Place. Here he restored some order amongst the Volunteers and got them to fall into a formation.[33] Pearse, MacDiarmada and Connolly, carried on a stretcher, were amongst those who followed McLoughlin. Sean MacDiarmada spoke to McLoughlin and expressed his fears that all seemed lost. 'My God', he exclaimed, 'we are not going to be caught like rats and killed without a chance to fight'. McLoughlin reassured MacDiarmada. 'There is no need to panic', he told him, 'I can get you out of here, but there will be only one man giving the orders and I will give them.'[34] MacDiarmada spoke to Connolly. Connolly, apparently impressed all week by McLoughlin's 'activities, resourcefulness and soldier-like qualities'[35] immediately agreed that control should be passed to him. McLoughlin knew the situation to be desperate, but felt that if they could get past Henry Place and across the Moore Lane opening, they might be able to take refuge in the tenements of Moore St. He began to look for ways of erecting a barricade behind which this manoeuvre could be attempted[36]. A motor van was soon pulled from the yard of a nearby mineral water factory and pushed across the mouth of Moore Lane. As protection from British bullets it was no use, but it did partially screen the Republicans from the British line of fire at the end of the lane, giving them the chance to dash across the opening and into the tenements. The Volunteers were then brought through the enfilading fire in small groups and filtered slowly into the Moore Street buildings.[37] The chaos again was acute here. Many Volunteers, unnerved by the ferocity of the British attack and the sight of their comrades being hit, tried to hide in Henry Place, almost frozen with fear. McLoughlin was in charge here[38] and, according to one source, 'stood out like a rock' amidst all the confusion.[39]

All of the Republicans, over 300 in total, eventually made it into Moore St. A new HQ was set up, initially in a grocers shop at the corner of Henry Place and Moore St. McLoughlin then instructed a mixed Irish Citizen Army/Volunteer unit to begin breaking through the adjoining walls of the tenement buildings, in order to diffuse their forces as widely as possible. The British were encamped behind a barricade at the end of the street, but for now made no attempt to mount an offensive. McLoughlin reckoned that this temporary calm was due to the sizeable number of Republicans now in Moore St: 'I had the feeling that the British were surprised by the unexpectedly large body of men and that our immunity, strange as it may seem, lay therein, at least for the time being.'[40]

The 'Death or Glory' Squad

On Friday evening, a meeting was held of HQ staff. Those present included Padraig Pearse, James Connolly, Sean MacDiarmada, Tom Clarke, Joseph Plunkett and Harry Boland. MacDiarmada proposed that McLoughlin be given the military command, commenting that he was 'the only one likely to get us out of here'.[41] Connolly, the Commandant-General, seconded this and insisted McLoughlin hold his rank.[42] McLoughlin's main task now was to organize a retreat from Moore Street. He was acutely aware of this, feeling that it was only a matter of short time before the British attacked and recognizing that if they began burning the Moore Street buildings, escape might well be impossible. In conversation with Connolly, who asked if he had any ideas for such a retreat, McLoughlin pointed out the weakness of the present position, and outlined roughly his thoughts on how the situation might be rectified:

> We are now paying the penalty of not having a line of retreat. We ought to have gone the other way, as I told you earlier, down Henry St, towards the Four Courts and that is what we shall do as soon as the men are rested…we shall move as soon as daylight comes.[43]

During the evening, McLoughlin ensured the continuation of the digging work, through the connecting walls of the Moore St tenements. Officers were appointed and instructions given that the work was to continue through the night. For McLoughlin, this task was essential to republican escape hopes:

> I told them we must burrow as far as possible before daylight; that to evacuate Moore St the men would have to be spread out over the widest possible front; that in any movement out of an enclosed position, the close bunching of the men was a gift to the enemy as they could be mown down en masse. Scattered, they presented a smaller target and offered a greater maximum of safety.[44]

The units engaged in this task worked Trojan-like and by daybreak had reached the break in the street at Sackville Lane. The British appeared unaware of this. McLoughlin stepped out into Sackville Lane to survey the situation. There he discovered the body of the O'Rahilly. After being hit by a blast of gunfire from the top of Moore Lane, the O'Rahilly had crawled up Sackville Lane, where he died. McLoughlin covered O'Rahilly's face with a handkerchief, and the same was done for his dead companions by those other Volunteers who had now joined McLoughlin in the lane. McLoughlin now felt it was time to move; he regarded a British attack as inevitable and feared that unless the Republicans took the initiative they would be burnt out of Moore St and destroyed. After discussing the situation with MacDiarmada in Sackville Lane, McLoughlin met with the HQ staff, which was now based in Hanlon's fish shop, 16 Moore St.

Initially, McLoughlin had toyed with the idea of releasing flammable liquid from a nearby hardware store, directing it towards the British lines, and setting it alight before attacking.[45] His eventual plan, though, was more straightforward. McLoughlin proposed an attack on the British barricades carried out by a 'death or glory' squad of between twenty to thirty Volunteers. This would be a diversionary assault and would allow the main garrison, spread throughout the Moore St buildings, to break out and run towards a large warehouse in Henry St. Here, forces would be re-assembled and would move down past Capel St onto the Four Courts, where they would 'fight it out' alongside Ned Daly.[46]

Pearse had reservations about the plan. Many civilians had already lost their lives, and he was concerned that more deaths would occur if such a mass retreat took place. 'I am sorry, I cannot help that', replied McLoughlin, 'this is a military operation and I can only make it successful if I don't think about such things.'[47] Pearse seemed to accept this point and the plan was ratified by all of the Provisional government leaders. McLoughlin set 12 o'clock mid-day as zero hour and began recruiting for the 'death or glory' squad. Seamus Robinson, later an IRA Commandant in county Tipperary, volunteered for the squad and remembered McLoughlin, with a yellow band on his tunic signifying his new rank, organizing it.[48]

Surrender

McLoughlin moved his unit out into Sackville Lane and gave each man his instructions. The signal for the attack would be a bomb thrown by McLoughlin towards the British barricades. As McLoughlin was in the middle of these preparations, however, he was approached by Sean MacDiarmada and told to return to HQ. There he ran through his plan in great detail again with Connolly and Pearse. But Pearse's concerns about civilian casualties had now increased as he had witnessed the British army mowing down an entire family in Moore St shortly beforehand.[49] Although making it clear that he was in no way critical of the plan, and conceding that it might yet need to be implemented, Pearse instructed McLoughlin to delay his attack one hour, pending further reconsideration of the entire situation. McLoughlin took his squad into one of the houses and listened on as rumours about a surrender began to permeate the ranks. When he returned to HQ, McLoughlin was told that the Rising was over. 'I am sending a message to the British to end this fight', Pearse informed McLoughlin flatly. 'Does it mean surrender?' asked McLoughlin. 'I don't know until we have heard from the British', was Pearse's final reply.[50]

McLoughlin disagreed with Pearse's decision. His chief concern was for the fate of those Volunteers, originally based in Kimmage, and known as 'The Refugees'.[51] This group contained a mixture of English, Scots, and a large number of Irishmen who had returned from Britain to avoid conscription. McLoughlin feared that they might be singled out for special punishment by the British army. He sat with Tom Clarke and made clear his opposition to the decision to seek terms. Clarke spoke to him, pointing out that he had done his best, whilst James Connolly urged him to look to the future:

> Connolly beckoned to me from the bed and said "you must not take it so hardily. You are young. You will see a lot more struggles before you die." I said, "I know". He said "there is no hope for me; all those who signed the Proclamation will be shot." I said "are you sure of that". He said "certain. The British can do no worse and we do not expect any mercy." And I said, "what about the rest of us?" He said, "The rank-and-file will probably be imprisoned and later released. You must keep quiet about the part you played. You will still be needed. You will have plenty to do in the future, if you keep quiet." He said, "We have done our best; it was better than we hoped. It has not ended as it might have,

in disaster."[52]

Pearse himself, accompanied by Elizabeth Farrell, went to the British HQ to seek terms for the ending of hostilities. He was then taken into custody. A message was sent back to Moore St, informing the garrison of the British terms. Briefly, they were that all insurgents should lay down their arms and march behind an advance party bearing white flags to Findlater's on Sackville St, where the surrender would be taken. After lining the garrison up, McLoughlin informed them of the decision to surrender and of the British terms. He reminded them to make 'religiously certain' that they had nothing of value on their persons, 'however legitimately acquired', in case they were shot as looters.[53] Despite the British instructions to the contrary, McLoughlin insisted that the men march to the place of surrender with their unloaded rifles in hand. For one participant, Joe Good, McLoughlin's instructions here allowed Republicans to end hostilities in a dignified and honourable fashion, and not humiliated, marching with their hands on their heads.[54]

It was McLoughlin who led the main column,[55] two deep and around 320 strong, to Findlaters, where he ordered them to lay down their arms, one line at a time, followed by a two-pace step back. The sight of McLoughlin acting in such a fashion, and the fact that the Republicans had carried their arms, roused the ire of the British commanding officer, General Lowe. 'Who the hell gave you the authority to give orders here', shouted Lowe to McLoughlin, 'I told you to leave your bloody arms in Moore St. I'll have you damn well shot.' McLoughlin, though, did not seem intimidated. He pulled out a sword that he had been carrying as an indicator of his rank and slammed it to the ground in front of Lowe. Lowe, who also lost his cool with Joe Good and attempted unsuccessfully to strike him with his riding cane, [56] 'seemed astounded' by this, but took no further action.[57] From Findlater's, the Republicans were marched to the gardens in front of the Rotunda hospital, where they remained until the following morning. McLoughlin sat through the night in the company of a group of Provisional government leaders and commandants including Clarke, MacDiarmada, Plunkett and Ned Daly. Daly, in particular, was both puzzled and upset about the decision to surrender, feeling that his garrison still had plenty of fight left in it.[58]

The following morning the Republicans were marched through the smoking ruins of Sackville St to the Richmond Barracks in Inchicore. Here, they were searched and interrogated by 'scrutineers' from police and military intelligence. It was at this point in Richmond Barracks that a curious incident occurred. A British military intelligence captain, apparently struck by McLoughlin's youth, took him aside, looked at his Commandant tabs and as he removed them, said in an 'enigmatic' fashion, 'you have now lost your rank.' 'It took me some time to understand the remark and the gesture', McLoughlin reflected many years later, 'that man was no enemy.'[59] McLoughlin may well have been correct here. In Richmond Barracks there were three lines of intelligence officers through which the prisoners passed; British military, Castle authorities, and the local detectives or G men. The incident between McLoughlin and the British captain occurred when he was being marched along the first line. This was significant, because it happened before McLoughlin reached the G men, some of whom, and in particular Henry Bruton and Johnny Barton, knew McLoughlin well. Barton, in fact, on seeing McLoughlin greeted him sarcastically as 'one of the gallant scouts'.[60] Basing his views on his own pre-Easter intelligence work, Barton did not accord McLoughlin senior status. Had McLoughlin marched past him wearing a commandant's insignia, however, Barton's response may have been different, and McLoughlin might have joined the seven others of that rank who ended up in front of firing squads. It is possible, therefore, that the action of the British captain saved McLoughlin's life.

Later that evening, McLoughlin was amongst the hundreds herded onto a steamer and shipped over to England for imprisonment. Unknown to him at this point, both his parents were beaten in their home by British troops as a 'punishment' for his activities.[61] This particular act of vengeance, however, was far from the worst that British troops perpetrated in North King Street during the Rising; earlier in the week soldiers from the 2/6th South Staffordshire regiment had shot dead thirteen innocent civilians, in a quite deliberate fashion. [62]After arrival in England, McLoughlin was sent to Knutsford prison, near Manchester. It was here, whilst in solitary confinement, that he learned from a friendly Sergeant in the Dragoons of the executions that had taken place. McLoughlin was not surprised that Connolly, Pearse and all of the other signatories of the Proclamation were shot; he knew that the men themselves had been reconciled to this fate. But the executions of men like Willie Pearse, Ned Daly, Con Colbert and Sean Heuston, all of whom he had known and some, like Heuston, to whom he had been close, clearly shocked McLoughlin. He later said that he 'never dreamed for a moment' that they would be executed and maintained that they had been so purely to 'placate the fury of stupid men'. [63]

From Knutsford, McLoughlin was sent to Frongoch internment camp in Wales and then to Wormwood Scrubs in London. Sean Hynes was part of the same group of prisoners who were sent from Frongoch to Wormwood

Scrubs. He recalled McLoughlin getting into a heated exchange with other prisoners, who seemed to doubt his promotion to the rank of commandant by James Connolly.[64] Hynes maintained that he was certain McLoughlin was telling the truth, but this would not be the last time that McLoughlin's role during the Easter Rising would be subject to dispute by those who had not actually witnessed it. McLoughlin was eventually released from prison in December 1916. This brought to an end one of Easter Week's most remarkable stories, but was only the beginning for McLoughlin and his struggle against British rule in Ireland. In the period ahead objective conditions in Europe would change and become more favourable for those seeking revolutionary change. All over the continent, the most marginalized and oppressed peoples and classes would for the first time step onto the stage of history and demand a new and more humane order. In an Ireland gripped by growing conflict and the harsh backlash that followed the crushing of the Rising, it too would become an era of revolution and one that offered opportunities for advance to those, like McLoughlin, who sought to complete the task begun in Easter 1916.

Notes

1   For two examples of this, see FSL Lyons, *Ireland Since the Famine*, (London: 1973), pp. 348-9 and WK Anderson, *James Connolly and the Irish Left*, (Dublin: 1994), p. 72.
2   For an example of this, see Moran 'Patrick Pearse and The European Revolt against Reason', *Journal of the History of Ideas*, I, 1989, quoted in Charles Townshend, *The Easter Rebellion*, (London: 2005), p. 114.
3   According to Colonel Eoghan O'Neill, the British had 6,000 mobile combat troops in Ireland with almost 2500 permanently stationed in Dublin, 'The Battle of Dublin 1916: a Military Evaluation of Easter Week', *An Cosantoir*, Volume XXVI, no. 5, (1966) p. 216.
4   This point, taken from Chinese General Sun Tzu's *Art of War*, written 3000 years ago, was quoted in Colonel Eoghan O'Neill,'s 'Battle of Dublin 1916, a Military Evaluation of Easter Week', *An Cosantoir*, Vol XXVI, no. 5, 1966, p. 215. For another analysis, which argues that the planning for the Rising was sound militarily, see Colonel PJ Hally, 'The Easter 1916 Rising in Dublin – The Military Aspects', *Irish Sword*, Vol 7, no. 29, 1966.
5   For a brief narrative of the main events of the Rising, see McArdle, *The Irish Republic*, pp. 158-68.
6   Sean McLoughlin, 'Memories of Easter Rising', *Camillian Post*, (Spring

1948) p. 3.
7   National Library Ireland, (NLI), 36, 147, Paddy Stephenson, 'Heuston's Fort', (unpublished memoir of 1916) p. 12.
8   John M. Heuston, 'Headquarters Battalion- Army of the Irish Republic, Easter Week 1916', *Nationalist*, Carlow (1966) p. 39. He was the brother of Sean Heuston and took the name John upon his ordination into the priesthood.
9   NA, Dick Balfe, Statement to the Bureau of Military History, WS 251, p. 5.
10 Sean McLoughlin, 'Memories of Easter Rising', p. 6.
11 Paddy Stephenson, 'Heuston's Fort', p. 22.
12 NA, Sean McLoughlin, p. 12.
13 NA, Dick Balfe, p. 6.
14 JJ Brennan, 'Mendicity Institution Area', in *Capuchin Annual* 1966, p. 191.
15 Paddy Stephenson, 'Heuston's Fort', p. 27.
16 Desmond Ryan, *The Rising, the Complete Story of Easter Week*, (Dublin: 1949) p. 155.
17 NA, Sean McLoughlin, pp. 13-14.
18 Sean McLoughlin, 'Memories of Easter Rising', p. 9.
19 See: NA, Mary McLoughlin, Statement to the Bureau of Military History, WS 934.
20 A British soldier, unaware of her involvement in the Rising and seeing her as a child who shouldn't be wandering the streets, eventually took Mary McLoughlin custody. She was taken to Court, the following day and asked why she had been found so close to the fighting. McLoughlin answered simply that she had been going home from school and had become caught up in the situation. She was given a pass from the Judge, Lord Powerscourt, and allowed to return home to North King St.
21 Colonel Eoghan O'Neill, 'The Battle of Dublin 1916', p. 219.
22 NA, Michael Staines, Statement to the Bureau of Military History, WS 284, p. 17.
23 Sean McLoughlin, 'Heritage of Easter Week', *Irish Worker*, 19-4-24
24 'Inside the GPO', by the Two Participants, in Roger McHugh (ed), *Dublin 1916*, (London: 1976) p. 201.
25 Sean McLoughlin, 'Heritage of Easter Week'.
26 Peter De Rosa, *Rebels*, (London: 1991) p. 345; Ryan, *The Rising*, pp. 146-7.
27 Sean McLoughlin, 'Memories of Easter Rising 1916', p. 10.
28 Thomas Coffey, *Agony at Easter*, (London: 1970) p. 207.

29 NA, Sean McLoughlin, p. 21.
30 Sean McLoughlin, 'Memories of Easter Rising 1916', p. 12.
31 Ibid.
32 NA, Sean McLoughlin, p. 21.
33 Interview with Jim Ryan, RTE, 14-4-1966
34 Ibid., p. 22.
35 Roddy Connolly interview, RTE, 14-4-1966; this point was also made by Ross Connolly (Roddy's son) in an interview with the author, 9-4-2002.
36 Jim Ryan, interview, RTE 14-4-1966.
37 Max Caulfield, *the Easter Rebellion,* (Dublin: 1963) p. 260.
38 Frank Henderson, *Frank Henderson's Easter Rising,* (Cork: 1998), p. 63.
39 Caulfield, *The Easter Rebellion,* p. 261.
40 Sean McLoughlin, 'Memories of the Easter Rising 1916', pp. 13-14.
41 NA, Sean McLoughlin, p. 23.
42 NA, Sean McLoughlin, p. 23; NLI, Seamus Scully, 'Moore Street 1916', paper to the Old Dublin Society 14-12-83, part of uncatalogued segment of Hanna Sheehy Skeffington papers; Interview with Ross Connolly 9-4-2002; Prionsas Mac Aonghusa, 'The leader that history has forgotten', in *Seven Days: The Sunday Independent Easter Rising Commemorative Supplement,* 17 April 1966.
43 NA, Sean McLoughlin, p. 24.
44 Ibid.
45 Joe Good, *Enchanted Dreams,* (Dingle: 1996), p. 61.
46 NA, Sean McLoughlin, p. 27.
47 Ibid.
48 NA, Seamus Robinson, Statement to the Bureau of Military History, WS 156.
49 Conor Kostick/Lorcan Collins, *the Easter Rising 1916,* (Dublin: 2000), p. 119.
50 NA, Sean McLoughlin, p. 28, also Coffey, *Agony at Easter,* pp. 233-42.
51 NA, Sean McLoughlin, p. 30.
52 NA, Sean McLoughlin, p. 29.
53 NA, Sean McLoughlin, p. 31.
54 Joe Good, *Enchanted Dreams,* p. 64.
55 Ibid., p. 72.
56 Ibid., p. 73.
57 NA, Sean McLoughlin, p. 32.
58 Sean McLoughlin, 'Memories of the Easter Rising 1916'.

59 Ibid.
60 NA, Sean McLoughlin, p. 34.
61 I am obliged to Sean McLoughlin's family for this information.
62 For more on this atrocity, and the half-hearted military inquiry that followed it, see Charles Townshend, *The Easter Rebellion* , pp. 292-294.
63 Sean McLoughlin, 'Memories of the Easter Rising 1916', p. 19.
64 *Evening Herald*, 24-5-1966.

3

The Emergence of a Socialist Republican, 1917-1921

Introduction

The years 1917-21 saw the onset of the Irish Revolution. The British State in Ireland would be rocked to its foundations during this period by a series of explosive challenges from the forces of both labour and republicanism. At several points during this period, it looked as though there could be no future for British rule in Ireland, and that an independent Irish Republic would be the outcome. These years would also prove to be crucially important for Sean McLoughlin. It was during them that his politics moved further in a socialist direction. As a result, his objective was no longer merely an independent Irish republic, but a socialist Irish republic. In consequence, McLoughlin developed a critique of Irish nationalism that focused on the class interests of those at the head of the independence struggle. In line with the ideas of James Connolly, McLoughlin adopted a class analysis, and argued that this leadership was hamstrung by British imperialism and would eventually seek to compromise with it. Only through socialism, McLoughlin argued, could Irish republicans achieve their objectives. McLoughlin would also become strongly influenced by the new revolutionary socialist thinking that began to spread throughout Europe following the Bolshevik revolution in October 1917. Before long he would be playing a leading role in both the Irish and British communist movements, and would be attempting to develop greater unity of action between them.

Return to Dublin

McLoughlin was amongst those released in December 1916, and arrived home in Dublin just following Christmas. The returning prisoners received a warm welcome from the crowds, showing that there was already a considerable degree of support amongst the population both for them and for what they stood for. This would soon be felt in the political field. After his return, McLoughlin had a period of rest and recuperation. He appeared to become ill as a result of prison, suffering from what he later termed a 'weakness of the left lung'.[1] McLoughlin was unable to work because of this, prompting his family to apply for financial assistance from the newly formed Irish National Aid and Volunteer Dependent's Fund. This had been set up in 1916 to provide aid to the families of the executed, dead, injured and imprisoned of the Rising. McLoughlin's family, however, do not appear to have received aid from this organization. His application was noted, along with the comment that he was suffering from a 'weakness and not wounded', but there is no mention of any money being paid out to him or his family.[2]

At around the same time, McLoughlin's brother Danny was blinded permanently in a mustard gas attack at the Battle of Passchendaele. Married just a few months earlier to childhood sweetheart Mary Jessop, he was now, at the age of just twenty-three, forced to contemplate the rest of his life with the most restricting of disabilities. Danny McLoughlin returned to Ireland soon after and was trained by the St Dunstan's organization, which had been set up to provide such assistance to blind ex-servicemen. By all accounts a quite vivacious character, he would later form a band that would become a well-known fixture in dance halls around Ireland and would even try his hand as a magician. His decision to join the British army in the first place, however, and his apparently consistent anti-IRA outlook, resulted in him being shunned by the rest of the family for the remainder of his life. The only exception here appears to have been Sean McLoughlin himself who, it would seem, did continue to have a relationship with his older brother after his return to Ireland. Sean McLoughlin was the most politically committed republican of his family, but this retention of a friendship with Danny is not as surprising as it might appear given the affinity they had had with each other from early boyhood and the apparent support that Danny expressed for the Labour movement.

After recovery from his own illness, McLoughlin began to re-involve himself in political activity. His first contact was with Michael Collins, who was already emerging as the leading figure within the republican re-organisation process. Collins suggested that McLoughlin should help restore the Fianna, pending re-involvement in the Volunteers itself. At the 1917 Fianna Convention, held in a St Enda's that had been 'torn to bits' by the British, McLoughlin was elected Commandant-General of the organization.[3] But McLoughlin's actual activity within the Fianna was minimal. At around the same time, he was re-initiated into the IRB. The threads that had been broken in 1916 were rapidly being repaired. The objective situation now, however, was very different. In February 1917, the father of executed Joseph Plunkett defeated the Irish Parliamentary Party at a by-election in Roscommon. It was the clearest sign yet that the long hegemony of home-rule nationalism was coming to an end.

Labour sidelined

The Labour movement had an opportunity at this stage to emerge as the leading political force in Ireland. That it did not do so was due partly to the outlook and programme of its leadership. At the first post-Rising gathering of Labour, the Irish Trades Union Congress and Labour Party (ITUCLP) Conference of August 1916, Labour leader Tom Johnson played the music of the future when he mourned the loss of James Connolly as a friend, but refused to discuss the motivations that had led him to the GPO. 'This is not a place to enter into a discussion as to the right or wrong, wisdom or folly of the revolt'. Johnson went on to compare those who had died during the Rising with British troops killed during the war, and concluded his address with a clear message of support for the British war effort, linking the victory of the British with the cause of freedom and liberty the world over.[4]

Johnson was an English socialist of ILP vintage, who shared many of the preconceptions extant within the socialist movement of that country. He adopted a mechanical approach to the relationship between nationalism and socialism and regarded the existence of a national question as an unfortunate problem to be dealt with by other agencies, as opposed to a reality that had to be faced and solved by socialists. As O'Connor put it, Johnson 'assumed a tension between nationalism and socialism' and treated Ireland's right to self-determination 'as if it were an item of foreign policy'.[5] Johnson's political approach, and that of ITGWU supremo William O'Brien, who counterposed the construction of a strong union to involvement in the national struggle, as opposed to combining it in the fashion of Connolly, was arguably one that both weakened the Labour movement and allowed Sinn Fein – almost moribund in 1916 but reorganised in 1917 – to assume a position of unrivalled leadership within the national struggle.

McLoughlin and the rebuilding of the Irish Volunteers

After meeting again with Collins, during which Collins expressed his own concerns about McLoughlin's health, McLoughlin was dispatched to the north of Ireland. His task was to investigate the potential for a reorganisation of the Volunteers. McLoughlin stayed in Newcastle, County Down and lodged with Bella Burns, aunt of Garry Holohan. From there he visited Belfast, where he made contact with Rory Haskins and IRB President Denis McCullough. McLoughlin was not overly optimistic about Volunteer prospects in the north, but soon had to leave in any case: after addressing what he believed was a private gathering at St Mary's Hall in Belfast, he learned that a warrant had been issued for his arrest. He was soon back in Dublin.[6]

McLoughlin contacted Collins on his return and arranged to meet him in Harcourt Street. On this occasion he took along with him James Connolly's son, Roddy. Roddy Connolly, five years McLoughlin's junior, was also a veteran of the Rising and had become acquainted with McLoughlin through membership of the Fianna. Connolly's recollections of that meeting are interesting and provide a glimpse of the relationship that existed between McLoughlin and Collins. As Connolly and many others have pointed out, Collins had an aggressive and robust personality which left those he encountered 'either all for or all against him'.[7] Garry Holohan's comment about Collins – that he was no more than a 'rude, bouncing bully'[8] – would certainly seem to back up the Connolly summation. McLoughlin, however, belonged to the former camp. According to Connolly, McLoughlin and Collins were good friends to the point that it seemed more a case of 'mutual admiration'. McLoughlin was willing to ignore 'any weakness or madcap deficiency' in Collins' make-up, so impressed was he by the 'tireless energy' and organizational ability of the man. Collins, for his part, remembered the role McLoughlin played during the Rising, and defended his right to the rank of Commandant against those volunteers who had tried to belittle or minimize the significance of McLoughlin's Easter Week promotion.[9]

The meeting, at which Harry Boland may also have been in attendance, was called to discuss reorganisation plans for the South. Although pointing out that he was 'a Dublin jackeen, who wouldn't know one end of a cow from the other', Collins asked McLoughlin to be O/C representing GHQ in this task.[10] McLoughlin soon left for the South. Before beginning his reorganisation work he accompanied Constance Markievicz on a short speaking tour in county Clare. This was a few months after de Valera's victory in East Clare, which further underlined the changes taking place within nationalist politics.[11]

Following on from his tour with Markievicz, McLoughlin travelled to Tipperary and began his work. He contacted Frank McGrath, a leading republican in the area and himself already beginning the rebuilding process in the north of the county.[12] McGrath, who was also a senior county hurler, found McLoughlin lodgings in Nenagh. McLoughlin remained there six months and during this time he helped organise Volunteer companies from the Limerick border through to Templemore and Toomevara. There McLoughlin worked with 'Wedger' Maher, another famous hurler and captain of the local Toomevara Volunteers. McLoughlin's method of organizing was to bring together a group of potential recruits, address them on the aims and objectives of the organization, drill them and teach them military formations, appoint officers, conduct training operations, and forward the affiliation fee, 10/- per company, to Dublin.[13]

McLoughlin enjoyed success in his work but ran into serious difficulty in January 1918. This happened as a result of a botched arms raid at the house of a British soldier named Sheehan, near Nenagh. The plan was to steal Sheehan's rifle after he had left his house. Unknown to the three Volunteers who carried out the raid, however, Sheehan's father, a 76-year-old ex-soldier, was in the house. After the three entered the property, a struggle broke out, leading to the old man being shot dead.[14] The shooting brought a swift reaction from the RIC and British army, almost crippling Volunteer activity in the area. McLoughlin, although not involved in the actual raid, had authorized it, and was by now a figure well-known to the military authorities in the area. Aware that he was in all probability a wanted man, he left Tipperary and returned to Dublin for a period, in order to let the situation calm down.

After a short spell in Dublin, during which he was appointed by Collins as a full-time Volunteer organizer, McLoughlin returned to Tipperary. This time, though, he based himself in Thurles and set about organizing mid-Tipperary. McLoughlin made contact with James Leahy, who was O/C of the Second Tipperary Brigade. Leahy would become a good friend of McLoughlin. On 10 February 1918, McLoughlin attended a large Gaelic league gathering in Drombane and, in a 'trenchant address', urged the young men gathered to 'join the national army and not stand idly by in shameful cowardice whilst Ireland's cause needed defending'.[15] Three weeks later he delivered a lecture on the Easter Rising at the town hall in Nenagh, which 'was eagerly followed by a large audience and loudly applauded all through'.[16] Again, though, during this spell McLoughlin had to go on the run. This was after the British military prohibited drilling, effectively outlawing the work he was involved in so openly. A local RIC Inspector, the appropriately named D.I. Hunt, made several unsuccessful attempts to arrest McLoughlin.

McLoughlin, the Volunteers and the threat of conscription

McLoughlin had what he termed a 'short holiday' in Dublin following this, but was soon back organizing in South Tipperary.[17] This period of work coincided with the peaking of the conscription crisis. This had been a growing concern for some time in Ireland, as the British state braced itself for one final offensive on the Western Front. On 16 April, a bill was passed in the Commons extending conscription to Ireland. Implementation of the act, however, was delayed after a mass, one-day general strike, observed throughout most of the country with the notable exceptions of Belfast and Derry, forced the British into retreat. The strike was organized by the labour leadership and was an exemplary display of working-class power. As such, though, it tended to highlight the more general failings of that leadership and its inability, or unwillingness, to claim for labour an ongoing central and commanding role in the national struggle.

McLoughlin took the threat of conscription seriously. He organized a conference of all the Volunteer units he had helped establish from North Tipperary to Cork and East Limerick to Waterford. In order to bluff the British authorities, he organized a series of meetings in various towns, whilst secretly instructing the Volunteers to proceed to Thurles. A large meeting in Tipperary town, at which he was billed to speak, was the main cover for this and a letter was read out on his behalf, urging all young Irishmen to join the Volunteers.[18] McLoughlin held his conference of Volunteer officers in the Sinn Fein Hall in Thurles, which was located behind Connell's pub, where Leahy worked. He then held a large parade of over 1000 Volunteers through Main St in Thurles. There he addressed the organization and, brandishing a revolver, asserted, 'only in this way can we prevent the British from making slaves of us'.[19]

McLoughlin drew up a detailed military plan to oppose conscription. Feeling that any attempt to resist the British in open combat 'could only lead to disaster', given their formidable military resources, McLoughlin advocated the establishment of smaller, more mobile guerilla units. At a conference of all company officers held in Galbally during the summer of 1918, McLoughlin outlined his idea of how the units would operate. All companies and battalions would be broken up into groups of around forty men and further divided into two groups of twenty. These sub-groups would each have different responsibilities; one would be tasked with quarter mastering, first aid and demolition duties, the other, armed and mobile, would seek to engage the British in hit and run tactics.[20] Liam Manahan, the O/C of the Galtee Battalion, worked with McLoughlin during this period, and remembered him as a 'good organizer [with] a good deal of military training, gained through his involvement in the Fianna'. At the same time, however, Manahan also recalled that McLoughlin's urgent manner 'did not always appeal to the rather easy going countrymen', and that some of his ideas were seen 'as a bit too spectacular'.[21]

Manahan took McLoughlin's plans to the Volunteer executive in Dublin, but they appeared to meet with a cool response.[22] McLoughlin met with the executive himself soon after and outlined the details. Nobody objected and no alternatives were offered, but concerns were expressed about one aspect of it, namely the seizure of all privately held arms. McLoughlin had already authorized such a policy in South Tipperary. It was proving controversial but, whilst recognizing it was open to abuse, McLoughlin defended the policy, seeing in it the only way for many Volunteers to get the necessary arms. McLoughlin was also asked what he proposed to do about the threat of aeroplanes and tanks, a question to which he replied that that was as much the leadership's problem as his. In any case, there were, he felt, 'ways and means' to at least meet the problem of tanks. No conclusions were reached and McLoughlin left the meeting dissatisfied and of the opinion that he would have to solve all of these problems himself. Before leaving Dublin he met with Collins, who informed him that in the event of conscription he would be appointed O/C for the entire South Tipperary, North Cork and East Limerick area.[23]

McLoughlin returned to South Tipperary and set up HQ in a small house above the Galtees. He appointed Manahan as Adjutant of the area and placed Con Maloney, Denis Lacey (later killed during the Civil War by Free State troops) and Dan Breen in charge of Tipperary town. By the summer of 1918, however, the conscription crisis was passing, as the British government, aware of the ferocious reaction it would provoke, recognised its inability to enforce it. With its passing, Volunteer activity slackened. But the threat of the measure and the campaign it led to had strengthened tremendously the demand and movement for republican independence, in the process weakening further British rule in Ireland. It had also been another important period for McLoughlin and one where his leadership skills had been further developed. His activities in Tipperary and Limerick are valuable in that they show clearly the actual methods by which the Volunteer organization rebuilt itself following 1916.[24] Significant, too, was the military plan he formulated to resist conscription. It represented one of the earliest attempts by an Irish Volunteer to map out a new strategy based on the principles of guerrilla warfare. Also important was McLoughlin's idea of deploying smaller units. He made it clear that he was opposed to the reformation of the larger brigades and battalions, which again were more designed for the type of set piece engagements won by the British during Easter week.

Towards the end of 1918, McLoughlin fell victim to the raging influenza epidemic that killed millions throughout Europe. Believed to be in a 'dying condition', he was taken to North Brunswick St hospital, where he remained until after the close of the war.[25] McLoughlin did pull through but was left in a weakened condition from which it took several weeks to recover. As such, he missed out in the general election campaign, held in the immediate aftermath of the war, and which resulted in a spectacular victory for Sinn Fein; 73 of the available 106 seats were scooped up by the Republicans, exposing the scale of the crisis now facing British rule in Ireland.

After recovery, McLoughlin had a spell organising in Leitrim, before returning to Dublin around the beginning of March 1919. He was arrested soon afterwards, on the day after a republican rally in the Mansion House, held to commemorate Robert Emmet. The rally had been well advertised, with highlights including a performance by Frank Mullings, a world-famous tenor.[26] Following Mullings' third or fourth song, Sean McGarry appeared on stage. McGarry had recently escaped from Lincoln jail along with de Valera, and his appearance was the cue for the G men in the crowd to start making arrests. Two G men, Bruton, again, and Hoey (who had pointed out Sean MacDiarmada to the British in Richmond Barracks in 1916, and who would be shot dead in September 1919 as a result on Collins' orders), tried to arrest McLoughlin, but were thwarted when he produced a revolver. They picked him up the following day, however, at his home in St Ignatius Avenue and brought him to the Bridewell.

McLoughlin was charged with conducting an illegal assembly and making a seditious speech in county Tipperary. At the trial, held before Justice Swifte, RIC Sergeant Donohoe testified that on 11 April 1918 McLoughlin had drilled a party of '48 or 50 men', near the village of Bansha, at which he 'used words of command of a military character', and explained to the men 'how they were to fire and retire'. Moreover, McLoughlin was alleged to have declared 'England will not win the war, England is beaten…if England conscripts us we shall resist, and the day England fires the first shot, we will shoot too'. McLoughlin was remanded for sentencing and reacted angrily ordering Swifte to 'cut the farce out' and deliver the sentence. After this outburst, a young girl in the gallery applauded McLoughlin, much to Swifte's displeasure.[27] He eventually was to receive a two month sentence to be served at Mountjoy.

Shortly after beginning his sentence, McLoughlin was examined by a doctor and sent to hospital. Once more his lung problem had reappeared. Despite this, McLoughlin went on hunger strike, along with the rest of the Republican prisoners in Mountjoy.[28] After his release, McLoughlin visited Michael Collins who, shocked at his poor physical appearance, took him immediately to a doctor in Merrion Square. The doctor advised McLoughlin to travel to California, which he said was the only place where proper treatment for his condition was available. Collins insisted that McLoughlin heed this advice, but McLoughlin decided to remain in Ireland for the time being.[29]

The Limerick Soviet

During McLoughlin's stint in jail a momentous event had occurred in Limerick that contrasted the considerable power of Irish labour with the timidity of its leadership. Limerick was Ireland's fourth largest city with an economy based largely on food processing. A recruitment drive by the ITGWU within these industries had brought in around 3000 new members, radicalizing the stance of the local Trades Council. In 1918, Limerick workers had celebrated May Day for the first time, with around 15,000 taking part in the parades.[30] Republicanism was also on the rise, with around 4500 Sinn Fein members and 1600 Volunteers in the city.

After the British authorities declared Limerick a Special Military Area, forcing all people to obtain special permits, the trades Council called a general strike. The call received 100 per cent support and the entire running of the city's life passed into the hands of the strike committee. This included the printing of its own currency, a move that, as one writer remarked, 'places Limerick in a unique position in labour history'.[31] Workers rule was now a reality in Limerick, with the British state powerless to prevent it. As the importance of Limerick became greater, so too did the pressure on the labour leadership to broaden out the struggle. Tom Johnson hinted that this might happen, when he spoke of how 'it was no longer a Limerick fight, but a fight of workers against military domination and imperial forces'.[32] Also, two days before the soviet was established, the Labour party journal *The Voice of Labour* had expressed its support for this type of structure. 'Again, we say Ireland's best and most effective answer is the immediate establishment of the Soviets, the instruments which will bring about the dictatorship of the Irish proletariat'.[33] Despite these sentiments, however, such action was not forthcoming. The Limerick leaders wanted a national general strike, but this demand, necessary to the soviet's survival, was rejected by the labour leaders and after fourteen days the soviet was wound down. Another opportunity to place Irish workers at the centre of the independence struggle had passed.

The move towards socialism

It is now, in the early spring of 1919, that the first clear evidence of socialism can be seen in McLoughlin's thoughts and actions. During this period, McLoughlin joined the Socialist Party of Ireland (SPI). As we have noted, McLoughlin's father was an ITGWU activist and may well have influenced him in a socialist direction from a young age. At the very least Ruggie McLoughlin must have developed in his son, indeed in all of his children, support for the Labour movement and the struggles of the working class.

We have also seen how Paddy Stephenson noted that McLoughlin had 'identified' with Larkin during the Dublin Lockout. Stephenson further maintained that McLoughlin, in joining the SPI in 1919, 'was returning to his old allegiance'.[34] This suggests a longer-standing commitment to socialism on McLoughlin's behalf. But whilst all of this points to the conclusion that McLoughlin was a socialist long before 1919, it is here in the early spring of that year that we see for the first time evidence of this commitment in McLoughlin's own words and actions. It is from this point, therefore, that Sean McLoughlin's involvement in socialist politics can properly be dated.

In March 1919, just before his arrest McLoughlin penned a letter to the *Socialist*, newspaper of the Glasgow-based Socialist Labour Party (SLP). In it, he defended James Connolly's involvement in the Rising and maintained that had it been successful, there could be 'no possible doubt' that it would have marked 'the first victory in the world for a socialist republic'. The remainder of McLoughlin's letter showed just how marked the influence of socialist ideology had become on McLoughlin's thinking:

> Most of us who fought in 1916 are still carrying on, never to cease until we have established the co-operative commonwealth controlled by the workers for the workers and doing all in our power to lend a hand to all who struggle with us for the overthrow of reaction and capitalism.[35]

McLoughlin concluded his letter by wishing the SLP 'every success' for the future.

The Socialist Labour Party and the development of communism in Ireland

The SLP were a revolutionary socialist organization. James Connolly had been the party's first national organizer and chaired its foundation conference in 1903.[36] This was following a split in the Social Democratic Federation that had its roots in the question of socialist involvement in capitalist governments. Inspired initially by the industrial unionism of Daniel de Leon's American SLP, the party was doctrinaire and had difficulty in working with other, less pure, socialist organizations. During the War, however, the SLP was transformed and, through its ceaseless activity, found for itself a place at the head of the most militant section of the British working class.

SLP leaders like Arthur McManus, (who had led an important strike at Singer's sewing machine factory in 1911, one of the few disputes organized by the syndicalist Industrial Workers of Great Britain union[37]) and Willie

Paul and Tom Bell (both of whom had been active with Connolly when the SLP was founded), all held leading positions within the Clyde Workers' Committee (CWC). The CWC had been set up in 1915, and was the most significant rank-and-file workers organization in wartime Britain. It led many strikes and protests, both against the war and in support of wage increases for those workers involved in the munitions industries, which dominated Clydeside. During these years the SLP activists worked closely with other socialists, notably Willie Gallacher, and the outstanding figure within the Scottish socialist movement, John MacLean. This helped the party to slough off its previous isolationist approach and allowed it to develop strongly.[38]

This process was also aided by the party's Marxist education classes, which were a hallmark of Clydeside wartime socialist agitation. So popular were these classes that it was estimated that more workers were attending them than there were students attending university in Glasgow.[39] In addition, there was the impact of the 1917 Bolshevik Revolution. Unlike many other socialist organizations, the SLP had supported the Bolsheviks before they took power and, at a time when the Kerensky government was popular in the eyes of many left wing bodies throughout Europe.[40] In the aftermath of October, the SLP became increasingly influenced by Bolshevik thinking, and began to discuss new theories such as that of the role of the revolutionary party. This soon led to negotiations with other British socialists with a view to creating such an organization in Britain. The party press in Glasgow also reproduced many Marxist classics and, in May 1918, became the first British publisher of a translated Bolshevik work when it published Trotsky's *War or Revolution*.[41]

Bolshevik theory may have sat uneasily with de Leonism, considering the different role each accorded to the political party, but both were discernible in the thinking of the SLP in, and for some members far beyond, the 1918-19 period. They were also visible in the outlook of McLoughlin. In June 1919, McLoughlin authored an article in the *Voice of Labour* entitled a 'New Programme for the Socialist Party'. The new measures advocated industrial unionism 'in order to prepare the foundation of the economic life of the Workers' Republic'; a broadening of the role of the party to include that of seizing political power – 'we refuse absolutely to accept that the functions of a socialist party are purely educational'; and the establishment of a socialist press, 'owned and controlled by the workers to propagate the ideas and principles of revolutionary action'.[42] All of these measures were strongly influenced by traditional, and current, trends in SLP thinking.

It is difficult to ascertain how or by what means the SLP began to influence

McLoughlin. There were strong links between the party and Ireland; not only had Connolly helped to found it, but the *Socialist* provided regular coverage of political developments in Ireland and occasionally provided speakers. It is possible that this contact between the SLP and Irish revolutionaries may have introduced McLoughlin to the party and stimulated an interest in its ideas. A more satisfactory explanation, however, lies in McLoughlin's association with Roddy Connolly. As we have seen, McLoughlin regarded Connolly highly enough to take him to a meeting with Michael Collins in 1917. Roddy Connolly, like McLoughlin, had also joined the SPI. In 1918 he went to work in Glasgow and whilst there became strongly influenced by the SLP. Connolly befriended prominent SLP leaders like McManus, Paul, and Tom Clark, all of whom had been disciples of his father. Clark, who lived in Bridgeton and was a leading shop steward in the Parkhead Forge where Connolly worked, was said to have had a 'considerable influence' over the young man. He was also chairman of Connolly's engineering union branch.[43] Russian Bolshevik thinking had had a powerful impact on the SLP by this stage, and when Connolly returned to Ireland in the spring of 1919, he was fired up with a determination to spread the new gospel within the ranks of the SPI. It is possible, therefore, that Connolly was the conduit between other young socialist radicals like McLoughlin and the new revolutionary socialist thinking that was spreading through Europe, and which had been adopted by the SLP.

It is also possible that McLoughlin accompanied Connolly, at least for a spell, during the latter's time in Glasgow. The actual evidence for this is patchy but, according to one source, McLoughlin was in Glasgow with Connolly during these months.[44] As we will see, it does seem certain that McLoughlin was there at some point during 1918-19, although exactly when or with whom, if anyone, he travelled remains unclear. McLoughlin made no mention of any of this in his account to the Bureau of Military History, but this in itself is far from conclusive; he also omitted a later extended spell spent in Glasgow in 1920. It is also the case that McLoughlin's account is threadbare from the passing of the conscription crisis in the summer of 1918, to his illness around November 1918. Certainly, this is the only period he could have been away, and it coincides, in part, with the period Connolly was there. If McLoughlin linked up with Connolly in Glasgow during these months, then he too would have been exposed to and influenced directly by the SLP and the explosion of working-class militancy and socialist ideas on Clydeside throughout that year.

The Rise of the Irish Bolsheviks

Released from prison in early May 1919, McLoughlin and the recently returned Connolly soon organized a Bolshevik faction within the SPI. The aim was to seize control of the party, transform it into a revolutionary organization, and affiliate it to the Communist International (Comintern), set up by Moscow in March 1919. The two also joined the ICA during this period, with the intention of transforming it into a genuine Irish red guard. On 19 May 1919, Connolly was accepted into the army,[45] followed by McLoughlin seven days later.[46] But the task of inducing militancy into the ICA was difficult. Once a workers' army, and fighting with great distinction during Easter 1916, the ICA degenerated rapidly in the post-rising period, and became for some more of a 'social club'[47] than a socialist militia.

McLoughlin, who was far more involved in the ICA than Connolly, proposed various ideas in order to jolt the organization back into revolutionary activity. He offered to conduct military instructions for the members,[48] proposed the abolition of the ruling army council, suggesting it be replaced by an elected HQ Staff, and mooted that the army begin conducting manoevres in the open.[49] All of these ideas were rejected by an ICA leadership that appeared also to have abandoned the place gained for it by Connolly at the head of the independence struggle.

McLoughlin had more success in the SPI. He and Connolly were named amongst the organizers of a James Connolly birthday commemoration event in June 1919.[50] The rally was due to take place at the Mansion House, but was proscribed by the British at the last minute. The day was saved, however, when the organizers moved it to the Trades Hall in Capel Street.[51] McLoughlin could well have been part of the armed ICA guard that was dispatched to secure this replacement venue. The Connolly commemoration was the biggest public event the SPI had organized since its re-formation in 1917, and encouraged the communists to step up their activities.

The following month saw McLoughlin, Connolly and a third member of the faction, Michael O'Leary, elected onto the SPI executive at the half-yearly party Conference.[52] McLoughlin was also installed as chairman of the party propaganda committee. The committee's task was to 'wage a vigorous campaign' in the form of meetings and lectures.[53] It was soon active. Both John MacLean and Arthur McManus were promptly invited to address SPI public meetings.[54] McLoughlin spoke at the MacLean meeting, and his contribution impressed the Scottish socialist, who remarked in his Glasgow newspaper that McLoughlin had 'fought through the rebellion' and was a 'true follower' of James Connolly.[55]

Soon after this, McLoughlin also addressed large and successful SPI recruitment meetings in Naas and Newbridge.[56] This burst of activity culminated in McLoughlin being elected President of the SPI in September.[57] In addition, a decision was taken by the party to affiliate to the Comintern.[58] November saw McLoughlin's status as party president underlined when he chaired a large rally in the Trades Hall, organized by the SPI to mark the second anniversary of the Bolshevik Revolution. At that rally, McLoughlin 'dealt with the present position in Russia and the manner in which a European revolution would affect Ireland.'[59] This was the second SPI event of the weekend. On the previous evening the party HQ, 42 North Great George's Street, was host to an all-night social and dance to celebrate the Russian Revolution. There, McLoughlin delivered an address on the Bolshevik triumph to a large audience of families and friends.[60]

An Irish socialist in Scotland

McLoughlin, however, did not remain long in his new SPI post. Around November- December, he travelled to Glasgow to undertake a speaking tour that had been organized by the SPI and the Clydeside socialists, possibly the CWC.[61] It was a sudden departure as, simultaneously, McLoughlin had been named as one of two SPI candidates for the January local elections.[62] He was penciled in for the Mountjoy ward, whilst Walter Carpenter was selected for Fitzwilliam. Ultimately, Carpenter would be the sole SPI candidate. In his absence, McLoughlin lost his position as party president to Cathal O'Shannon.[63] This appears to have been the result of a determined effort on behalf of the former leaders within the party to regain control. All of the left-wingers lost their places on the party executive, including Connolly, who had accompanied McLoughlin to Glasgow. It was a damaging blow for the SPI Bolsheviks and meant that the party was once more headed by a leadership which, although sympathetic to Russia, balked at the two demands of the left: the formation of a revolutionary party and affiliation to the Comintern.

There was another factor behind McLoughlin's departure. On 7 January 1920, he married 21 year-old Isabella Barr at Oswald St registry office in Glasgow. Connolly was his best man and, along with SLP activist EG Carr, one of the two specified witnesses to the event.[64] It is not clear where or when McLoughlin met Barr, whose father was a wealthy businessman but may also have been involved in socialist politics. Although not impossible, it is extremely unlikely that the marriage would have been the result of a whirlwind romance begun when McLoughlin arrived in Glasgow just a few weeks earlier. This, of course, adds weight to the possibility that McLoughlin did spend some time in Glasgow with Connolly a year or so earlier, perhaps meeting his future wife whilst there, and establishing through Connolly direct links with the Socialist Labour Party. Certainly, it suggests very strongly that the trip to Glasgow in late 1919 was not his first to the city.

McLoughlin's speaking tour lasted until the summer of 1920. During this time, he and his new bride lived in Downs St, Springburn in Glasgow. Connolly was there for the first week or two, and between 5-11 January they addressed a string of meetings in Glasgow, Paisley and Duntocher.[65] This included a very large gathering at Main St in the Gorbals, alongside Willie Gallacher of the CWC. At the first of these meetings, held in Kingston Halls, Paisley, McLoughlin insisted that Ireland was 'ready for revolt' but would be unable to maintain her freedom as long as a 'fully armed and powerful capitalist state' was 'crouched on her rear, ready to crush her'. 'We must bring about the workers' republic not only in Ireland but in Great Britain,' he continued, 'and it is the duty of every Irishman to get into every revolutionary organization in Great Britain to bring about the overthrow of the capitalist system'.[66] The basic theme of this speech, which stressed the link between the revolutionary struggles in Ireland and Britain, was one that would inform much of McLoughlin's activity in the months ahead.

These initial meetings McLoughlin addressed were organized by the Irish Labour Party, Glasgow (IrLP G) which had been recently formed. The IrLP G was an independent body and not under the authority of the party in Dublin. But, like the Irish Labour Party itself, it married a verbal commitment to socialism with an acceptance of and deference to, Sinn Fein as the rightful leaders of the national struggle. The new party welcomed the large crowds and finance that the McLoughlin/Connolly meetings had brought it, with branch secretary James McAuley anticipating an 'augmentation of membership' as a result.[67] And he was not to be disappointed. In the aftermath of the tour, branches of the party were set up in Cowcaddens, Shettleston and Paisley.[68]

This connection between Irish revolutionaries and Scottish socialists did not go unnoticed by the authorities. As we have seen, the Directorate of Intelligence had already observed the 'negotiations' between the two that had brought 'extremists' from Ireland to Glasgow. The British state was worried about these developments. It was aware of the strength of the workers' movement in Glasgow, and also considered that city to be 'the most dangerous center of Sinn Fein activity in Britain'.[69] In December 1919 it had noted with concern how, amongst a crowd of 5000 'extremists' in Glasgow attending a 'Hands off Russia' event, there was a large number of 'Sinn Feiners'.[70] This link between the Irish and British revolutionaries was personified in McLoughlin's work and over the next few months a close watch was kept on him and his 'notoriously violent' speeches.[71]

McLoughlin joined the IrLP (G). Before long, however, divisions became evident between him and the leadership. These related to a parliamentary by-election, which was held in Paisley in February 1920. Liberal leader Asquith, who had been Prime Minister of the wartime coalition government until December 1916, but had subsequently lost his seat at the 1918 election, stood in Paisley, hopeful of securing a quick return to the Commons. Paisley was a town with a large Irish population. It was estimated by one source that it contained around 5,000 catholic voters, the majority of whom were 'directly associated with or closely identified in the future of Irish politics'.[72] McLoughlin intervened in the campaigning and in his pre-election propaganda meetings in Paisley he savaged Asquith as an imperialist, noting how his hands 'were red with the blood of Connolly and Pearse', and concluding that 'only a reptile of the lowest order' would vote for him.[73] But unlike the IrLP (G) leadership, McLoughlin was also opposed to the Labour candidate, John Biggar, and condemned him too in word and print:

> The thing that must be realized by all the advanced elements in the workers' fight is this: that sooner or later the gauge of battle must be thrown down by the revolutionary elements, not only to the Asquiths, Churchills etc., but to their **"smoke screens"** and **apologists**, The [Arthur] Hendersons, [Jimmy] Thomases and the Mr Biggars. Mr Biggar does not believe that there is ever and always an industrial war between the working class and capitalist class...He is too respectable for such things. He is in favour of Labour – **when somebody else does the labour.** He is a Co-operator – and wants the workers to co-operate. Well; we would advise the workers to co-operate – and throw him out along with Asquith and the rest.[74] (McLoughlin's emphasis)

McLoughlin concluded that the SLP should have stood in the election, in order to turn what was a 'little picnic', into a 'real fight'.[75]

This was not the position of the IrLP (G), leadership, who felt that Biggar, as a Labour candidate, should be supported in what appeared a winnable seat.[76] McLoughlin, however, rallied his supporters and at a specially convened meeting on 8 February was elected President of the party. McLoughlin then declared to all gathered that he was 'out for rebellion in Ireland, and if he could manage it, in Scotland as well'.[77] This was a step forward for McLoughlin in his attempts to bring together the two revolutionary struggles, but it was not to last. The old leadership, headed by former Irish clerical workers union executive member William Drew, resented his election. Drew enlisted the support of various, unnamed Sinn Fein leaders back in Dublin, who informed him that they did not 'recognise' McLoughlin, and that he had 'assumed' the title of commander during the Rising 'without authority'.[78]

This action by the Sinn Fein leaders, which is interesting in that it shows how early the process of re-writing the history of the revolutionary period began, was used by Drew in an attempt to discredit McLoughlin. McLoughlin eventually split from the party, but took with him both the Springburn and Duntocher branches in to a new organization that he called the 'Irish Workers Republic Party'.[79] As police intelligence noted, McLoughlin orientated his little organisation towards the SLP, or IWW, as they sometimes called it,[80] suggesting perhaps that this had always been his objective in relation to the IrLP (G) as a whole.

McLoughlin soon became a prominent figure on SLP platforms. March saw him both speak alongside Tom Clark at a mass 'hands off Ireland' meeting held in Clydebank[81] and receive an 'excellent reception' from 'the local extremists' in Edinburgh, following a meeting there.[82] McLoughlin next travelled to the Vale of Leven, just north of Glasgow. This was a town with a vibrant socialist tradition, but one where the main source of employment, textile dyeing, had been ravaged by the post-war economic slump.[83] The Vale of Leven workers had responded to this in fighting fashion, however, by setting up an unemployed organization in 1919. McLoughlin's lecture was on the 'history of the Irish revolt', and they showed their interest in this question too, by turning up for it in large numbers.[84]

In April, McLoughlin attended the Independent Labour Party (ILP) conference, held that year in St Andrews Hall, Glasgow. It was a frustrating experience for him, and in a report he compiled for the *Socialist*, the party leadership were subjected to scathing criticism. After pointing out how Manny Shinwell had opposed ILP affiliation to the CWC, McLoughlin commented bitterly 'the slap on the head he received from a "peeler's baton" during the 40 Hours strike seems to have knocked out all the brains he ever possessed'. Criticised in strong terms too were Ethel Snowden, wife of ILP leader Philip Snowden, 'one felt a strong inclination to sprinkle the hall with Jeyes fluid or Keating's powder once she had finished', and Ramsay MacDonald, whom McLoughlin considered to be 'the most dangerous enemy of socialism in Britain today'.

The reason for McLoughlin's hostility to both McDonald and Snowden was their opposition to ILP affiliation to the Comintern. This was one of the most important questions facing the international socialist movement, and seen by the revolutionaries as an acid test for all organizations and leaderships that claimed to be socialist. Snowden opposed disaffiliation from the Second International which, as will be recalled, had been guilty, in socialist eyes, of national chauvinism and opportunism on the outbreak of war in 1914. She was due to go on a fact-finding mission to Moscow later in the year, but had evidently made up her mind already, regarding the Soviet Republic as neither socialist nor a workers' state. McDonald employed a more sophisticated approach. Sensing the opposition of the delegates to the Second International, he accepted the argument for ILP withdrawal but still opposed affiliation to the Comintern, arguing instead for the establishment of a 'new' International under the leadership of the [Second Internationalist] 'Swiss socialists'.[85] The eventual position adopted was quintessentially ILP; the party decided to withdraw from the Second International, but voted against Comintern affiliation, leaving it in something of a centrist halfway house.

Concluding his report, McLoughlin argued that the decision of the 'sickly, watery, sentimentalist' ILP had serious implications for the socialist movement in Britain:

> To think that after all the propaganda, all the education, all the lessons, all the blood that has been spilt on behalf of socialism, the furthest the ILP could get was a break from the Second International, it makes one almost despair. We are forced almost to the conclusion that socialism will come only to Britain on the points of the invading bayonets of a European Red Guard.[86]

In his public work during this month, McLoughlin delivered a lecture on the 'History of the Dublin Rebellion' at Partick Burgh Halls in Glasgow.[87] A similar lecture was delivered the following week at St Mungo's Halls in Govan.[88] McLoughlin then held a series of public meetings at various locations in Glasgow, including the Gorbals, West Regent St in the City centre, Vulcan St in Springburn, which was close to where he was living, and Steven St.[89] He rounded the month off with a week's work in Paisley.[90] Like Paisley, districts such as the Gorbals and Govan had large Irish immigrant populations, and in most of his speeches McLoughlin's subject matter was the situation in Ireland.

McLoughlin and the Irish and British Revolutions

In addition to this public work, McLoughlin also submitted a series of long articles to the *Socialist*, where he laid out in detail his views on the nature of the Irish revolutionary struggle and its relationship to that for socialist transformation in Britain. In 'Sinn Fein and Socialism' published on 26 February, McLoughlin exposed what he saw as the conflicting class interests locked within the national independence struggle and warned that the question of what class would rule in an Irish Republic would be 'the rock on which Sinn Fein will be wrecked'. McLoughlin pointed out that a capitalist Irish republic would not solve the problems of Irish workers. The revolution, he insisted, would need to go beyond this point, and involve also the economic and social question:

> Many people are consoling themselves today in Ireland, and out of it, with the idea that they have entered the Promised Land. With the taking over of the country by an Irish government, they will receive a rude shock...the working class and the employing class have nothing in common and it will come no easier to an Irish worker to toil for an Irish capitalist under a Republic than it did under a monarchy. Yet all these things can be avoided if in the process of revolution the Irish workers (or that class conscious section of them) are able to accomplish the same task as the Russians, who did not allow their revolution to stop at the point marked by their exploiters.[91]

McLoughlin recognized that the Irish bourgeoisie would resist this, 'we will be bitterly opposed...the fight to overthrow British power in Ireland may not be half as bitterly contested as the fight between the Irish working class and Irish middle class for control of the country'. To meet this, he advocated a dictatorship of the proletariat, pointing out that the bourgeoisie 'true to their class interests' would not 'fall into line', and understood only 'superior force'.[92]

McLoughlin displayed a similar analysis in a report he sent off to the Comintern Sub Bureau in Amsterdam, which was later published as an article in the *Socialist*. Here, his focus was on the various political organizations that dominated both the Republican and socialist movements in Ireland. McLoughlin began by dismissing the leaderships of both Sinn Fein, 'composed solely of people of a bourgeois outlook', and the ICA, 'incompetent...narrow and very reactionary'. Similarly condemned was the leadership of the ITGWU and SPI. It was criticized by McLoughlin both for being sympathetic to the Second International, and for acting as a mere 'tail end' of Sinn Fein. The individuals within this leadership were, McLoughlin claimed, 'more concerned with a big membership and big bank balance', and 'anything but socialists'. The ITGWU rank-and-file, were different, though, and for McLoughlin there were elements there sympathetic to the idea of the workers' republic.

The body that McLoughlin held out the most hope for was the Volunteers, which would soon become the IRA. McLoughlin identified within the organization a rank-and-file with a 'proletarian outlook', few of which were hostile to the goal of the workers' republic. Most, he argued, had contempt for Arthur Griffith 'and the reactionary groups in Sinn Fein', as a result of his support for Murphy during the Lockout. Overall, McLoughlin considered this rank-and-file to be 'the factor' in Irish politics. He felt that they could 'sway Ireland as they wished', and could be won to a position of active support for socialism. 'They are out for a Republic, but if it were once established, the majority could be relied on to see that the Republic would be controlled by the workers.'[93]

McLoughlin's analysis displayed clearly his belief that the national struggle needed to be transformed into a social struggle, in order to free the Irish workers. It was an analysis that sought to expose the class divisions within the national movement, and held out the hope that the proletarian interests of the republican rank-and-file would eventually come to the fore. McLoughlin's analysis explains why, despite his joining the SPI, he was still part of the Volunteer movement. He clearly believed that it was important for socialists to be active in this organization, in order to promote change from within. In fact, in addition to his socialist propaganda activities, McLoughlin may also have been involved in arms smuggling on behalf of the Volunteers during this period.[94] McLoughlin's view, that the rank-and-file of the Volunteers constituted a fertile ground for the development of socialism, would remain central to Irish communist thinking and strategy throughout and beyond the revolutionary period.

On the relationship of the Irish revolutionary struggle to that of the socialist struggle in Britain, McLoughlin was clear; the two were linked together through being directed against the same ruling class. McLoughlin surveyed the ground initially in his article 'Standing up for Ireland'. Here, he bemoaned the fact that there had been no attempt to unite British workers with their counterparts in Ireland, or with Irish immigrant workers in Britain. McLoughlin pointed out that on the conscription issue, 'Ireland had to fight for herself and won', and that so far the independence war had produced a similar story. Looking at Irish immigrant workers in Britain, he argued that historically they had been 'driven from sympathy' with their British counterparts, by the divide and rule tactics of the British bourgeoisie, which pitted them against each other. McLoughlin also considered that criticisms by British workers of the methods used by Irish revolutionaries had been a contributory factor to the negative relationship that existed between the two.

All of this had to change. Both sets of workers had to realize that they needed each other. Irish workers at home and in Britain had to see that there could be no such thing as a free working class in Ireland without a free working class the world over. British workers, on the other hand, had to view the struggle in Ireland in its proper light: as part of the world crisis of capitalism, and directed against the same ruling class that would soon be suppressing their class in Britain.[95]

McLoughlin returned to the question in far more detail in 'Britain and the Struggle in Ireland'. Here, and in line with the views he expressed about the British working class in his ILP Conference report, McLoughlin described Britain as the country where the revolutionary movement was 'least advanced'. He argued, however, that this could be altered if British imperialism was destroyed:

> If the British Empire can be broken up into its component parts and every country under the control of Britain can repudiate the empire and secure its own salvation the resulting economic crisis will precipitate a revolution in Britain.[96]

In no country, McLoughlin continued, was the struggle against imperialism succeeding so well as in Ireland. In line with his earlier views, he believed that this struggle could be turned in a socialist direction, and that a workers' republic was possible. An Irish workers' republic would not only detonate uprisings throughout the Empire and lead to its shattering, but result also in a revolutionary crisis in Britain itself, and one in which Irish immigrant workers would have a role to play. Unless similar developments took place in Britain, the Irish workers republic would not survive:

> If once a workers' republic was established in Ireland, the effect in Britain would be tremendous. It would practically mean that the same thing must occur in Britain. The Irish workers might have to assist in bringing this about… If they were not successful, there would have to be war because Ireland could never exist as a workers republic whilst Britain and America remained in the hands of the capitalist class. There **must be unity of action** between the conscious Irish and British workers, if they are to succeed.[97] (McLoughlin's emphasis)

McLoughlin's argument was neat. Both struggles were linked and both sets of workers needed each other. A workers' revolution in Ireland would help break up the empire and induce a revolutionary crisis within Britain itself, thus strengthening socialist prospects there. It was in the interests of British workers to support in every way possible – and McLoughlin later advocated a British general strike to withdraw troops from Ireland – because by doing so they would be weakening their own class enemy at home. But Irish workers in Britain had to get involved. They too had a vested interest in the struggle for a British workers' republic. The power of British capitalism was such that an Irish workers republic would not survive unless it was overthrown. Therefore Irish workers needed to become active alongside their British counterparts in the fight for socialism in Britain. McLoughlin's work in Britain, therefore, had two purposes; to illustrate to Irish and British workers the true nature of the Irish revolutionary struggle and the need for it to be moved in a socialist direction, and also to hammer home to each set of workers, who were often hostile to each other, the mutuality of the Irish and British struggles, and the need for both to support and get involved in both the Irish and British socialist movements. This desire to link together advanced British workers and Irish immigrants in these struggles can be seen as the reason why McLoughlin devoted so much of his energies to this work in Britain.

Some of the thinking that underpinned this work was extremely innovative. Although the idea that a revolution in Ireland might have a radicalizing effect on the British proletariat was not new, and had been advanced by Marx, what was original was McLoughlin's belief that socialist transformation itself might occur in Ireland before Britain.[98] Whilst conceding that Irish socialism would need the support of British socialism to endure – a position that was internationalist – McLoughlin was convinced that such a revolutionary transformation would occur in Ireland first, and would be a powerful incentive for Irish workers to get involved in the British socialist movement. This was a clear reversal of the more traditional socialist view concerning the sequencing of the Irish and British socialist revolutions. It was indicative of the new thinking spreading through the international socialist movement as a result of the Bolshevik Revolution. October 1917 had shattered the belief that socialist revolution could occur only in advanced capitalist states and eventually brought home to socialists throughout the world the importance of the colonies as springboards to revolution in the metropolitan states. McLoughlin was clearly a pioneer of this view within both the British and Irish socialist movements.

Revolution and counter revolution in Ireland

In May, McLoughlin's activities were halted for a short spell through illness; once more his pulmonary problem had appeared, forcing him to cancel lectures and meetings.[99] After recovery, he returned to Ireland for a brief period. By now the revolutionary crisis was reaching new heights. During 1920, the IRA killed 230 British military personnel,[100] whilst British forces burned parts of Cork, Balbriggan, Mallow, Galway, Tuam, Feakle, Limerick, Templemore, Ennistymon, Lahinch and Milltown-Malbay.[101] The British forces now included the Black and Tans and Auxiliaries, special brigades deployed by Lloyd George to stave off a wholesale collapse of British power in Ireland.

Class struggle raged. Between January and June 1920 there were 864 agrarian 'outrages', provoked mainly by the slowdown in the work of the Congested Districts Board.[102] Spreading from Kerry into Tipperary and up through most of Connacht, Westmeath and Offaly, these 'outrages' took the form of land seizures and the breaking up of large ranches. In Limerick, the Cleeve's creameries were seized and the red flag hoisted over the central factory at Knocklong. Trade union membership grew dramatically; the ITGWU, for example, claimed 130,000 members by the summer of this year.[103] The labour leadership called a general strike to gain the release of the republican prisoners, and a six-month dispute on the railways, directed against the transport of British war material, also occurred.

Counter-revolution, though, was close at hand. The Sinn Fein leaders claimed that 'the common patriotism of all sections [proved] superior to all special class interests',[104] but this was not true. These elements, now representing also those class interests previously upheld by the parliamentary party, might have wished to eschew class struggle, but when it occurred they were forced to respond, and mainly did so to uphold the interests of the landed. This could be seen with the establishment of the Land Courts, set up in 1920. Nominally, these were set up to adjudicate the competing claims of the landed and landless, but in practice they were often used to prevent large scale seizures by the latter and stem an agitation that was sweeping through parts of Ireland 'like a prairie fire'.[105]

The Sinn Fein leaders did support land re-distribution – they had no choice but to support it given the intensity of the agitation – but only to a limited degree and, as far as was possible, under the control of the middle classes. As Fergus Campbell has shown, at a local level the republican organizations, drawn from the most exploited sections of the working class and peasantry, did advocate more radical land reform and took part in activity to this end.[106] For this, however, they were often criticized by their leaders in the

Dail and told to desist.[107] This shows clearly the class tensions and divides that existed within the republican movement. The upshot of this was that in the areas where land hunger and economic marginalisation was at its greatest, the West, active involvement in the independence struggle, headed by Sinn Fein, was weakest. Republican leaders, their verbal sympathy for the plight of Irish labour notwithstanding, also occasionally intervened in strikes against the interests of the workers. One example, criticized by communists, came when republican police forced striking Kilkenny workers to repair a damaged water main.[108] And of course in the north, Sinn Fein's mixture of catholic nationalism and economic protectionism was grist to the mill of the Ulster industrialists, who used it to argue that the interests of the protestant working class, economic and cultural, would perish in an Irish republic.

This power of Orangeism in the north and the support offered to it by the British state constituted itself a second, infinitely more fortified, bulwark of counter-revolution in Ireland. It was one addressed by McLoughlin after that class whipped up a series of anti-catholic riots and pogroms in the summer of 1920. He argued here that the source of the division between catholic and protestant workers lay in ruling class manipulation; just like the US bourgeoisie, which divided workers on the basis of colour, the British ruling class, in India and Ireland, did so on the basis of religion. For McLoughlin, the British ruling class was the most reactionary in the world and the biggest obstacle to the development of socialism globally. Not only had it supported counter-revolution in Germany and Hungary but had physically attacked the fledgling Bolshevik Republic in Russia. Its overthrow would give 'tremendous impetus' to world revolution. But it was precisely because of this that divisions were being sown in Ireland; the threat of revolution in Ireland was what lay behind bourgeois manipulation of a section of the Irish working class; it was the 'greatest fraud and humbug that had ever been foisted on any people'.

After exposing what he saw as the nonsense that lay at the heart of orange mythology, pointing out, like James Connolly before him, how the Williamite-Jacobite war was nothing but a 'sordid scrap for property', McLoughlin focused on more recent events. He showed how, during the forty hours strike in Belfast in January 1919, the 'loyal' orange employers had used the 'loyal' police to starve the 'loyal' workers back to work. For McLoughlin, orangeism was a 'yarn', the propagation of which enabled the bosses to continue their exploitation unhindered. It was kept going by such as the shipyard bosses for purely business purposes. He urged protestant workers to look around at their own poverty and misery and seek common cause with catholic workers in order to bring it to an end.[109]

McLoughlin's article did not examine in any detail any of the cultural factors behind protestant opposition to Irish independence. That said, his comment that there were 'bigots on both sides' but that protestant workers 'had nothing to fear' in a socialist republic, does suggest that he was both aware of and sympathetic to protestant concerns that bourgeois home rule may well mean Rome rule. Perhaps the main weakness of the article, though, was that whilst McLoughlin did identify the anti-working class character of orangeism, he did not locate the main material reason why a section of the protestant working class was willing to collaborate with the orange and British establishment classes in such a fashion – the reason being that it existed as a labour aristocracy with tangible, if marginal, advantages over the remainder of the working class [110] – or the implications this alliance had for socialist prospects in Ireland.

The Irish Communist Labour Party

The communists were clearly concerned about the lack of a revolutionary socialist leadership in the struggle against British imperialism and it was in connection with this that McLoughlin made a temporary return to Ireland. In March, McLoughlin had mentioned in his Scottish speeches that a communist party had been set up in Ireland.[111] He had touched on this theme also in his report to the Comintern, written about that time, and hinted that a new 'workers communist party' would soon be making its presence felt. May saw the formal launch of this new organization, which was eventually titled the Irish Communist Labour Party (ICLP). It was a step deemed necessary by the Irish communists because, in the months that had passed since the right wing regained control of the SPI, the organization had become inactive. Feeling that it was moribund, the communists became convinced of the need for this new departure, which they hoped might provide a lead to the Irish workers in struggle.

McLoughlin, elected Chairman of the new party, explained all of this in a report he sent to the Comintern in Moscow. In it, he accused the SPI leaders of adopting opportunist and reformist policies 'completely out of harmony with the teachings of Marx'. He maintained that after the success of the left wing in September 1919, there had been a flourish of party activity, which had provoked a reaction from press and pulpit, helping to restore the old leaders to power. By flooding the party with clerical workers and ITGWU officials, the right wing of the SPI, 'led by a catholic reactionary named William O'Brien and another of the same kind named O'Shannon', had consolidated their triumph, but virtually 'killed off' the party. This had compelled the revolutionaries to set up the new body.

McLoughlin informed Moscow that an 'ambitious programme' had been drawn up, involving an 'intense propaganda' campaign, and that he was 'hopeful' concerning communist prospects in the period ahead. McLoughlin did not offer any evidence to back up his arguments, but nonetheless contended that Irish workers were gradually becoming aware of the limitations of both bourgeois nationalism and labour reformism and were moving towards the view that only revolutionary socialism could solve their problems. McLoughlin felt that in order to aid this process, the new party needed funds for activity and a newspaper. He pointed out that speeches were not enough. The objective situation, where 'militarism stalks naked through the land', required more from the communists. 'Action and printed propaganda are the only things that will impress the workers', he concluded, 'and we appeal to the workers of the world to assist us with financial help where possible'.[112]

McLoughlin, though, did not wait around in Dublin for Moscow's reply, which did not seem to come in any case. Instead, he returned to Scotland to finish off his speaking tour, where his services had been booked until mid-July. McLoughlin first visited the SLP branch in Aberdeen, working there for a week, and concluded his spell in Scotland with another week's activity in Dundee. Dundee was a city with a substantial Irish immigrant population and, according to the local SLP branch secretary, McLoughlin's tour there was a big success; £10, 10/- was collected, £5 worth of literature was sold, and one of the meetings in particular, held on 4 July, was said to be 'a record, the best in years.'[113]

McLoughlin left Scotland for Dublin in mid July. The immediate purpose of his return was to help in the organizing of a one-day general strike of Dublin workers in protest against the jailing of Jim Larkin in the USA; Larkin had recently been given five to ten years for his communist activities, or 'criminal anarchy' as the US courts termed it.[114] In June, a Larkin Release Committee was set up in Dublin by his sister Delia,[115] and dominated by the pro-Larkin faction that controlled Dublin Trades Council. At a large demonstration called by the Committee on 11 July, a resolution was passed, calling on the ILPTUC to declare a general strike in support of Larkin for 21 July.[116] The ILPTUC leaders, many of whom were 'not... quite so anxious' to see Larkin return to Ireland [117] and who resented also the influence of his followers on Dublin Trades Council, rejected this demand.

The strike went ahead despite this opposition, and did involve a few thousand Dublin workers, mainly dockers.[118] McLoughlin helped in the organizing of picketing, and was aided here by a contingent of SLP members from Glasgow, who took advantage of the Glasgow Fair holiday to travel to

Dublin and help out.[119] McLoughlin addressed a large meeting in Beresford Square the following Sunday. There he hailed the action a victory, 'because it succeeded in bringing the workers out on strike in spite of Liberty Hall (ITGWU HQ), and despite the lies that were cited everywhere by the capitalist Press'. He also forecast more strikes in the near future. A Sinn Fein Ireland, he maintained, would be so weak in relation to other capitalist states that only by driving down the wages of the working class could its capitalist class hope to survive. The main lesson of this strike, therefore, was one that would stand the workers of Ireland in good stead for future battles: 'One point has emerged very clearly. That no matter who rules the working class can only rely on themselves and relying on themselves will play the last card and win.'[120]

McLoughlin remained in Ireland for the next few months, deciding to devote his energies to the building of the ICLP. Before he could do so, however, he became embroiled in a controversy with the ICA. In May, the organization's leaders had received a copy of the report sent by McLoughlin to the Comintern, in which he had dismissed them as 'incompetent' and 'reactionary'. McLoughlin and his report was the main subject of discussion at a number of ICA army council meetings.[121] Eventually a decision was taken to bring him before the body, to explain his conduct.

With McLoughlin being away in Scotland, it was not until 27 July that he could comply with this request. Even then, he only did so on the understanding that the meeting would not be held at Liberty Hall, the ICA HQ, but of course also that of the ITGWU, the leadership of which he clearly despised. At this meeting, which was eventually held in Marino, he was instructed by the ICA leaders to 'be careful', in the future, and 'not to give any information, no matter in what aspect without first consulting the council'.[122] McLoughlin's report to Moscow had carried within it an estimate of the size of the ICA, and it seems that it was this, as much as the biting political criticisms, that the leadership objected to. McLoughlin was not actually a member of the ICA at this stage; his membership had long lapsed, both as a result of his long spell in Scotland and of his feelings concerning the leadership. At this meeting he spoke about the possibility of re-joining, but never did so, and was never involved in that organization again.

On 29 August, the ICLP held its first public meeting. A 'good crowd' was said to be in attendance. Both McLoughlin and Paddy Stephenson spoke at it, and the 'communist idea was expounded in all its phases'.[123] An appeal was made for supporters to set up branches and further public meetings were held, discussing and debating such topics as the history of the Irish working class, and the merits of the workers' republic versus the political [capitalist] republic.[124] Progress remained modest, however, and the party did not find it easy to sway nationalist revolutionaries towards communism. It identified the land question as being important in an Ireland that was still mainly agricultural, and set itself the task of devising a detailed programme capable of winning over the most marginalized rural classes.[125] This ambitious objective, however, was well beyond the scant resources of the ICLP and no such programme was ever issued.

Irish Communists and the Second Comintern Congress

Although the majority of the Irish communists were involved in the new project, not all were. Roddy Connolly, Eamon MacAlpine, who was a former colleague of Larkin in the USA, and a handful of others, had formed a rival communist faction, later named the Communist Groups (CGs). The difference between the two bodies was tactical, not ideological. Connolly's faction felt that with the Tan War at its height, and the British military cracking down on all forms of open political activity, republican and labour, secretive underground work within these movements was the only option for Irish communists.

In a report he sent later to the Comintern, Connolly argued that any attempt to set up an open communist party would be to 'court instant disaster' and would lead to 'suppression, arrests...the total scattering of the socialist movement in Ireland'.[126] The creation of such an open party remained the aim of those who had formed the ICLP, explaining the division between the two. But although the ICLP was larger and better organized, Connolly had made contact with Sylvia Pankhurst in London. With her help and financial assistance from Captain Jack White, both Connolly and MacAlpine made it to Petrograd and participated in the Second Congress of the Comintern, which opened there on 19 July 1920.[127]

The Second Comintern Congress was in many ways the true foundation event of the organization and much larger and more important than that which announced the body in March 1919. Important directives were given to all communists active in colonial states, and in line with Lenin's growing appreciation of the revolutionary potential of the colonies, communists were instructed to work with their national independence movements, if they were truly revolutionary, and use such alliances to both weaken imperialism and build communist strength.[128] In Ireland – which Moscow regarded as significant due to its close proximity to its most aggressive enemy, Britain – the directives meant alliance with the IRA. This, of course, was already the Irish communist view and required no change of thinking on their behalf;

on the contrary, it could only have strengthened the Irish belief that they were already pursuing the correct path.

The ICLP initially welcomed the fact that Connolly and MacAlpine had participated in the Congress, feeling that they 'would do good work for the Irish proletarians'.[129] Ultimately, however, tensions developed between the two organisations because of their tactical differences. ICLP secretary Stephenson clearly thought that the Connolly/MacAlpine secretive strategy was simply an alibi for laziness; their lack of activity, he predicted, would lead Lenin to regret the time and 'tea and cakes' he had 'wasted' upon them.[130]

Return to Britain

McLoughlin did not seem to get involved in this dispute, and did not offer any public criticism of the small rival communist faction. In fact, McLoughlin's time in Ireland was once more coming to an end. Another tour had been planned for him by the SLP, but there were other factors behind his decision to leave. McLoughlin was finding it difficult to operate in Dublin; thanks to the attentions of Special Branch, his home was once raided several times in one day.[131] He had also been involved in a 'shooting affray' in Dawson St, when an attempt was made to arrest him by some G men.[132] In addition, McLoughlin was approached by Michael Collins, who apparently asked for his help in building active support for Irish independence amongst the British left; Collins was keen to win recruits in Britain from this quarter willing to engage in sabotage and smuggling, as well as propaganda, and saw McLoughlin as the ideal person to undertake the task of finding them.

For a variety of reasons, therefore, McLoughlin again left Ireland. This was on 24 November 1920, three days after the IRA shootings of senior British Intelligence officers and the Croke Park reprisals from the British. It was also just a few weeks after the birth in Dublin on 24 October of his son, named Terence MacSwiney Sean McLoughlin, as a tribute to the republican Lord Mayor of Cork who died in Brixton Prison after a 70-day hunger strike on 25 October.

Four years had now passed since McLoughlin's release from Frongoch. They had been years of importance in his political development and saw him embrace fully Bolshevik thinking and become part of the world communist movement. Through this influence, McLoughlin had been able to formulate a sophisticated critique of the independence movement, and a strategy for its success. He was still part of the IRA, but this was a tactical involvement, in line with, if not derived from, Comintern thinking on the matter. For McLoughlin such involvement was the only way that communists could open the eyes of the IRA rank-and-file to its own class interests and win it over. It was a strategy which, although logical from his perspective, had not yet prevailed. But McLoughlin was far from despondent. And in the period ahead the volatile Irish situation would change dramatically, filling him with hope that success might be close at hand and pulling him back into the heart of the revolutionary struggle.

Notes

1 NA, Sean McLoughlin, Statement to the Bureau of Military History, WS 290, p. 35.
2 NLI, Irish National Aid and Volunteer Dependent's Fund papers, 24, 362.
3 NA, Sean McLoughlin, p. 35.
4 Tom Johnson, *the Future of Labour*, (Dublin: 1916), pp. 1-6.
5 Emmet O'Connor, *Syndicalism in Ireland 1917-23*, (Cork: 1988), p. 88.
6 Ibid., p. 36.
7 Roddy Connolly, 'A glimpse of Collins', in Michael Collins Memorial Foundation Supplement, *Irish Independent*, 20-8-1966.
8 NA, Garry Holohan, Statement to the Bureau of Military History, WS 336, p. 2.
9 Roddy Connolly, 'a glimpse of Collins'.
10 Ibid.
11 A process which was aided immeasurably when, in October 1917, Sinn Fein was re-vamped and an unwieldy, if effective, coalition of nationalists and republicans from all classes was forged. It soon placed itself at the head of the independence struggle, plugging the gap that had lain vacant since the Rising, as a result of the sclerosis of the Parliamentary Party and the failings of Labour. There it would remain largely unchallenged for the duration of the conflict with Britain.
12 For more on McGrath, including his recollection of McLoughlin coming to Tipperary, see, NA, Frank McGrath, Statement to the Bureau of Military History, WS 1558.
13 NA, Sean McLoughlin, pp. 37-38.
14 Sean McLoughlin private papers, also for more detail on the raid see the *Tipperary Star*, 2-3-1918.
15 *Tipperary Star*, 2-3-1918.
16 Ibid., 9-3-1918.
17 NA, Sean McLoughlin, p. 39.

18 *Tipperary Star*, 20-4-1918.
19 NA, Sean McLoughlin, p. 45.
20 Ibid., p. 40.
21 NA, Liam Manahan, Statement to the Bureau of Military History, WS 456, p35, and UCDA, Liam Manahan in Ernie O'Malley notebooks, P17b/106/132.
22 Ibid., p. 36.
23 NA, Sean McLoughlin, pp. 41-2.
24 For more on the re-organisation of the Volunteers in the post-1916 period see Joost Augusteijn *From Public Defiance to Guerrilla Warfare*, (Dublin: 1996).
25 NA, Sean McLoughlin, pp. 43-4.
26 *Evening Herald* 5-3-1919.
27 The proceedings were covered in the *Evening Herald*, 6-3-1919, and *Evening Mail*, 6-3-1919. See also, *The Socialist*, 10-4-1919.
28 See file on John McLoughlin, NA, General Prison Boards Index, 1919/2051, and letter from Paddy Stephenson to the *Socialist*, 10-6-1920.
29 NA, Sean McLoughlin, p. 45.
30 Liam Cahill, *Forgotten Revolution: Limerick Soviet 1919*, (Dublin: 1990) p. 39.
31 Ibid., p. 77.
32 Ibid., p. 100.
33 *Voice of Labor*, 12-4-1919.
34 *The Socialist*, 10-6-1920.
35 *The Socialist*, 13-3-1919.
36 CD Greaves, *the Life and Times of James Connolly*, (London: 1986) pp. 164-65.
37 For more on this important dispute see: Glasgow Labour history workshop, *The Singer strike, Clydebank 1911*, (Clydebank: 1989).
38 H.R.Vernon, 'The Socialist Labour Party and the working class movement on the Clyde, 1906-23,' M Phil Thesis, (1967), Leeds University, p. 121.
39 Ibid., p. 202.
40 Ibid., pp. 194-95.
41 Walter Kendall, *Revolutionary Movement in Britain 1900-21*, (London: 1969) pp133-34.
42 *Voice of Labour*, 19-6-1919.
43 Mike Milotte, 'Communist Politics in Ireland, 1916-1945', PhD Thesis, QUB Belfast, (1977) p. 59.

44 Michael McInerney, 'Roddy Connolly, Sixty Years of Political Activity' in *Irish Times*, 27-8-1976.
45 Irish Labour History Archives, (ILHA) Irish Citizen Army Minute Book, 19-5-1919.
46 Ibid., 26-5-1919.
47 Brian Hanley, 'The Irish Citizen Army after 1916', *Saothar 28*, (2003).
48 Irish Citizen Army Minute Book, 23-6-1919.
49 Ibid., 5-10-1919.
50 A list of the organizers and sponsors is contained in the special commemorative programme issued for the event, copy in NLI.
51 *The Voice of Labour*, 14-6-1919.
52 Ibid., 26-7-1919.
53 Ibid.
54 *The Voice of Labour*, 2-8-1919, 30-8-1919.
55 Nan Milton, *John MacLean*, (London: 1973) p. 209.
56 *Voice of Labour*, 6-9-1919.
57 *Socialist*, 23-10-1919, 10-6-1920.
58 *Voice of Labour*, 20-9-1919.
59 *Voice of Labour*, 15-11-1919.
60 Ibid.
61 A November 1919 police intelligence report noted that the CWC had been 'negotiating' a visit 'from Irish extremists', British National Archives, Kew, (BNA) report on the revolutionary organisations in the United Kingdom, Directorate of Intelligence, Cab24/93/cp168, 20-11-1919.
62 *Voice of Labour*, 20-12-1919.
63 *Voice of Labour*, 10-1-1920.
64 Marriage Certificate of Sean McLoughlin and Isabella Barr, courtesy of Martha St Registrar, Glasgow.
65 *The Forward*, 3-1-1920 advertised the meetings in advance.
66 For McLoughlin speech in full see: *Glasgow Observer*, 10-1-1920, and BNA, report on the revolutionary organisations in the United Kingdom, Cab 24/96/cp429, 9-1-1920.
67 *Glasgow Observer*, 10-1-1920.
68 Ibid., 17-1-1920.
69 BNA, report on the revolutionary organisations in the United Kingdom, Cab 24/98/cp620, 2-2-1920.
70 Ibid., Cab 24/94/cp256, 4-12-1919.
71 Ibid., Cab/24/98/cp620, 12-2-1920.
72 *Glasgow Evening Times*, 2-2-1920

73 Sean McLoughlin, 'Bloody Asquith, Labour, and Paisley' in *the Socialist*, 12-2-1920.
74 Ibid.
75 Ibid., The SLP leadership had suggested that Willie Paul stand for the party, but he declined the nomination, *Glasgow Evening Times*, 23-1-1920.
76 *Glasgow Observer*, 7-2-1920. The 1918 result had been Sir John McCallum (Liberal), 7,542, John Biggar, (Labour and Co-Operative), 7,438, James McKean, (Coalition), 7,201. Asquith won the by- election, defeating Biggar by 14,736 votes to 11,902. McKean, a member of the Tory party, finished third on 3,795.
77 BNA, report on the revolutionary organizations in the United Kingdom, Cab 24/99/cp748, 26-2-20.
78 Ibid., Cab 24/98/cp620, 12-2-1920.
79 Ibid., Cab/24/99/cp 791, 4-3-20.
80 Ibid., The Industrial Workers of the World was a syndicalist trade union organization, based in the USA, but well-known throughout the world. The association of the SLP with syndicalism and de Leon was the reason that police intelligence described it in such a manner. This is notwithstanding the fact that there were fundamental political differences between de Leon and the IWW.
81 Meeting advertised in *The Socialist*, 26-2-1920.
82 BNA, report on the revolutionary organizations in the United Kingdom, Cab24/100/cp840, 10-3-20.
83 For more on the socialist movement in the Vale of Leven, see Stuart MacIntyre, *Little Moscows: Communism and Militancy in Interwar Britain* (London: 1980) pp. 79-112.
84 *The Socialist, 18-3-1920*.
85 ILP Conference Report, April 1920, pp. 70-71.
86 McLoughlin's report on the 1920 ILP Conference is carried in *The Socialist*, 15-4-1920.
87 *The Socialist*, 15-4-1920.
88 *The Socialist*, 22-4-1920.
89 Ibid.
90 *The Socialist*, 6-5-1920.
91 *The Socialist*, 26-2-1920.
92 Ibid.
93 'Report of the Political Organisations of the Working Class,' *The Socialist*, 27-5-1920, also, NLI, William O'Brien papers, 15,674, (3) part 9.

94 McLoughlin mentions that he was involved in such activity during his next spell in Britain from November 1920 onwards, NA, Sean McLoughlin, 'Statement to the Bureau of Military History', WS 290, p. 47. The spell of activity in Britain between December 1919-July 1920 is not mentioned in his account to the Bureau of Military History, but clearly, if he was still in the Volunteers and carrying out such actions after November 1920, he may well have been likewise engaged before November 1920.
95 Sean McLoughlin, 'Standing up for Ireland', in *The Socialist*, 25-3-1920.
96 Sean McLoughlin, 'Britain and the Struggle in Ireland', in *the Socialist*, 27-5-1920.
97 Ibid.
98 Of course, the logic of James Connolly's analysis that only the Irish working class could bring about independence through socialism shows that, like McLoughlin, he too considered such a transformation in Ireland could precede similar change in Britain. Connolly, though, unlike McLoughlin, did not address specifically the nature of the relationship between the two revolutionary struggles.
99 *The Socialist*, 6-5-1920.
100 See FSL Lyons, *Ireland since the Famine*, (London: 1973) pp. 415-20.
101 The American Commission on conditions in Ireland, interim report, (London: 1921) p. 37.
102 Paul Bew et al, *The Dynamics of Irish Politics*, (London: 1989) p. 22.
103 CD Greaves, *the ITGWU: The Formative Years, 1909-23*, (Dublin: 1982), p. 276.
104 Michael Laffan, *The Resurrection of Ireland*, (Cambridge: 1999), p. 258.
105 *Connacht Tribune*, 3-4-1920 quoted in Fergus Campbell, 'Land and Politics in Connacht, 1898-1909' PhD thesis, (University of Bristol: 1997) p. 461.
106 This was certainly true in parts of the West. For more, see Fergus Campbell, pp. 461-538.
107 Arthur Mitchell, *Revolutionary Government in Ireland*, (Dublin: 1995) p. 258.
108 *Workers Republic, 19-11-1921*
109 Sean McLoughlin, 'The Orange Fraud in Ulster' in the *Socialist, 8-7-1920*.
110 For more on the protestant labour aristocracy and its influence over the protestant working class as a whole see, Johnston/ Larragy/Williams,

James Connolly a Marxist Analysis, (Dublin: 1986) pp. 120-130.
111 BNA, report on the revolutionary organizations in the United Kingdom, Cab 24/103/cp1009, 30-3-1920.
112 Report of ICLP to the Third International, 20-5-20, 495/89/2-3, formerly the Institute for Marxism-Leninism, Central Committee, Communist Party Soviet Union, Moscow, now Russian State Social and Political Archives, Moscow, hereafter RGASPI.
113 *The Socialist,* 15-7-1920.
114 Emmet O'Connor, 'James Larkin in the United States, 1914-23', *Journal of Contemporary History,* Vol 37/2, (2002), pp. 191-2.
115 *The Socialist,* 24-6-1920.
116 Ibid., 22-7-1920. The ITUCLP changed its name to the ILPTUC in 1918.
117 *Irish Times,* 21-7-1920.
118 For an (extremely hostile) account of the strike, see the *Watchword/ Voice of Labour,* 31-7-1920.
119 *The Socialist,* 5-8-1920.
120 Ibid.
121 See, for example, ILHA, ICA army council minute book, 25-5-1920, 1-6-1920, 10-6-1920.
122 Ibid., 27-7-1920.
123 *The Socialist,* 16-9-1920.
124 *The Socialist,* 23-9-20.
125 Ibid.
126 RGASPI, Report to Comrade Kobietsky for the Comintern executive by Roddy Connolly, 3-2-21, 495/89/10-2/3.
127 For more on this see Charlie McGuire *Roddy Connolly and the Struggle for Socialism in Ireland,* (Cork: 2008), pp. 31-37.
128 For Lenin's views on the national and colonial question and communist tactics in relation to it, see: VI Lenin, *Speeches at the Congresses of the Communist International,* (Moscow: 1972), p. 57.
129 *The Socialist,* 14-10-1920.
130 Ibid., 18-11-1920.
131 NA, Sean McLoughlin, Statement to the Bureau of Military History, WS 290, p. 46.
132 Ibid.

4

The Triumph of Reaction, 1921-23

Introduction

The years 1921-23 were crucial, both to the fate of the Irish Revolution, and to the development of Sean McLoughlin's politics. In Ireland it produced the Truce, Treaty, consolidation of partition and eventual civil war. As such, it was a period that marked the defeat of the revolutionary struggle and the onset of reaction, north and south. For McLoughlin, too, it was a vital time. Although he began 1921 as a successful propagandist within the British socialist movement, the tumultuous nature of the events unfolding in Ireland eventually called him home to one last spell of involvement in the struggle for a workers' republic.

Like all Irish communists, McLoughlin's hopes were high during these years. This was particularly so after the outbreak of civil war. The move towards compromise by the nationalist leadership and subsequent rupture of the republican movement had long been predicted by communists and in the new situation they saw possibilities for revolutionary socialist advancement. Events would not turn out as they planned, but the communists would make an appreciable contribution to the anti-Treaty struggle. For McLoughlin, however, it was also a spell that would mark the end of his involvement within Irish republicanism. By the end of 1923, he would be arguing the necessity for a communist break from the IRA, if the revolutionary left were to have any chance of building a mass movement.

Back to the SLP

McLoughlin returned to Britain in November 1920. He travelled to Sheffield initially, and possibly stayed there for a short period. Sheffield was an SLP stronghold and it is probable that he had made contacts in the city during his previous spell in Britain. McLoughlin got in touch with local Irish Republicans, through the Sheffield Irish club, and had some degree of involvement in the smuggling of arms back to Ireland.[1]

Afterwards, he travelled to Dundee, a city with a substantial Irish immigrant population. There, with the help of a group of unemployed Irishmen, he broke up a meeting of the local city council, which had been planning to pass a resolution condemning the 'terrorist' actions of the IRA.[2] By the end of December, however, the SLP press was advertising his availability for speaking tours. Before long, he was once more working full-time in that capacity, but this time as a member of the party.

In January 1921, McLoughlin travelled to Motherwell in the west of Scotland and gave a 'very eloquent and able address' on the subject of socialism in Ireland.[3] The following week, he journeyed east to the mining town of Dunfermline. There, he addressed seven meetings in the course of a week that was described as the most successful the party had enjoyed:

> It would be no exaggeration to claim that no previous socialist propagandist had made the same impression on the minds of the workers of West Fife as comrade McLoughlin. His lucid, though scientific, analysis of the Irish and world situation from a Marxist point of view cannot fail to have had a good effect, even on the most confused Henry.[4]

Whilst at the first meeting the collection totalled 8/6, by the time of the seventh the intake per night had reached almost £11, showing the growing enthusiasm for McLoughlin's speeches. That there was a significant degree of support for the Irish struggle amongst particular sections of the Scottish working class could also be seen later that month, when miners in Giffnock, near Glasgow, downed tools for a one day strike 'against British military occupation of Ireland'.[5]

McLoughlin and the CPGB

Following on from this, McLoughlin had a further week's work around Edinburgh, holding four meetings in the Scottish Capital and one in each of the surrounding towns of Musselburgh, Broxburn and Leith. In addition, two lantern lectures were held in Pringle's Picture Palace in Edinburgh, and one in the local picture hall in Musselburgh. Again, the meetings were said to be a success:

> During the campaign many aspects of the class struggle were fully analysed and explained. The Irish Question was well explained and the history of Ireland both past and present was an eye-opener to many who attended the meetings. The comrade's handling of the unity stunt was really good and his exposition of the SLP attitude on the matter has cleared the air a bit in Edinburgh.[6]

The 'unity stunt' referred to in this report related to the moves that had been made by a section of the SLP leadership to join forces with other socialist organizations in Britain, in order that a single revolutionary party, affiliated to the Comintern, be created. This process began in early 1919, but it was not until the summer of 1920 that such a new party, the Communist Party of Great Britain (CPGB), was formed. The British Socialist Party (BSP), an organization that had contained a substantial reformist element, dominated the CPGB numerically. BSP insistence that the new party affiliate to the Labour Party, as it had done itself, was opposed vehemently by the far more militant SLP. Members were balloted, and whilst the vote was 395 –132 in favour of unity, 'on the general principles of the dictatorship of the proletariat, the Soviet system and the Third International', only 72 members were prepared to support affiliation to Labour, with 443 against.[7] Despite this opposition, however, the heavyweight SLP leadership, headed by McManus, Bell and Paul, eventually accepted Labour affiliation and was expelled from the party, taking with it many key activists from Clydeside. It was a split from which the SLP would not recover. Not only did it leave the party weakened organizationally, it also left it out of step with Moscow, a problematic position for any serious socialist organization to find itself in in 1920. Lenin, who appears to have been deeply misinformed about the benefits that would accrue to the new communist party through Labour affiliation, was strongly supportive of the measure and played a key role in persuading British communists to accept it.[8]

McLoughlin was critical of the developments that had led to the creation of the CPGB. Like most SLP activists he was deeply opposed to the Labour Party, regarding them as 'capitalist apologists' and 'social traitors'. But his critique went much further and deeper than the question of Labour affiliation. For McLoughlin, the unity process had been artificial and did not address the main weakness of the British socialist movement, which was its lack of influence among the organized working class and in the workplaces. He argued that with the exception of the workshop committees in Glasgow and one or two other places, 'the industrial movement, from a revolutionary point of view, [is] very disheartening'. As a consequence, McLoughlin considered that the 'only unity of real value' was not between various different socialist parties, but 'between the political and industrial socialists'.[9]

It was in this unity that McLoughlin saw the embryo of a future workers' state. He argued that all socialist parties should become involved in this type of activity within the workplaces, and use it to promote the establishment of soviets in the local areas. For McLoughlin it was irrelevant what actual parties took the lead in this; all that mattered was that in each locality a revolutionary council was set up involving socialists and organized workers. In the revolutionary crisis he thought inevitable, these organizations would not only give a lead to the working class, but would become a forum for the activities of all revolutionary socialists. Only when such a crisis developed could unity and a true communist party be constructed.[10]

McLoughlin's argument did expose some of the most serious shortcomings within the British communist movement. The movement did not have much of an influence amongst the organized working class, or in the workplaces. Without this influence, a socialist revolution was not possible, meaning that the task of developing it was, as McLoughlin indicated, a main priority for all communist activists. In some respects, McLoughlin's argument was similar to that advanced by Rosa Luxemburg at the foundation congress of the Communist Party of Germany (KPD) in December 1918. Luxemburg argued here that the most important task facing German communists at that point was to develop the strength of the workers' councils and wage class struggle and raise class consciousness within the workplaces. Until this was done, any talk of the German proletariat seizing power and setting up a workers' republic was premature, notwithstanding the collapse of the monarchy and undermining of bourgeois rule as a whole.[11]

At the same time, however, it can be argued that one of the additional factors behind the eventual defeat of the 1918-19 German revolution was that the KPD arrived on the scene too late to influence matters decisively. Luxemburg, who had previously downplayed the need for such a party, did recognize in late 1918 that such a party was a necessity. The task, though, of constructing a revolutionary socialist party in the middle of a revolutionary crisis proved immensely difficult. The party that emerged was immature in many respects and proved unable to lead the working class to victory. Rosa herself paid with her life in the counter-revolution that followed. McLoughlin's argument that a British communist party could not be created until a revolutionary crisis developed indicates that he was not aware of this as a possible factor in the defeat of the revolution in Germany.

Overall, McLoughlin's insistence that socialists build their forces and develop their influence in the workplaces, his support for soviets, both as a means of destroying the old order and establishing the new, and his belief that a communist party should be set up at some point in Britain, albeit not immediately, are all testament to the general impact of Bolshevism on his thinking. They also show that he was acutely aware of the weaknesses of socialist organization in Britain. His contention, though, that the formation of a single communist party in Britain was premature and the fact that he did not indicate clearly what, if any, specific function such a party should have were nonetheless significant. Both suggest that McLoughlin had not fully embraced the Leninist concept of the revolutionary party, which argued a dialectical relationship between the party and the masses and which accorded the party a central role in the destruction of capitalism and establishment of a socialist society.

'The greatest propaganda speaker I have ever heard'

February saw McLoughlin undertake a spell of work in the west of Scotland. He first had a week's tour in and around Clydebank, addressing meetings in the town, and in nearby Duntocher and Old Kilpatrick. His final meeting, held in Clydebank, was said to be 'rousing' and he made an appeal on behalf of the dependents of Irish political prisoners. A sum of £7 was raised.[12] McLoughlin then held a series of meetings in Glasgow on the 'Tragedy of Ireland'. These included addresses in St Mungo's Hall, Springburn Public Hall, and the Louvre Picture House in Parkhead. The Clyde Workers' Band was an accompaniment at these meetings, adding greatly to the entertainment value of the proceedings.[13]

After his week in Glasgow, McLoughlin travelled east again back to Dunfermline. His meetings had gone down exceptionally well there, and the local branch was keen to get him back, this time for a month. During this four-week spell, McLoughlin spoke at large public meetings in Inverkeithing, as well as Dunfermline itself, and organized a large protest demonstration against 'murder in Ireland, the reduction of wages and the imprisonment of communists in England'.[14] McLoughlin also travelled to nearby Cowdenbeath, another mining town, and held several meetings there. It was noted at this stage that the local CPGB were 'boycotting' McLoughlin's meetings, evidence of the growing hostility between the SLP and a party it regarded as renegade. McLoughlin's speeches reflected this development, and he became increasingly critical of the CPGB, dubbing them 'tinpot revolutionaries, who see themselves directing red divisions – from behind'.[15] As before, McLoughlin's spell in Fife was a great success, the 'most successful' spell of work, in fact, in the Branch's history. As a result, Dunfermline SLP nominated him for the position of full-time SLP National Organiser.[16] After Dunfermline, McLoughlin made the short journey back to Edinburgh, where he again conducted a week's work in and around the city. This concluded with a lantern lecture at Pringle's Picture Palace, the report of which not only gives an insight into McLoughlin's political views and perspectives but also his actual style of speaking which was proving so attractive to audiences everywhere. It was a lecture delivered in a real Irish fashion with a little bit of humour to lighten the tragedy of Ireland and then on the back of the humour, the real stuff was rammed home. The appeal to them to realize that the Black and Tans of Ireland today may be the Black and Tans in Britain tomorrow seemed to find a ready response from the audience, who were then told not to wait on it coming, but to get organized on a revolutionary class basis and be prepared to meet the attack of the Ruling Class and to end it all by carrying through the social revolution in this country and thus smashing forever British Imperialism. By these means only can we help the people of Ireland, Egypt, India and elsewhere.[17]

As before, McLoughlin was connecting the revolutionary struggle in Ireland to that in Britain, in order to hammer home to British workers their inextricable links. In addition, he was bringing into focus the struggle of other subject peoples against the British Empire, again with the intention of raising the consciousness of the British workers and the central role they could play in the destruction of imperialism and capitalism. That all of this was delivered in a style which ordinary workers could relate to and appreciate marks McLoughlin out as one of the most skilled socialist propagandists of his era.

McLoughlin's focus, however, was not solely on this relationship between the British working class and those toiling in the colonies. McLoughlin also dealt at length with issues that specifically affected British workers in Britain itself. This was particularly so with the crisis in the mining industry, which reached a peak in the spring of 1921, and which affected working-class communities in many of the places McLoughlin visited, such as Dunfermline, Inverkeithing, Cowdenbeath and Musselburgh.

The crisis in the mines had occurred when the industry, which had been nationalized during the war, was returned to private ownership. Wage cuts and the breaking up of centralized bargaining machinery soon followed, provoking an angry backlash from the miners and a demand for strike action. Since 1914, the miners union – the Miners' Federation of Great Britain – had been part of the Triple Alliance, along with the National Union of Railwaymen and the Transport and General Workers Union. After initially agreeing to a strike, the rail and transport unions pulled out of the planned action, breaking up the Triple Alliance and leaving the miners isolated. This event, which took place on 'Black Friday' 15 April, was one tailor-made for an effective propagandist like McLoughlin and he exploited it to the full. His analysis of reformism and what he considered to be the consistently treacherous role played by the British trade union and Labour leaders appeared to strike a harmonious chord in many of those mining communities he visited in Scotland, and may even have been a factor in the eventual development of the 'sack the leaders' movements that emerged later that year.

'Black Friday' was also significant for another reason. It represented a new stage in the offensive that had been waged by the British employers against the working class since 1920. With the slump having bitten hard into the British economy, the interests of capital had demanded an onslaught against the limited improvements in wages and conditions that British workers had won during and after the war. And it had quickly come. Between June 1920 and February 1921, for example, the Boot and Shoe Operatives Union paid out £73,887 in unemployed benefits to its members, compared to a figure of only £86,468 for the thirteen years preceding.[18]

The situation was to get worse. The miners, isolated and left to fight on their own, were defeated and forced back to work in early July. This was a massive boost to the British employers, who feared the power and militancy of the miners, and came just weeks after 500,000 cotton workers were locked out and compelled to accept a 4/5-pay cut.[19] No section of the working class was now safe, and by the end of the year 1.73 million were unemployed, with another 255,300 on short time.[20] In March 1922, another important battle was lost when engineers were forced to accept pay cuts following a 14-week lockout.[21] Objective conditions were changing for the worse, as far as the prospects for socialist development were concerned. The capitalist offensive would become relentless throughout 1921-22, giving the organized working class what one socialist leader would later describe as the 'severest hammering' in modern history.[22]

This, though, may not have been apparent to McLoughlin and other socialists active in the spring of 1921. In fact, before demoralization set in, the changing conditions of the working class provoked an initial bout of militancy, in the form of strikes and agitation amongst the unemployed, which provided a fillip to their work. This was certainly the case with McLoughlin. After leaving Edinburgh, he travelled south for a two week speaking tour in and around Dewsbury in Yorkshire, and again was a standout success. At one meeting, held in Dewsbury market place, it was estimated that 10,000 people attended.[23] Several of his other meetings, including some in nearby Batley, attracted crowds of between 2-3000 each time.[24] McLoughlin then travelled down to Sheffield and held four meetings on consecutive nights. Again, his subject matter was widened out beyond the Irish question, and again the message he delivered was well received. Such was McLoughlin's impact in Yorkshire that fifty years later one old ex-SLP member was moved to comment:

> He was the greatest propaganda speaker I have ever heard. He was able to draw the largest crowds and hold them. I think he outshone AJ Cook who too was a mass orator of the biggest calibre.[25]

The old SLPer, Batley man CH Burden, in a later interview also recalled 'his histrionics were marvelous. He could tell the tale, you know, repartee if there was any heckling. He was a marvelous fellow, McLoughlin.'[26]

From Sheffield, it was down to Coventry in the English Midlands. The response was identical:

> Our comrade Sean McLoughlin has arrived and everyone knows it. Huge meetings have been held, audiences spellbound, finance rolling in, so we all want our comrade to stay another week and here he will be...verdict: Sean McLoughlin is the best we have had in the City.[27]

McLoughlin's next port of call was Aberdeen. In June, he conducted a 'vigorous fortnight's propaganda' which was said to have made a 'big impression' on workers in the Granite City. Large meetings were held every night which, to the glee of the local branch secretary, 'completely swamped' those being conducted nearby by ex- SLP leading figure Davie Kirkwood, now of the ILP.[28] But it was not only the ILP meetings which were 'swamped'; the local CPGB in Aberdeen also made reference to the 'McLoughlin opposition', when pointing out the poor collections at their meetings and the fact that they still had 6 dozen copies of the *Communist* unsold.[29] By contrast, McLoughlin's meetings in Aberdeen provoked 'tremendous interest', with many local workers 'hearing for the first time, the truth about Ireland'[30] After Aberdeen, McLoughlin visited Clydebank again, for a 'very successful' week of meetings in and around the town. The response of local branch secretary Finlay Hart was enthusiastic:

> I strongly advise every branch to secure the services of Comrade McLoughlin at the earliest opportunity, as he has the knack of decoying the poor 'Henry' and then hits him so hard that if he does not reason things out better when he is finished with him, it is a surgical operation he needs, not knowledge.[31]

It was at this point, early July, that McLoughlin's activities were brought to a temporary halt. He took ill whilst in Edinburgh, and spent a short period in hospital. It appears that McLoughlin had suffered a recurrence of his previous lung problems.[32] After a period of recuperation, however, he was back on the road. In August, McLoughlin was in Yorkshire, for a three-day engagement in Sheffield,[33] and he then spent a week in Leeds. 'Needless to say', pointed out the secretary of the Leeds branch, 'the message of the SLP has been convincingly put and has been received by the audiences that have gathered round to listen clearly'[34]

McLoughlin also continued to write for the *Socialist*. His articles during this period displayed a strong internationalist flavour and showed that he believed capitalism to be in its death throes. 'Drifting', published on 3 March, characterized the objective situation in Europe as one where 'capitalism and communism are in death grips'. In every country, McLoughlin continued, there were 'tremendous struggles between the labouring masses and the forces of reaction'. Pointing out how the Russian communists themselves realized that their success or non-success would be decided by the fate of the European Revolution, McLoughlin located the victory of this in the defeat of both British and French imperialism. The defeat of either or both these ruling classes was, for McLoughlin, a pre-requisite for the development of communism throughout Europe. It gave an added importance to the socialist struggle in Britain, and pointed out the need for British socialists to stop wasting time on their infighting, and start to prepare resolutely for an 'organized attack on the forces of capital'.

These were themes that McLoughlin returned to in 'Counter Revolution in Europe' three weeks later. Here, he argued that the recent deployment of French troops into the Ruhr[35] should not be seen as a renewed attack on the German ruling class. On the contrary, McLoughlin contended, the German bourgeoisie secretly supported this occupation because they knew it was directed against the German working class that dominated this, the industrial heartland of the country. For McLoughlin, it was evidence that a new war was being planned, 'not against the German militarists, but against the revolutionary working class in Europe'. McLoughlin viewed this as part of the inevitable collapse of capitalism, the rumblings of which could be heard 'from Vladivostok to Galway'.

With McLoughlin considering that the objective situation in Europe was at such a critical juncture, it was no surprise that he sharpened his attacks on the leaders of the British Labour movement. These elements were not only 'weaklings, traitors and cowards', but in the event of a revolutionary crisis would show their true class interests and move to 'sabotage and destroy any attempt to secure freedom' on the part of the workers. McLoughlin, though, had faith that the European bourgeoisie and their reformist backers would not succeed. Prior to the First World War, he argued, the working class had little idea of the power it could wield. The idea of using armed force 'or even economic power' was, he maintained, 'entirely foreign to their minds'. Now the situation was different. 'Years of the red hell of war has given them new ideas,' McLoughlin continued, 'and men who have been accustomed to wield guns and bombs on behalf of capitalism will not hesitate to again use the same weapons against capitalism when the need arises'.

In these articles McLoughlin showed his revolutionary outlook, his belief that a confrontation between capital and labour in Britain was looming, and his determination to engage and confront the British bourgeoisie in such a struggle. His consideration that socialist revolutionary opportunities were in evidence for the European working class seemed somewhat at odds with that of the Comintern leaders, who were tending more to the view that a temporary period of reaction, caused by setbacks such as the defeats of revolutions in Germany and Hungary, was more likely. For Moscow, the overall revolutionary nature of the period was unquestioned, but it was felt that the temporary capitalist stabilization ruled out socialist victory in the immediate present.[36] McLoughlin, enjoying success with his speaking tour, and perhaps not fully aware of the traumatic effects economic slump would have on workers struggles in Britain, clearly believed that socialist revolution was still possible. His articles here are important. The manner in which they explicitly linked socialist revolution in Britain to the salvation of the Russian Revolution and overall victory of the European working class identifies McLoughlin as a socialist internationalist, and provides a further important reason for his activity in the British socialist struggle.

Expulsion from the SLP

By September, McLoughlin's work in Scotland and England had lasted almost nine months and had been tremendously successful. His meetings had attracted massive crowds, most of whom appeared keen to learn more, both about the situation in Ireland, and the causes of and solutions to their own often miserable conditions of existence at home. The regular reports sent in by local branch secretaries, grateful as much for the swelling coffers as for the swelling crowds that accompanied McLoughlin's meetings, are evidence of the impact he had as an activist within the British socialist movement.

Unlike before, McLoughlin joined the SLP during this spell of activity. By the summer of 1921, he was regarded by many as an important figure in the party, and its most able propagandist by a considerable distance. With the party still shaken by the departure of its former leaders into the CPGB,

McLoughlin's impact seemed to offer to party activists grounds for optimism and hope for the future. All the more surprising, then, that the 15 September edition of *The Socialist* should contain the following terse statement 'To whom it may concern. Sean McLoughlin is not now a member of the SLP, having being expelled by the NEC at a meeting on September 10'.

The actual reason for Sean McLoughlin's expulsion from the SLP was never publicized, but it soon transpired that elements within the SLP leadership had either accused him of being a police agent, or believed such accusations made about him by others.[37] That this was untrue can actually be seen from a survey of contemporary police intelligence reports; during the same month that McLoughlin had been expelled from the SLP for being an agent of British intelligence, the Directorate of Intelligence at Scotland Yard was itself attempting to have him prosecuted by the DPP for a string of 'violent speeches' he was said to have delivered in Yorkshire.[38] Whilst there may be various different ways of running agents in order to maximize their usefulness, having them gaoled and removed from the very organizations they have been instructed to infiltrate, is not usually one of them. C.H. Burden, commenting on McLoughlin's expulsion, 'did not think that there was anything in it'.[39] Moreover, Burden recalled that the very weekend McLoughlin's expulsion from the SLP was noted in the *Socialist*, the local branch in Dewsbury had arranged a speaking tour for him. The branch was then contacted by SLP central office and told of the reason for his expulsion. Rather than abandon the tour, however, which would have been the probable course of action taken had the story been believed, Burden's branch held back from selling the paper for a few days, so that it could avail itself of McLoughlin's considerable propaganda activities![40]

But whilst Burden had his doubts about the expulsion, he made some other interesting points that go some way to explaining why such an event had occurred. According to Burden, 'most people' he knew in the party reckoned McLoughlin was 'buying and selling arms'. He recalled an unnamed Irishman, introduced to him by McLoughlin in the Dewsbury Socialist Club in Victoria Rd, attempting to sell pistols to local SLP members, arguing that they would soon be needed 'for the Revolution'.[41] This appears to have had a disconcerting effect and may have sowed the seeds of doubt about McLoughlin in the minds of local socialist activists. Burden also recounted a tale about McLoughlin that appears to have been doing the rounds at the same time. According to this story, there was a Volunteer in the Easter Rising named O'Loughlin who had been sent with some others to knock out the telegraph exchange, in order to hamper British communications. After setting off, however, O'Loughlin absconded and was never heard of again. Burden, his doubts about the expulsion notwithstanding, wondered if ' O'Loughlin' was really McLoughlin,[42] with the obvious inference being that he had been at best unreliable and at worst a traitor. The story was of course a fiction from beginning to end and simply did not happen, but if such tales were becoming common currency in the SLP, it is understandable that McLoughlin was expelled.

In truth, when looking at McLoughlin's background and all of the activities he was involved in at this point, it becomes clear that although he was in the SLP he was never really 'of' the SLP. By his own testimony, he remained in contact with Cathal Brugha throughout this period, and was involved in arms smuggling to Ireland.[43] This gives credence to Burden's story about the Irishman in Dewsbury Socialist Club, and it may have been that he and McLoughlin were attempting to sell some pistols in order to raise money or buy better arms for the IRA. Alternatively, it may have been that McLoughlin, who, as we have seen, believed that revolution was now the order of the day throughout Europe, simply wanted to prepare the British socialists for it. Whatever his motivations, whilst being in close proximity to arms and planning for armed attacks against the British government was second nature to Irish revolutionaries like McLoughlin, it was not to most British socialists. There were a few exceptions, mainly amongst the Clydeside socialists, some of whom did have considerable contact with Irish revolutionaries. However, on the whole, the overwhelming majority of British socialists, products of a very different political environment, were unused to such practices. This was particularly so in places like Dewsbury, where the SLP was said to be 'more a mutual admiration society'[44] than a vanguard party of the working class. To such people, McLoughlin may have appeared as reckless or extreme and possibly an agent provocateur.

It is also the case that although McLoughlin was an outstanding propagandist and the best draw the SLP had, he was not part of the SLP leadership. McLoughlin was not on the SLP executive, and never received a nomination in that direction. Dunfermline SLP put his name forward for the position of National Organiser, but this fell through when, at the 1921 Conference, the party voted against the establishment of such a full-time post.[45] McLoughlin's absence from the SLP leadership, at a time when the party was bereft of any outstanding figures, suggests perhaps that he did not have both feet in the SLP and that the existent leadership knew this to be the case. In small revolutionary organizations, composed of principled people, such a situation can, and often does, lead to mistrust and misunderstandings.

The demise of the Socialist Labour Party

McLoughlin's departure from the SLP came at a bad time for the party. The split, and more significantly the effects of the deepening economic slump, demoralized the SLP, inducing a severe crisis within the organization. As a result, party membership slumped and debts mounted. In the eleven months between the 1920 and 1921 conferences twelve branches resigned and seven were disbanded. Only six were established in their place. A full 796 members had resigned, been expelled, or simply lapsed into inactivity, with only 434 new entrants replacing them.[46] When it is considered that the party began 1920 with only 1258 members,[47] the scale of the trauma becomes clear. The party tried to put on a brave face, hailing the 1921 conference held in Dewsbury as the best it had ever had. The fact, however, that only 23 delegates, representing 22 branches, turned up perhaps tells another story.

Relations with Moscow were also difficult. In the summer of 1921, James Clunie travelled to Russia for the Third Comintern Congress, but was initially refused entry, having previously been instructed to take the party into the CPGB.[48] Clunie was eventually allowed entrance as an observer, but left in no doubt as to what was expected of him and his party by Moscow. On Clunie's return, however, the SLP began to distance itself from the Comintern. Soon after, it criticised what it considered to be the 'absurdity' of the organization 'in imposing its psychological outlook upon the rest of the countries where conditions dictated otherwise'.[49]

This retreat from Moscow was matched, and in many ways bound up with, a more general and fundamental SLP return to the isolationist outlook of its early days. C.H. Burden, for example, recalled that in his locality the party eschewed involvement in the day-to-day struggles of workers, viewing them as a 'distraction' from the 'real struggle' for the overthrow of capitalism.[50] Such an approach did not seem likely to recruit many workers, the only class capable of winning the 'real struggle'. That the party appeared now to have just one branch in Glasgow, which itself was advocating entry into the CPGB, in order to strengthen the hand of the revolutionary 'anti-Labour Party affiliation' element within that organisation,[51] was also testament to both a sharp decline in influence in Clydeside and discontent there amongst the remaining activists with this isolationism of the leadership.

By early 1922, the SLP was at death's door. Although claiming 1100 members at the time of the Third Comintern Congress,[52] the real figure, certainly of activists, was much lower and considerably dwarfed by the 5000 or so in the CPGB. Financially, the party was in 'a desperate position',[53] again unlike the CPGB, which received a generous subvention from Moscow, keeping it afloat in the stormy seas whipped up by the economic recession.

British intelligence certainly did not see the SLP as much of a threat and focused almost all of its attentions during this period on the CPGB and its links to the worldwide revolutionary movement.[54]

In 1922, the *Socialist* moved from a weekly to a monthly production, before disappearing altogether amidst claims that senior party figures had been using the party press in Glasgow to build up a printing business.[55] The party was never officially wound up, and from time to time there would be attempts to conduct some form of socialist agitation under its banner.[56] For its activists, however, 1922 marked the end, and those who remained in politics did so mainly in organizations like the National Council of Labour Colleges, where they could continue the deliverance of socialist education to workers. Most ex-members appear not to have joined the 'renegade' CPGB.[57] On the whole, it was an ignominious end to one of the British socialist movement's most important organizations, a party co-founded by James Connolly, and one that had been deeply influential in the political development of Sean McLoughlin.

McLoughlin post-SLP

Although expulsion from the SLP was an obvious blow to McLoughlin's revolutionary ambitions, it was one he reacted to in a positive fashion. He remained active in socialist politics and towards the end of that month, September 1921, conducted a series of meetings throughout Yorkshire.[58] It is not clear which, if any, organization he was now working with, but it may have been the unemployed workers' movement; a few months later, it was noted that McLoughlin had addressed a string of unemployed workers' meetings all over the north-east of England, including Gateshead, Newcastle, South Shields, Jarrow and West Hartlepool.[59] As will be seen, he also kept in close contact with an Irish communist movement that had changed much since his departure in November 1920.

This period in McLoughlin's life, however, would apparently soon be scarred by a deep personal tragedy. It began with the break up of his marriage. Isa McLoughlin had not accompanied her husband to Britain, but remained in Dublin, continuing to live in the house they had shared in Ballybough. Eventually, tired of waiting for him to return, she went back to Glasgow. Some time later, Danny McLoughlin's wife, Mary, who had been close to Isa, asked her brother, who was off on a trip to Scotland, to check up on her. When he reached the Barr home he was given short shrift and pointed in the direction of the family graveyard. There, he found the grave of Isa and Terence. As to the causes of the deaths, he was simply told that Isa had died of a 'broken heart', following the death of her infant son.

How or when McLoughlin received this news is unknown; as far as can be established, it was a loss to which he never referred at any point in his life.[60]

The Communist Party of Ireland and the slide to civil war

Back in Ireland, the political situation was changing rapidly. In July 1921, the IRA and the British state concluded a truce, pending negotiations 'on how the association of Ireland with the commonwealth of nations known as the British Empire may be reconciled with Irish nationalist aspirations'.[61] This led to the prospect of more relaxed political conditions and encouraged most communists to sink their differences, come out into the open, take over the dormant SPI, and apply for affiliation to the Comintern. This was achieved by early October and was followed a couple of weeks later by a change of name, to that of the Communist Party of Ireland. (CPI). Roddy Connolly, who had met Lenin at the Third Comintern Congress in Moscow and received his support for all of these moves, was installed as President of the new party, as well as editor of its journal, the *Workers' Republic*.

The CPI predicted that the Republican leaders would compromise with British imperialism and accept a deal that would fall short of the Republic. At this stage, it did not consider that civil war would occur, but that a 'good lot of discontent' from hard-line republicans would be 'channelled in a communist direction', helping to create a healthy communist opposition party in any new legislative assembly.[62] The first part of this perspective was borne out in December 1921, when the Irish republican leaders did accept such a compromise deal with the British government. Although a degree of fiscal autonomy was conceded, in most other respects the Treaty seemed to thwart republican aspirations. Partition was copperfastened, notwithstanding the promise of a boundary review. Control of Irish ports, a key British strategic objective,[63] was retained by London. The new 26-county Free State was not fully independent but still under the authority of the Crown, to which all elected representatives had to swear an oath of loyalty. Finally, the fledgling Irish exchequer was forced to contribute its share of the British national debt, as well as pay the pensions of ex-RIC members. In addition were the land annuity payments. It was little wonder, therefore, that Lionel Curtis, an adviser to the British government on colonial matters, described the Treaty as 'one of the greatest achievements of the Empire'.[64]

The CPI reacted with hostility to the Treaty and became the first political party to publicly oppose it. It was a 'shameful betrayal' that, in return for a 'hollow mockery' of their aspirations, Irish people were now compelled to become 'lackeys of the Empire and an ally of the most hateful tyranny history has produced'.⁶⁵ Michael Collins was dismissed by the CPI as 'a traitor, an opportunist, an imperialist careerist,' ⁶⁶ whilst Arthur Griffith was likened to Thiers, 'the puppet minister of the French Monarchists [during the period of the 1871 Paris Commune]...the hangman of the first workers' revolution.'⁶⁷ In an ominous revision of the second part of its pre-December perspective, the party now warned of 'civil war and social hell' if the Treaty was accepted.⁶⁸

Missing from the CPI discussion was the question of partition. The party clearly felt that the defeat of British rule in Dublin would end its control throughout the whole of Ireland and as a result directed most of its attention towards the relationship that existed between the republican leadership and the British. It was an understandable position to take, perhaps, as it did appear to most that events in Dublin were more significant than those in Belfast at this moment. But this, the omission of the institutionalization of a divide in the working class, and the reining in of its most important section behind reaction, constituted a serious theoretical oversight and weakness for the party. Undoubtedly it was one caused partly by the lack of a CPI base in Belfast, a situation that the party did try to rectify, albeit to no avail.⁶⁹

McLoughlin was in England at this point, but kept a close eye on these developments. He appears not to have expected quite such an agreement as the Treaty⁷⁰ and, like all other Irish communists, considered it to be obnoxious. Shortly after the Treaty was signed, McLoughlin wrote a long article in the *Workers' Republic* in which he displayed not only his anti-Treaty standpoint, but also his support for the new communist party. McLoughlin began by describing the Treaty sarcastically as 'Lloyd George's Xmas gift' to the Irish people. In accepting this 'gift', however, and making Ireland 'a grand country...for dividend hunters', the weak Irish bourgeoisie was at once exposing the class divisions, hitherto concealed, within the national movement, and signaling that movement's death knell:

> With the signing of this Treaty between the blood-stained imperialist butchers and the representatives of Ireland, the working class can now transfer their allegiance from the national representatives and give it to their own class. Soon the bitter truth enunciated by Marx nearly 74 years ago will be realized: "the workers' have no country. What they have not got, cannot be taken from them". With the definite establishment of the Irish Free State, the class struggle enters.⁷¹

McLoughlin also praised the establishment of the CPI, saying that it had come onto the world political stage 'at a most momentous time', and asserting its right to lead the Irish working class in the struggle against British imperialism:

> The Communist Party of Ireland now claims the allegiance of the Irish proletariat. It calls to the slum dwellers of the cities and towns of Ireland. To the poverty stricken agricultural workers, the ex-soldiers of the British and Irish Republican armies, here is the party of your class. Come into it. Help us to put an end to the careers of Lloyd George and his like. Give them the only Xmas box they deserve. When the rubbish of kings and presidents has been shot into the dustbin of history, the road to the Workers Republic is clearer.[72]

In Ireland, the CPI attempted to expose the class interests that lurked behind the Treaty, and warned the anti-Treaty majority within the IRA of the consequences should it fail to do so. CPI leader Connolly believed that this propaganda was working and that the IRA 'in large numbers' was drifting in the party's direction.[73] Whilst there was no evidence to sustain this claim, made in connection with an appeal to the Comintern for funding, three senior IRA officers – Liam Mellows, Joe McKelvey and Peadar O'Donnell – were sympathetic to the CPI,[74] with O'Donnell actually joining it[75] and winning for it some influence in his brigade.[76]

In addition, Connolly made contact with Rory O'Connor, the leader of Mellows, McKelvey and O'Donnell, and head of an IRA faction regarded by Connolly as the most militant in the entire organization. Connolly placed the services of the CPI and its newspaper at his disposal.[77] When civil war did finally erupt in June 1922, partly as a result of the British government's scuppering of the Collins-de Valera pact and its dismissal of the draft Free State constitution, considered by Churchill as too Republican,[78] the CPI felt the time had come for it to step on to the Irish political stage.

The CPI, IRA and the Irish Civil War

It is easy to understand why the CPI was so optimistic when civil war began. Since its inception in 1919, the Irish communist movement had been attempting to crack open the national revolutionary movement, expose the shortcomings of its middle-class leaders, and win over its proletarian and peasant-based rank and file. The CPI considered that the signing of the Treaty validated its analysis by highlighting the previously obscured bourgeois class interests upheld by the Republican leaders. Linking these class interests to the move by these elements towards compromise with imperialism, the CPI felt that it had taken a step towards success. The subsequent outbreak of civil war strengthened CPI optimism. With the supposedly monolithic national movement now split, the CPI hoped that the bewildered IRA majority that opposed the Treaty, but lacked any coherent analysis of, or strategy for dealing with, the new situation, might look to it for guidance. Moreover, the CPI also felt that the IRA would avail itself of the help that would be offered to it by Moscow and that this in turn would boost communist credibility in republican eyes. As a result of all these factors, the CPI participated in the civil war fighting and saw several of its members imprisoned. This was the volatile scenario to which McLoughlin returned in July.

It was Roddy Connolly who brought McLoughlin back to Ireland. Connolly had taken part in some of the fighting before being summoned to London to meet with the CPGB – the British party had a fostering role in relation to the CPI, similar to that of the German party over the Austrian and Swiss CPs [79] – and leading Comintern representative Mikhail Borodin. After attending a special meeting of the CPGB executive, which discussed the changing conditions in Ireland and the tasks of Irish communists therein,[80] Connolly and party treasurer George Pollock were interviewed closely by Borodin in order to devise an actual means of intervening in the Civil War. Borodin, keen to mobilize a broad anti-imperialist front, suggested that the Irish communists travel to Cork, still under anti-Treaty control, and present the IRA with a social programme. May had seen an extensive seizure of factories by workers and the establishment of soviets in several towns and cities in Counties Limerick, Tipperary and Cork.[81] The tiny CPI had itself intervened in one of these, at the Cleeves creamery combine in Limerick. Following an attempt by management to cut wages by one-third, the Cleeves workers had taken over the running of the creamery and the CPI agreed to assist them in the distribution of 60 tons of butter. Unfortunately for the communists, however, the ITGWU learned of this arrangement and pressurized the Cleeves workers to end their association with the CPI.[82] Overall, there would be 80 such occupations throughout Ireland in 1922.[83] The hope was that the Republicans would set up a provisional government, publicise the programme, and with the increased support this would bring from these militant workers and peasants, turn the tide of war against the Free State and its British backers.[84]

Connolly had another reason for travelling to England. He had been approached by anti-Treaty leaders Sean T. O'Kelly and Austin Stack and asked to bring McLoughlin back to Ireland in order that he might help in the organisation of the anti-Treaty forces in the field.[85] McLoughlin appears to have been living in Sheffield at this point, for that, it seems, is where Connolly contacted him.[86] McLoughlin agreed to return to Ireland, and became the CPI's director of organization.

McLoughlin and the Civil War

McLoughlin's involvement in the Civil War was nearly ended before it had begun. He and Connolly were almost arrested soon after their arrival in Dublin. A police officer recognized McLoughlin on Abbey St and shouted to a passing troop of Free State soldiers to detain him. McLoughin, though, kept his cool, claimed a case of mistaken identity, and was let go.[87] After surviving another scare on North King St, where he again was almost apprehended,[88] McLoughlin travelled with Connolly to Fermoy, Cork. There they presented IRA leader Liam Lynch with the social programme drawn up by Connolly and Borodin. For Borodin, this ten-point document was a mere temporary measure. As a leading Bolshevik activist for over twenty years, he was steeped in a political and intellectual tradition that placed the utmost importance on facts as the basis of strategy. Consequently, he instructed both the CPI and CPGB to carry out an exhaustive analysis of Irish social and economic structures, particularly those of rural Ireland, and envisaged the drafting of a far more detailed social programme when this had been completed.[89] To help with this ambitious task, Borodin decided also to introduce to the Irish communists the programmes of communist parties of other predominantly rural countries, such as Russia and Bulgaria. For now, though, the temporary document taken by Connolly and McLoughlin to Cork got the message across well enough. It was deeply radical, including such measures as nationalization of industry and finance; confiscation and re-distribution of ranch land; abolition of all rents and mortgages; a shorter working day; municipalisation and free use of all public services; and the arming of the workers.[90]

According to Connolly, Lynch was sympathetic in principle but more concerned with organising a military campaign to defeat the Free State.[91] This, though, was not the end of the CPI/IRA collaboration. Both McLoughlin and Connolly were heartened by this sympathetic attitude of the IRA leader. They believed that if they could show their worth to the IRA militarily, communist political influence over the army would increase.[92] To this end, the communists embarked on a sustained bout of activity. Connolly travelled to Germany and then Moscow in an attempt to put together an arms deal for the IRA.[93] McLoughlin, with far more military experience, decided to join the IRA and spread the communist message from within. He left Connolly at Thurles and travelled to Clonmel to meet Seamus Robinson,[94] one of the volunteers in his 'death or glory' squad of 1916, and now O/C of the IRA's Second Southern Division. Robinson also had left-wing views and described himself as a 'social republican'.[95] He appointed McLoughlin to the post of Commandant of an IRA flying column, which based itself initially in Glenbrohane, above Ballylanders in county Limerick. From there, McLoughlin began to organize the republican campaign and 'kept the Free State on edge from North Cork, to Tipperary and into Limerick City'.[96]

Shortly after his move into the IRA, McLoughlin submitted two lengthy articles to the *Workers' Republic*, outlining his views on the Civil War and ways of winning it. In the first of these articles, 'How the Republicans may win', McLoughlin highlighted the weakness of the Republican strategy in the immediate post-Treaty period. 'De Valera', he maintained, 'had been in the clouds' and his 'vacillation' had left Republicans weak. This was in contrast to the Free State, which was building its forces and preparing for the fight. All, though, was not lost. McLoughlin argued that as the Civil War unfolded, it was becoming 'more and more clear that the Free State [was] merely a puppet state, controlled and manipulated from London'. The new Free State government, bound hand and foot to imperialism, was 'nakedly and unashamedly a bourgeois and capitalist government, hostile to labour and carrying its hostility into action'. In these circumstances, a class-based challenge to the Free State was the only option. The mobilization of the full power of the Irish working class and marginalized rural classes was possible, but only if the Republican leaders adopted a social programme; such workers would not be moved 'by the sentimental appeals of a capitalist republic in which they would be wage slaves'. McLoughlin concluded with a ringing declaration:

> The way is clear. Victory lies with the side that can attract to itself the masses, the workers of the towns and cities and the landless peasants... the programme would be based upon the present needs of the masses, comprising confiscation of the land, the big estates and ranches... social ownership of creameries, confiscation of all heavy industries etc, land and housing to be in the hands of councils elected by workers and peasants. Republicans, here is your chance. With the workers behind you, the Free State relapses into the black hell from whence it came.[97]

In the second article, written the following month, McLoughlin surveyed the situation as it then stood, almost two months into the Civil War. He pointed out that whilst the Republicans appeared to be holding their own and that morale was good, this in itself would not lead to victory. The Free State was well organized, he maintained, had a clear and coherent programme, and was enthusiastically supported, not just by the British but by the capitalist class, the landowners, ranchers, shopkeepers and the Press as well.

Economic conscription of a half-starved working class was a further factor in the growing strength of the Free State. By way of contrast, McLoughlin focused on republican inability to win over the urban and rural workers, large sections of which remained apathetic and indifferent to the outcome of the war. Again, he stressed the importance of the social programme. Just as the Free State had rallied its supporters around a coherent programme, so too must the Republicans:

> No party in the world today can exist without formulating its programme in a clear and lucid manner. The Free State provisional government has outlined its programme and policy, both harmonizing with the policy and programme pursued by the imperial government of Great Britain. Government by the few for the many, exploitation of the poor and weak and aggrandizement for the powerful and rich, the bayonet and prison cell for those who disagree. This programme will not attract the masses. It remains for the Republicans, by outlining just and equitable proposals and an honest and fearless economic policy to capture the people and so win the present struggle.[98]

Militarily, McLoughlin was busy during this period. According to Free State intelligence, McLoughlin became the leader of the Republican forces in Kilmallock, close to Ballylanders in county Limerick.[99] In the early days of the Civil War, Kilmallock was a large centre of anti-Treaty resistance. It was taken by the IRA on 13 July, and was the scene of a Free State reverse towards the end of that month.[100] There had also been the establishment of a soviet at the local creamery in the town, which had been in operation from May to June 1922.[101] By early August, however, the situation had changed. The successful Free State sea landings in Cork and Kerry drew most of the several hundred or so IRA fighters away from the town, making relatively straightforward the advance of Free State commandant Eoin O'Duffy into it.[102] From that point on, IRA flying columns were established and began a campaign of sabotage and harassment in the surrounding areas. This included sniping attacks on Free State army barracks,[103] post office raids,[104] and attempts to blow up the railway bridges that linked Kilmallock to Knocklong.[105]

In McLoughlin's flying column was Liam Manahan, whom he had met some years earlier during his spell as a Volunteer organizer in Tipperary and east Limerick. According to Manahan, McLoughlin had a 'good command' and appeared to be carrying out a 'good fight' in a situation that was 'a bit wild at times'.[106] McLoughlin may also have had some success in his endeavours to promote socialism within the ranks of the IRA. In a report sent to the Comintern in late 1922 it was noted that:

> The Director of Organisation was sent to the south among the republicans and for the time being he has won the position of Commandant in one of the most active flying columns. This gives him a very useful influence among the republican worker fighters. He has reported good success and widespread sympathy for the social programme everywhere among the proletariat in the South West.[107]

Having lost control of all cities and towns in Munster by mid-August, however, the Republicans became increasingly hard-pressed and were gradually worn down. As McLoughlin himself pointed out when appointed Second Southern Division O/C for operations, 'there was nothing to operate'.[108] The position became worse and on 7 December disaster struck McLoughlin's unit, when Free State troops killed one of its members, Hugh O' Donnell, and arrested Liam Manahan near Kilfinnane.[109] McLoughlin and the rest of the flying column managed to stay on the run, but not for long. On 18 December they were all captured by a joint patrol of Free State soldiers, operating from both Limerick City and Doon. It appears that the republicans were surrounded in a house with no chance of escape. At the time of his capture, McLoughlin had been ill and was confined to bed. For the Free State army, South West Command, the arrest of McLoughlin was a coup and it immediately sent off a dispatch to the centre, informing them that the 'red-flagger from Dublin, and leader of the Die-hards in Kilmallock' was now in their custody.[110]

McLoughlin was sent to Limerick Jail, where he joined several hundred other republican prisoners. He faced an uncertain future. In October, the Free State government had passed a regulation establishing Military Tribunals, empowered to pass sentences of death on any republican found in possession of guns and bombs, including 'articles to be used in the manufacture of bombs'.[111] Again, it was possible to detect the hand of the British in this new development; in September, Samuel Hoare, writing on behalf of the Home Office to the Secretary of State for the Colonies, had complained bitterly that the Free state seemed to be 'hand in glove' with the IRA, and that what was needed 'if the Provisional Government is to survive', was 'a really great effort to wipe out the Irregulars'.[112] This advice was given the moral sanction of the Catholic Church, which simultaneously issued a pastoral that effectively denounced republicans as murderers and assassins.[113] In November, the executions began and almost immediately included men, like Mellows, Barrett, McKelvey and O'Connor, who had been imprisoned long before the new regulation had been introduced and had not been tried in front of any court. By the time of McLoughlin's arrest, thirteen men had been shot, and the day following another seven were executed in Dublin.

Immediately upon his arrival, McLoughlin was elected O/C of the IRA prisoners in Limerick jail.[114] Conditions in the jail were appalling: according to one local newspaper, it had only sixty cells but held over six hundred republican prisoners.[115] In addition, it lacked basic sanitation facilities. As a result of this, and the difficulties of the republican struggle at that point, morale amongst the prisoners was said to be 'collapsing'.[116] According to Manahan, McLoughlin 'very quickly got things organised', including the repair and installation of toilet facilities on all wings.[117] McLoughlin also put in place a command structure and appointed Bob de Courcy, who was elected mayor of Limerick later that year, and Liam Cripps as his Adjutants. Before long, he had managed also to get arms smuggled into the jail.[118]

At this point, though, a series of courts martial took place in Limerick jail, presided over by General McManus. Death sentences were passed on several IRA members, including McLoughlin. These were not carried out. During the Civil War, the final decision on whether to execute prisoners lay in the main with local commanders. So far, there had been no executions in Limerick Jail. McLoughlin claimed that he had a meeting with the prison governor, Hughes, and informed him that should any execution take place, he would make the situation for Hughes 'so costly, as not to be worth the while'. McLoughlin also brought an end to the practice of using IRA prisoners to clear mines. McLoughlin maintains that three men were later executed in Limerick jail but that their presence at the prison had been unknown to the rest of the Republicans, and that in the aftermath he warned McManus what to expect if he tried this again. McManus apparently gave an assurance that there would be no more executions.[119]

It is difficult to corroborate all of this, especially in light of other comments attributed to McLoughlin, where he seemed to indicate that the Labour leadership in Dublin had played some role in having his death sentence postponed.[120] McLoughlin appeared to make this point in order to show that the Labour leaders held sway over the Free State government, and were, as a result, guilty by association in relation to all of those death sentences that were carried out. Some of McLoughlin's comments, however, were in line with events as they unfolded at Limerick. There were no executions in Limerick prison until 20 January 1923, although it was two men, Cornelius McMahon and Patrick Hennessy, rather than the three McLoughlin spoke of, who eventually faced the firing squad. After this there were no more Civil War executions in Limerick. This suggests that McLoughlin's recollections might have been accurate and that a possible reason Limerick jail had so few executions was this pressure placed on the authorities by the prisoners. One further factor, not mentioned by McLoughlin but touched upon by Manahan, was the attitude of the local people in Limerick; Manahan maintained that the executions were unpopular and that the local population 'kicked up a row' about them.[121] This pressure from the outside would certainly have been felt by the Free State authorities in Limerick and may well have been another factor in their decision to suspend the executions.

At the same time as these events were taking place, McLoughlin's sister Mary took out a writ of Habeas Corpus, directed to both the governor of Limerick Jail and Free State army Adjutant General Gearoid O'Sullivan, in order to clarify the precise legal basis of his detention and have his rights as a POW upheld. The application was heard in Dublin on 22 January 1923 at the Kings Bench Division, before Lord Justice O'Connor. Alexander Lynn, on behalf of McLoughlin, argued that since 6 December 1922, the day the Free State Legislature became active, there had been no laws passed under its auspices granting to the Military the quite exceptional powers they now possessed. Lynn pointed out that he was not questioning the Free State army's right to detain. In the absence, however, of any law passed through the proper channels outlined in the Constitution that created new crimes and fixed extraordinary penalties to them, (like those crimes tried and sentences handed out by the Military Tribunals), the Free State was compelled to treat IRA prisoners as prisoners of war. This, according to Lynn, was the sole aim and purpose of his client's writ. The Free State's policy of executions would have been thrown into jeopardy had this application succeeded. O'Connor, however, rejected the application, describing the basis on which it had been made as 'absolutely unsustainable'. Ignoring Lynn's argument entirely, O'Connor concluded that the application had questioned the right of the military to detain and threw it out on the grounds that the courts 'had nothing whatever to do...with the adequacy of the grounds upon which detention was exercised'.[122]

As we have seen, however, McLoughlin's life had already been spared, at least for the time being. In the ensuing period, he continued with his work in improving the conditions within the jail. He also became involved in that perennial activity of incarcerated Republicans, the organizing of jail breaks. Generally this was achieved through tunneling, although on some occasions it also included impersonation, where prisoners on less serious charges about to be moved elsewhere, would allow those facing possible death sentences to take their places. In such instances it took weeks or months for the Free State authorities to track down the men concerned. By the time they did, the prisoners had often been released or had escaped from other jails. McLoughlin was involved in helping at least one prisoner to escape and was said to be in contact with republicans on the outside, in preparation for a mass breakout.[123]

McLoughlin's position in Limerick jail at this point was that of a respected leader who had the confidence and support of the men. He had shown an ability and willingness to not only introduce discipline within the ranks and improve organization, but also to alleviate partially the hardships imposed on the men by prison life, as well as helping some to freedom. That this was achieved at a time when Republican morale was plummeting inside and outside the jails is again indicative of his leadership qualities. But it was a position of authority that was soon to be challenged. Before long, McLoughlin would become entwined in a controversy that was not only divisive and undermined him in the eyes of some in jail, but also acted as a catalyst for his eventual departure from the IRA.

Dealing with defeat: McLoughlin, the peace moves in Limerick jail and the Liam Deasy proposals

The seeds of this controversy were sown during McLoughlin's period of involvement in the Civil War fighting. Although he was said to have been active and had a good command, McLoughlin himself was deeply unhappy about the manner in which the war was being fought. The unwillingness of the IRA leadership on the outside to adopt a social programme had, for him, left the struggle isolated from the urban and rural workers, depriving it of some much needed class muscle. Communists had made strenuous and sustained efforts to remedy this situation and at times had felt close to success. Some months before his execution, Liam Mellows had written to the IRA's Assistant Chief of Staff in Leinster and Ulster, Ernie O'Malley from Mountjoy jail, outlining the need for a social programme based on that of the CPI, and for the establishment of a Provisional republican government to popularize it. Mellows, who according to the CPI had, along with Joe McKelvey, indicated a desire to join the party, warned that the Free State meant capitalism and imperialism and that only a turn towards the working class could topple it.[124]

In addition, leading CPI member George Pollock recalled how at a meeting he attended with CPGB and IRA leaders in Dublin, IRA Quartermaster General Tom Derrig promised the support of the army to any provisional government set up by the communists in Cork.[125] An agreement was signed by the IRA and CPGB leaders committing the Republicans to the type of social programme outlined by McLoughlin and Connolly earlier.[126] Meanwhile, Roddy Connolly had travelled to Moscow, albeit unsuccessfully, in order to procure arms for the republicans and Ernie O'Malley had expressed an interest in using the CPI for IRA intelligence work.[127] Republicans in Glasgow, under the leadership of Seamus Robinson's brother Joe, were also said to be working closely with the Clydeside communists.[128] In spite of these positive developments, however, most of which show that the CPI did influence the outlook of some within the IRA, the leadership on the outside refrained from implementing the social programme, preferring instead to dig in for a protracted, if scarcely winnable, guerrilla war. As a result, the class militancy, particularly of the rural workers and smallest farmers of the west and south, which was bound up with an anti-Treaty outlook, was left untapped by the republican struggle.

In addition, McLoughlin was not impressed by the apparent military incompetence and indiscipline of the IRA. In a speech he delivered shortly after release from jail, he highlighted some of the difficulties he had faced from both the leadership and some of the rank-and-file as well. On occasion, local commanders who had disagreed with his instructions had 'cleared off' with contingents of men to carry out 'stunts' which, according to McLoughlin, 'usually ended in inglorious defeat'. At other times, McLoughlin found it simply 'impossible' to get the rank and file to obey instructions. He contrasted the chaos and lack of organisation within the IRA to what he saw as the well structured and disciplined Free State army, and identified it as a further reason for the rout inflicted by them.[129]

After his imprisonment McLoughlin had more time to reflect on these views and develop them. As he saw it, the IRA had two choices: it could either organize a mass breakout from the jails for a last stand battle against the Free State, or it could call an end to all hostilities.[130] Following discussions and exchanges of views with prisoners and republicans on the outside, McLoughlin eventually plumped for the latter; the war should be ended. Shortly afterwards, he drew up a peace document and presented a copy of it to both Free State General McManus and Major-General Brennan. Briefly, the proposals were that the Free State grant a temporary parole to four prisoners in Limerick Jail, McLoughlin being one of them. The four would meet with the IRA leadership, and put it to them that the conflict be ended. The document stressed that it was not possible to state in advance what measures might secure such peace; only those on the outside could decide that. It was suggested that the Free State stop all executions for the duration of the initiative, and that the IRA too cease the 'punitive measures' it had adopted, which had included assassinations of Free State politicians and officials. The proposals, which were endorsed by all of the republican leaders in Limerick jail, concluded with a stark warning: if the war continued much longer, Ireland would be a 'land of blood and ashes'.[131]

Unknown to McLoughlin and the Limerick prisoners, however, more significant developments were unfolding elsewhere. After his arrest and court martial on 25 January 1923, IRA Deputy Chief of Staff Liam Deasy undertook 'to accept and aid in an immediate and unconditional surrender of all arms and men as required by [Free State] General Mulcahy'. Deasy had been considering this step before his arrest and concluded his statement with an appeal to the remainder of the IRA leadership to issue a general surrender and give themselves up to the Free State.[132] Deasy's proposals were different to those outlined by McLoughlin. McLoughlin was asking for an opportunity to meet with the IRA leadership, to put forward the view that the war be ended and discuss ways in which this might be done; Deasy, on the other hand, had committed himself to aiding in an immediate and unconditional surrender. Deasy later stated that his original request was merely to be granted facilities to contact the IRA on the outside, in order to impress on them his view that the conflict be ended, but that this was rejected by the Free State, which insisted that he call publicly for surrender and aid actively in its implementation. The alternative was the firing squad.[133]

Having rejected Deasy's initial request to be allowed leave to visit the IRA leaders, there was little chance of the Free State acceding to the similar one made by McLoughlin and the Limerick republicans. In fact, sensing an opportunity to exploit these favourable developments, the Free State military attempted to intimidate the Limerick prisoners into accepting the Deputy Chief of Staff's proposals. McLoughlin claimed that a gun was held to his head, and that he was both told that the IRA leadership on the outside had surrendered and warned that if he did not give his support to the Deasy document, wholesale executions of prisoners would begin in Limerick.[134] McLoughlin's response, however, was not to sign the Deasy proposals, but to convene a meeting of the Limerick prisoners, where the issue was discussed. McLoughlin then wrote to Deasy. He wished from Deasy the full facts of the situation: had Deasy agreed to an unconditional surrender, and was this the policy of the IRA GHQ? Although McLoughlin agreed with Deasy that the war should be ended, he made it clear that unless GHQ backed any such proposals, he would neither support nor vouch for them. To attempt to influence the Limerick prisoners in order that they accept the Deasy proposals, without GHQ ratification, would be to betray the 'trust and confidence' that they had in him. McLoughlin made it clear that he 'would rather go to the grave' than do this, no matter what his own view on the situation was. He concluded his letter to Deasy by wishing him luck in his endeavours to bring about an honourable peace, and predicted that the Limerick prisoners would accept any agreement endorsed by the IRA leadership. In a final point, McLoughlin stressed the need for unity; for the sake of the movement, any decision needed to be 'unanimous'.[135]

McLoughlin's last point about the need for unanimity was significant because in Limerick jail divisions were beginning to open up. McLoughlin's decision to convene a meeting that discussed such a proposal as unconditional surrender, even though he was not advocating it, was not universally popular. When the Deasy proposals were leaked another meeting of the prisoners was held, and again divisions were evident. McLoughlin appeared to want a discussion on Deasy, but according to Liam Manahan this was rejected by a majority of the prisoners. Manahan, who had supported McLoughlin's original plan of obtaining parole in order to meet with the IRA leaders, opposed McLoughlin himself here, arguing that there 'should be no consideration of the Deasy proposals'.[136]

The situation became more strained for McLoughlin when it emerged that 'Roddy Brown' (Roddy Connolly) may have contacted him and suggested that he convince the Limerick jail authorities to let him out, to enable him to take part in talks Connolly had arranged with the Labour Party designed to end the war. It is not clear when this message was received but, judging from Manahan's account, it appears to have happened in the midst of all these other events and might have included the suggestion that McLoughlin sign the prison promise. This was the pledge to refrain from armed struggle against the Free State, necessary if release from prison was to be gained. The Comintern leadership in Moscow was now insisting that imprisoned Irish communists sign it to get them out of jail and the party more involved in the class struggles of Irish workers.[137] McLoughlin was deeply opposed to this directive,[138] but if it is true that Connolly did so contact him, it might partly explain his later comments about the Labour party preventing his execution. Added to the controversy over the Deasy proposals, however, it served to widen the distance between McLoughlin and his opponents, who saw it as evidence that he was 'becoming friendly with the Free State'.[139] As a result of all of these events, McLoughlin's position as leader was undermined.

The decision of the Free State to publish both the Limerick and Deasy proposals, along with reports of IRA units surrendering in Kanturk, in the same edition of the *Irish Independent*,[140] made matters worse for McLoughlin. It seemed as though his proposals and Deasy's were linked, and part of a groundswell of Republican opinion in favour of surrender.

The situation hardly improved for McLoughlin when the IRA leadership rejected Deasy's appeal and criticized the Limerick proposals, stating that they were providing 'propaganda for the enemy'.[141]

McLoughlin reacted angrily to the way in which his proposals had been linked to those of Deasy. He argued that the Free State had deliberately misrepresented him and that he had pointed out to Deasy the need for GHQ ratification of any ceasefire plan before it could be acceptable. McLoughlin also maintained that the Free State had tried to coerce the Limerick prisoners into accepting the Deasy proposals, and had lied by telling them that Liam Lynch, IRA Chief of Staff, had surrendered. He concluded by stressing that all of the actions he had taken in response – the holding of meetings etc. – had been done to prevent a wholesale collapse of the IRA in Limerick jail.[142] The IRA leadership, however, remained of the opinion that the action of the Limerick prison leaders had been detrimental to the Republican struggle. It accepted that the action was motivated by a desire to bring about an 'honourable' end to the war, but nonetheless represented gross indiscipline on behalf of the jail leaders; they knew that the regulations of the IRA forbade members of the organization 'from taking part in matters connected with peace negotiations', and that such matters 'rested with the Government of the Republic and Army Executive'. By way of conclusion, it was suggested that they be court-martialled on release.[143]

All of these unofficial peace initiatives by the various IRA factions in early 1923 eventually came to nought. The Free State was so dominant that by this stage it had no need to seek any form of compromise or acquiesce in any settlement that afforded even a modicum of honour to its opponents. The IRA leadership, on the other hand, although in receipt of an ongoing battering, and with its army rapidly being degraded to the point of destruction, did not yet believe that all was lost. On the contrary, its leaders continued to hope that the tide might yet be turned and opposed all talk of a ceasefire. By May, however, they would finally be disabused of these notions, and forced into an unconditional surrender – precisely the scenario that McLoughlin and others in Limerick had tried to prevent three months earlier.

McLoughlin remained O/C on the main wing in Limerick prison, but his authority was damaged by the entire peace move controversy. Manahan appears to have been elected as O/C for his wing, and relations between him and McLoughlin became strained. According to Manahan, McLoughlin occasionally visited his wing, but was asked by Manahan to stay away. This led to a heated row between the two, with Manahan recalling 'he was not an easy man to argue with'.[144] McLoughlin, for his part, maintains that he retained the support of most of the prisoners, that they 'backed him to the end' and that those who 'misunderstood and reviled' him and his allies were 'all sorts of queer creatures'.[145]

Departure from the IRA, towards a new strategy for Irish communism

Although McLoughlin retained support amongst some of the IRA prisoners, his involvement in the organization was coming to an end. The dissatisfaction he already felt with the IRA leaders could only have been exacerbated by their decision to keep the war going, when all hope of victory had gone. This gave the Free State the pretext it required to continue with the executions policy. Between February and May, 22 republican prisoners were shot, with nine of these executions coming on 13 and 14 March. The arrival of Dan Breen and Con Lehane in Limerick Jail added to McLoughlin's dissatisfaction; he did not 'see eye to eye' with this pair and after a dispute, details of which are unknown, McLoughlin resigned as prison O/C. McLoughlin states that he still had the backing of the prisoners, but shortly afterwards was moved to Mountjoy jail.[146]

McLoughlin was taken to Mountjoy on Friday, 1 June 1923. Mountjoy held most of the imprisoned IRA leadership, all of whom were doubtless aware of McLoughlin's role in the Limerick peace controversy. This, though, did not seem to affect or bother McLoughlin. In fact, soon after arriving at Mountjoy, he embarked upon a sustained bout of communist propaganda activity. He organized political education classes and lectures for the prisoners, where he attempted to introduce them to the basics of Marxism, as applied to Irish conditions. There were a handful of communist prisoners in Mountjoy, but McLoughlin was noted by Peadar O'Donnell to be the most active of the group.[147] During his months in Mountjoy, McLoughlin delivered 27 lectures on socialism, all of which, he said, were followed with 'rapt attention' by rank-and-file Volunteers.[148] This enthusiasm, however, did not extend to the IRA 'big guns'. It appears that the IRA leadership in Mountjoy jail were unhappy about McLoughlin's communist activities and 'made every effort' to prevent his meetings.[149] By this stage, though, McLoughlin was unaffected by such actions or opinions. The Civil War was over, and with it had gone the constraints and heavy responsibilities of leadership that he had shouldered in Limerick Jail. To McLoughlin's eye, fundamental shifts in strategy were now necessary if the Free State was to be defeated in the future. A turn to class politics was the only way forward. But the republican leaders were incapable of this. Not only were they militarily incompetent, they could also be reactionary on social issues. Austin Stack, for example, was dismissed by McLoughlin as 'never likely to be of any use to the working class', whilst PJ Rutledge and Frank Aiken, who replaced the deceased Lynch as IRA Chief of Staff, were dubbed a 'pair of rotters' towards the workers.[150] Whilst in Limerick, McLoughlin had recognized and upheld the IRA leadership's right to decide on important policy issues, in the new post-Civil War situation in Mountjoy he cared little for its views or opinions on any matter. It was an estrangement that would widen out further in the weeks ahead.

McLoughlin became convinced that a new movement would emerge when the jails were opened. He argued that the IRA rank and file would not take up arms again 'except for a workers' republic' and that they would overthrow their current, failed leadership in order to do so.[151] At the same time, McLoughlin identified some senior republicans who he thought would move in a socialist direction. Included here were Mick Fitzpatrick, Michael Kilroy, Sean Lehane and Sean Fitzpatrick, all of whom, he maintained, had expressed support for communism.[152] These men would be to the fore of the new movement envisaged by McLoughlin. Seamus McGowan, another CPI/IRA prisoner who had been ploughing the communist furrow since his arrest in July 1922, expressed similar views. 'I did a lot of propaganda work amongst them', McGowan pointed out in January 1924, 'and find that the IRA in general and some high and low ranking officers are very strong for a workers' republic'.[153]

As a result of the development in McLoughlin's views, and his growing confidence that the CPI could shape the future of the anti-Treaty struggle, he would soon be advocating a communist break from the IRA and open opposition to its leaders in order to win over this disaffected rank-and-file. Republicanism would remain a key political base for communist development, but in McLoughlin's eyes the method of approach would have to be altered. In consequence, McLoughlin dropped his objections to the prison promise and signed it.[154] He was released from Mountjoy jail on 13 October 1923. Despite the tribulations of the previous two years, McLoughlin left prison with great optimism. He saw favourable opportunities coming the way of the communists and was filled with a determination that they could and would be exploited. It would be this positive perspective that would inform all of his activity in the turbulent period ahead.

Notes

1   NA, Sean McLoughlin, Statement to the Bureau of Military History, WS 290, p. 46.
2   Ibid., pp. 46-7.

3   *The Socialist*, 13-1-1921.
4   *The Socialist*, 3-2-1921. 'Henry Dubb' was the hapless worker created by US socialist cartoonist Ryan Walker. Dubb's unquestioning acceptance of his miserable conditions of existence and the absurd logic offered by the capitalists to justify it formed the basis of many of Walker's satirical strips. Normally published by the US Socialist Party, the sketches were popular among British socialists. McLoughlin on occasion also referred to the unfortunate 'Henry' in his public speeches.
5   BNA, report on the revolutionary organizations in the United Kingdom, CAB 24/119/cp2451, 3-2-21.
6   *The Socialist*, 3-2-1921.
7   RGASPI, Report of the Socialist Labour Party of Great Britain to the 3rd Congress of the Third (Communist) International, 490/1-3/7.
8   See: Raymond Challinor, *Origins of British Bolshevism*, (London: 1977), pp. 215-34. The irony, of course, is that when the CPGB finally applied for affiliation to the Labour Party, it was summarily rejected.
9   Sean McLoughlin 'Unity, Ireland and the Revolution' in the *Socialist*, May Day supplement, 1920.
10 Ibid.
11 For Rosa Luxembourg's views on this question, see Chris Harman, *The Lost Revolution, Germany 1918-23*, (London: 1997), pp. 64-65.
12 The *Socialist*, 17-2-1921.
13 The *Socialist*, 24-2-1921.
14 The *Socialist, 14-4-1921*.
15 BNA, report on the revolutionary organisations in the United Kingdom, CAB 24/ 123/cp2938, 12-5-21.
16 Final SLP Agenda of 18th Annual Conference, Dewsbury, March 1921.
17 *The Socialist*, 14-4-1921.
18 BNA, report on the revolutionary organisations in the United Kingdom, CAB 24/121/cp2765, 23-3-21.
19 JT Murphy, *Preparing for Power*, (London: 1934) pp. 212-14.
20 BNA, report on the revolutionary organizations in the United Kingdom, CAB 24/131/cp3579, 22-12-21.
21 JT Murphy, *Preparing for Power*, pp. 212-14.
22 JT Murphy quoted in Challinor, *Origins of British Bolshevism*, p. 262. Murphy was a leading figure in the CPGB.
23 The *Socialist*, 21-4-1921.
24 The *Socialist*, 28-4-1921.
25 C.H. Burden quoted in Challinor, *Origins of British Bolshevism*, p. 267. AJ Cook was the leader of the Miners' Federation of Great Britain.

26 Peter Brearey interview with C. H. Burden, 1975. I am obliged to Raymond Challinor for a copy of the tape.
27 The *Socialist*, 5-5-1921.
28 The *Socialist*, 7-7-1921.
29 BNA, report on the revolutionary organisations in the United Kingdom, CAB/127/cp3252, 18-8-21.
30 The *Socialist*, 7-7-1921.
31 The *Socialist*, 7-7-1921.
32 Sean McLoughlin private papers.
33 The *Socialist*, 25-8-1921.
34 The *Socialist*, 8-9-1921.
35 This took place on 8 March 1921, in response to the German government's opposition to paying the sum of 226,000 billion gold marks in war reparations. The eventual sum agreed upon was a still-ruinous 133,000 billion gold marks.
36 For more on Comintern outlook and strategy in this period, see McDermott/Agnew *The Comintern: a History of International Communism from Lenin to Stalin* (Basingstoke: 1996), pp. 27-32.
37 Peter Brearey interview with CH Burden, 1975.
38 BNA, report on the revolutionary organizations in the United Kingdom, CAB24/128/cp3350, 29-9-21.
39 Peter Brearey interview with C.H. Burden, 1975.
40 Ibid.
41 Ibid.
42 Ibid.
43 NA, Sean McLoughlin, p. 47.
44 Peter Breary interview with CH Burden, 1975.
45 Socialist Labour Party of Great Britain, *Report of 18th Annual Conference, Dewsbury, March 26-27, 1921*, (Glasgow: 1921).
46 Ibid.
47 Socialist Labour Party of Great Britain, *Report of 17th Annual Conference, Carlisle, April 3-4 1920*, (Glasgow: 1920).
48 *The Socialist*, 25-8-1921.
49 *The Socialist*, 27-10-1921.
50 Peter Brearey Interview with C.H. Burden, 1975.
51 The Glasgow and Woolwich branches moved a resolution to this effect at the 1921 party Conference, but were defeated by 17 votes to 5, SLP, *Report of 18th Annual Conference, Dewsbury, 26-27 March 1921*, (Glasgow: 1921).
52 RGASPI, SLP report to Comintern, 490/1/3-29.

53 BNA, report on the revolutionary organizations in the United Kingdom, CAB 24/136/cp3917, 31-3-22.
54 In the fortnightly reports compiled by British intelligence throughout this period, the SLP received only brief and occasional mentions. This was in contrast to the CPGB, which was the subject of a detailed analysis, sometimes 4 or 5 pages long, in virtually every report.
55 Peter Brearey, interview with C.H.Burden, 1975.
56 Including the SLP set up by Arthur Scargill in 1996. This party described its establishment as a 're-formation' and traced its lineage back to James Connolly.
57 Peter Brearey interview with C.H. Burden, 1975.
58 BNA, report on the revolutionary organizations in the United Kingdom, CAB 24/128/cp3350, 29-9-21.
59 Ibid, CAB 24/136/cp3983, 16-5-22.
60 I am grateful to the Shiel family for this information. It seems that it has been passed down through the generations since the 1920s. Unfortunately, however, it is information that I have yet to verify. A search through the records at the GRO in Scotland failed to reveal any such deaths in this period. In the case of Terence, there still has been no death registered in Scotland of anyone of that name who was born in or around 1920.
61 Dorothy McArdle, *the Irish Republic*, (London: 1968) p. 480.
62 See 'Peace or War in Ireland?' by Roddy Connolly, written in August 1921, and published in the *Workers' Republic*, 17-12-1921.
63 See: T. Ryle Dwyer, *Michael Collins and the Treaty*, (Cork: 1991) pp. 59-61 for British strategic interests and their importance to the British negotiators.
64 Kieran Allen, *Is Southern Ireland a Neo-Colony?* (Dublin: 1990) p. 18.
65 The *Workers' Republic*, 17-12-1921.
66 The *Workers' Republic*, 29-4-1922.
67 The *Workers' Republic*, 25-3-1922.
68 For more on the CPI in this period see: Charlie McGuire, *Roddy Connolly and the Struggle for Socialism in Ireland*, (Cork: 2008), pp. 47-57.
69 The CPI tried to link up with the ILP in Belfast, which was a militant organization having formerly been home to leading socialists such as Jack Hedley and Simon Greenspon. The party, though, for unstated reasons, was unable to complete the merger, and never formed a branch in Belfast, RGASPI, CPI, (section of the Third International), report, 9-11-21, 5/3/581/22.

70 Sean McLoughlin private papers.
71 *Workers' Republic*, 24-12-1921.
72 Ibid.
73 RGASPI, Roddy Connolly, Report to the Comintern on the Irish Party, Berlin, 12 April 1922, 495/89/16-18.
74 RGASPI, Theses on Irish Policy, 495/89/11-26.
75 RGASPI, CPI to ECCI, August 31 1922, 495/89/12-43.
76 RGASPI, Borodin interviews delegates from Irish party, 15-7-22, 495/89/13-8 refers to a CPI member who was a Commandant-General of the IRA, and who had 'a great influence in his brigade', taking large quantities of the CPI newspaper for it. It could only have been O'Donnell.
77 RGASPI, Borodin interviews delegates from Irish party, 495/89/13-17.
78 The Collins-de Valera pact was conducted prior to the June 1922 Free State Constitutional Convention election as a means of shelving the question of the treaty from that election and keeping the door open to future re-unification of the republican leadership. It angered deeply the British government, as did the draft Constitution, drawn up by Collins in order to placate the anti-Treatyites. For more on British government attitudes to the pact and the draft constitution, see: T.P. Coogan, *Michael Collins*, (London: 1991), pp. 322-326, Calton Younger, *Ireland's Civil War*, (London: 1968) pp. 285-96, T. Ryle Dwyer, *Big Fellow, Long Fellow*, (Dublin: 1999), p. 309, DG Boyce, *Englishmen and Irish Troubles*, (Cambridge: 1972), p. 179 and Bew et al, *Northern Ireland 1921-94*, (London: 1995), p. 29.
79 Emmet O'Connor/Barry McLoughlin, 'Sources on Ireland and the Communist International 1920-43', *Saothar, 21*, (1996), p. 103.
80 BNA, report on the revolutionary organizations in the United Kingdom, CAB 24/138/ cp4132, 27-7-22.
81 C.D. Greaves, *Liam Mellows and the Irish Revolution*, (London: 1971), pp. 317-18.
82 See McGuire, 'Roddy Connolly', p. 54.
83 Emmet O'Connor, *Syndicalism in Ireland, 1917-23*, (Cork: 1988), p. 104.
84 RGASPI, Borodin interviews delegates from Irish party, 15-7-22, 495/89/13-6/23.
85 *Irish Press*, 29-1-48. Letter written by Connolly in response to McEntee red scare tactics during 1948 General Election campaign.
86 Mike Milotte, *Communism in Modern Ireland*, (Dublin: 1984), p. 60.

87 Mike Milotte, 'Communist Politics in Ireland 1916-45', PhD thesis, QUB, (1977) p. 110.
88 Sean McLoughlin private papers.
89 RGASPI, CPI report to ECCI, October 1921 to October 1922, 495/89/16/40-72. See also Borodin interviews delegates from Irish party, 15-7-22, 495/89/13/6-23, and BNA, report on the revolutionary organizations in the United Kingdom, Cab 24/138/cp4132, 15-7-22. Unfortunately for the Irish communists, however, Mikhail Borodin was arrested by police in Glasgow in August 1922, sentenced to six months in Barlinnie jail and deported upon his release. The dynamism and focus he had given to British and Irish communist activity was lost as a result, and no such comprehensive study or social programme ever emerged.
90 For full details of the CPI Social Programme see *The Workers' Republic*, 30-9-1922.
91 See: Roddy Connolly, 'Past and future policy' in the *Workers' Republic*, 6-1-1923 and RGASPI, resignation of Roddy Connolly, to the Secretary of the ECCI, 19-2-23, 495/89/22-8.
92 Ibid., (RGASPI). For more on the CPI view of this important question see also: RGASPI, Borodin interviews delegates from Irish party, 495/89/13-18, and Report of the Communist Party of Ireland to the ECCI from October 1921 to October 1922, 495/89/16-63.
93 RGASPI, Roddy Connolly to Luise, Berlin 22-8-22, 495/89/12-36.
94 Sean McLoughlin private papers.
95 Roddy Connolly, *Republican Struggle in Ireland*, (Dublin: 1966) p. 51.
96 Sean McLoughlin private papers.
97 McGuire *Roddy Connolly*, p. 63.
98 *The Workers' Republic*, 19-8-1922.
99 Military Archives, (MA) South West Command daily report, CW/ops/2b/18-12-22.
100 Michael Hopkinson, *Green against Green*, (Dublin: 1988) pp. 150-1.
101 Conor Kostick, *Revolution in Ireland*, (London: 1996) pp. 188-9.
102 Hopkinson, *Green against Green*, p. 152.
103 *Limerick Leader*, 13-11-1922.
104 MA, South West Command daily report, CW/ops/2B, 21-11-22.
105 Ibid.
106 UCDA, Liam Manahan testimony, Ernie O'Malley notebooks, p17b/106/p24.
107 RGASPI, report of the Communist Party of Ireland to the ECCI from October 1921 to October 1922, 495/89/16-61.

108 Sean McLoughlin private papers.
109 UCDA, testimony of Liam Manahan, O'Malley Notebooks, P17b/106/ p.24.
110 MA, South West Command, daily report, CW/ops/2B/18-12-22.
111 See: *Limerick Leader*, 11-12-1923 for a copy of these regulations.
112 BNA, Samuel Hoare, Memo to the Secretary of State for the Colonies: The Position of the Irish Provisional Government, CAB 24/139/cp4226, 21-9-22.
113 See The *Free State*, 14-10-1922.
114 Sean McLoughlin private papers and UCDA, testimony of Liam Manahan, O'Malley Notebooks, P17b/106/ p25.
115 *Limerick Leader*, 20-11-1922.
116 Sean McLoughlin Private Papers.
117 UCDA, testimony of Liam Manahan, O'Malley notebooks, P17b/106/ p. 25.
118 Sean McLoughlin Private Papers.
119 Ibid.
120 UCDA, Communist Party of Ireland, 6-11-23, Report to Minister of Defence, Mulcahy Papers, P7a/87/98.
121 UCDA, testimony of Liam Manahan, O'Malley Notebooks, P17b/106/ p. 26.
122 *Limerick Chronicle*, 23-1-1923.
123 UCDA, testimony of Liam Manahan, O'Malley Notebooks, P17b/106/ p. 27. This mass escape, however, does not seem to have come off.
124 *Irish Independent*, 22-9-22.
125 See George Pollock's letter to Sean McEntee in response to McEntee's red scare tactics during the 1948 Free State general election, *Irish People*, 14-2-48.
126 For more on this see: RGASPI, report From Communist party Great Britain to ECCI October 1921 to October 1922, 495/8913-82 and J.T. Murphy, *New Horizons*, (London: 1941) pp. 184-86.
127 For O'Malley comments see UCDA, O'Malley to Adjutant General, 22-7-22, Sighle Humphries papers, P106/1954 (2).
128 BNA, report on the revolutionary organizations in the United Kingdom, CAB24/158/cp15, 11-1-23.
129 For a report on the CPI meeting at which McLoughlin made these comments, see UCDA, Office of Directorate of Intelligence to Minister of Defence, re Sean McLoughlin, 9-1-24, Mulcahy papers, P7b/140/182.
130 Sean McLoughlin Private Papers.

131 UCDA, Sean McLoughlin to Major General Brennan, 3-2-23, Ernie O'Malley papers, P17a/46.
132 *Irish Independent,* 9-2-23 and Liam Deasy, *Brother against Brother,* (Cork: 1999), pp. 109-126.
133 Ibid.
134 UCDA, McLoughlin to Father O'Leary, 9-2-23, Ernie O'Malley papers, P17a/46.
135 UCDA, Sean McLoughlin to Deasy, Ernie O'Malley papers, P17a/46.
136 UCDA, testimony of Liam Manahan, Ernie O'Malley Notebooks, P17b/106/p28.
137 Mike Milotte, 'Communist Politics in Ireland, 1916-45', pp. 119-20.
138 Ibid.
139 For more on this aspect of the controversy see UCDA, testimony of Liam Manahan, O'Malley Notebooks, P17b/106/pp27-28. It should also be noted, however, that Sean McLoughlin did not make any reference to any such contact from Connolly in his letters to IRA leaders during this period, or his brief personal notes on the matter drawn up many years later.
140 *Irish Independent,* 9-2-1923.
141 UCDA, Deputy Chief of Staff (IRA) Conn ua Maoldhaomhnaigh, to Sean Fitzpatrick, Adjutant general Second Southern Division, (IRA) Ernie O'Malley papers, P17a/46.
142 UCDA, McLoughlin to Father O'Leary, 9-2-23, Ernie O'Malley papers, P17a/46.
143 UCDA, HQ Dublin Brigade, copy of special bulletin issued by GHQ, 24-2-23, Ernie O'Malley papers, P17a/46.
144 UCDA, testimony of Liam Manahan, O'Malley Notebooks, P17b/106/p.29.
145 Sean McLoughlin Private Papers.
146 Ibid.
147 Peadar O'Donnell, *The Gates Flew Open,* (Cork: 1965), p. 79.
148 UCDA, Sean McLoughlin lecture, 'My prison experiences and the possibility of communism in Ireland' Communist Party of Ireland, 6-11-23, report to Minister of Defence, Mulcahy Papers, P7a/87/98.
149 Ibid.
150 Ibid.
151 Ibid.
152 Ibid.
153 UCDA, Seamus McGowan, P34/D/20, Cowan papers.
154 UCDA, Notes on communism in Ireland, P67/528, McEntee papers.

5

One Last Push for the Workers' Republic, 1923-1960

Introduction

After a recurrence of the lung illness that saw him hospitalized again following his release from jail,[1] McLoughlin threw himself into political activity. He had high hopes for the future of the Irish communist movement, and was prepared to devote all of his energies towards the building of it. McLoughlin was quickly brought onto the executive of the Party and later became the final editor of the *Workers' Republic*.[2] This activity was soon noted by Free State intelligence, which had placed an informant in the tiny CPI.[3] A report from this source pointed out how McLoughlin had 'not wasted much time in getting into business again'[4] and was the 'strong man' of the movement.[5]

But despite McLoughlin's hopes and his best efforts, the Irish communist movement did not enjoy success in the period ahead. On the contrary, as a result of objective and subjective factors, the tiny CPI was only weeks away from extinction. In the aftermath of its demise, McLoughlin would engage in a further spell of socialist activity in the Larkinite movement, which was the only path now left for Irish communists to take. Failure here, however, would mark the end of his involvement in Irish revolutionary politics. This, coupled with sustained harassment and intimidation from the Free State, drove him out of Ireland altogether, and into an exile from which there was no return. McLoughlin would continue with his socialist activities for a period in England, but in a less intense fashion. The strain of involvement in the Irish revolution affected his health badly and left him old and worn-out before his time. As a result, he would slowly fade from political activity. His life thereafter was quiet and anonymous, spent with his family in Sheffield. But McLoughlin did not grow indifferent to the causes that he had served with such energy in his youth. He remained a socialist and looked forward to a day when the struggle he and others had given themselves to in Ireland many years earlier would finally be brought to a successful conclusion.

McLoughlin and the new communist strategy

McLoughlin's first campaign after release was focused on the IRA hunger strike, which had begun just as he left Mountjoy prison. He was concerned that little was being done to publicise it, and his criticism was aimed at both the Republican and Labour movements for their failings on the issue. McLoughlin appeared at the Sinn Fein Ard Fheis three days after his release and, in a powerful speech, outlined the harsh conditions prisoners were enduring in Mountjoy. This included 24-hour lock-ups, overcrowding, the absence of washing facilities, outbreaks of scabies and vermin infested cells. McLoughlin expressed particular concerns about the health of IRA leader Ernie O'Malley, who had been shot several times during his arrest in November 1922 and had spent several months in hospital as a result. McLoughlin thought he resembled a 'living skeleton'.[6] McLoughlin, himself admitted to hospital for two days the following week, insisted that Republicans and the Labour party organize a mass campaign, including pickets at the prisons, in order to pressurize the Free State government on the issue. This did not happen. In response, McLoughlin wrote two articles in the *Workers' Republic*. The first of these, published on 3 November, urged the republicans to 'give over weeping and wailing', and instead do something to get the prisoners out. 'Too long now have the revolutionary workers been with you', continued McLoughlin, 'too many opportunities have you been given'. Again, he predicted that when the IRA prisoners were released 'a new chapter' would open. This would see workers rally under the banner of the CPI and 'fight the only fight that matters, the class struggle.'[7] The following week, McLoughlin pointed out to the Labour leaders that they had decisive class power and insisted they use it in support of the prisoners. If they failed to act and men died, it would be on their heads. 'The working class will come to power some day,' McLoughlin warned 'and they will remember even if you forget.'[8]

Again, however, although trenchant in his support for the prisoners, McLoughlin was deeply critical of the IRA leadership and its role in the hunger strike. According to McLoughlin, a ballot on the proposal of a hunger strike had been conducted amongst prisoners in Mountjoy. A majority rejected it. Rather than respect this decision, however, the IRA leaders had 'compelled' the men to go on hunger strike anyway, a decision that had caused much dissent in the jail.[9] McLoughlin's younger brother, Patrick, a former captain of B Company, 2nd Dublin Battalion IRA,[10] may have been among those who resigned from the army as a result of this.[11] The hunger strike was eventually called off after 41 days.[12] Two prisoners had died but the Free State was unmoved. It was another defeat for the IRA.

For McLoughlin, the hunger strike and the role of the IRA leadership in starting it, as well as the eventual outcome, underlined the need for a communist break from the organization. He now believed more firmly than ever that the IRA rank-and-file was ready to split from its leadership en masse, and that they could be won over by the CPI. This was a view he began to press strongly within the CPI and it led to a series of discussions within the party in early November over how best to approach the republicans. Here, McLoughlin argued that the IRA leadership had betrayed its members and that the movement was 'about to collapse'. To continue supporting the IRA was a 'suicidal' policy for the CPI to adopt. Instead the CPI needed to formulate its own coherent and detailed socialist programme. This would appeal to the IRA rank-and-file, the discharged Free State soldiers, the small farmers (who, for McLoughlin led a 'horrible existence' of exploitation by the large landowners), the unemployed, currently 'wandering about like a lot of lost sheep', and the 'revolutionary element of the working class'.[13] With such a programme in place and the adoption of an independent stance, the party could go it alone and assume leadership of all classes exploited by capitalism and imperialism.

As will be seen, the CPI had been inconsistent on this question throughout 1923. By this late stage, however, it was clear that most of the party membership shared McLoughlin's views. His argument was strongly supported at these meetings. One young CPI member, Pat Breslin, captured the prevailing mood with his dismissal of de Valera and Stack as a 'pair of flag-wagging fools'.[14] Roddy Connolly, though, was not convinced. He considered that the best strategy for communists was continued alliance with the IRA based 'on certain conditions'. What these conditions were, Connolly did not say. He did argue, however, that the republican movement was split and that the CPI should support only the 'advanced revolutionary section' of the IRA, as opposed to Sinn Fein. This section, which Connolly indicated would become a separate party, could be influenced by the CPI to accept the goal of the workers republic and would itself become the main revolutionary force in Irish politics.[15]

The nature of the debate was clear. Connolly believed that a new revolutionary republican party was emerging, and that communists should seek to work within it, whilst McLoughlin felt that the time was now right for communists themselves to challenge for the leadership of this constituency. Both saw the republican rank-and-file as crucial to communist development, but differed in their thinking about how best to approach it. The matter was eventually decided at an executive meeting on 16 November. Agreement, it would seem, was reached. Republicans were to be given one last chance. Either they formulated a socialist programme, or the communists would split from them. A new orientation towards working-class struggle was also envisaged, with all members instructed to join a trade union and no non-union members now accepted.[16] Over the following month or so, McLoughlin made strenuous efforts to recruit disillusioned republicans to the CPI. This was soon picked up by Special Branch, who noted that both McLoughlin and Connolly were 'frequent visitors' to the Sinn Fein HQ in Dublin.[17]

The demise of the CPI

Despite McLoughlin's efforts, however, and the hopes that underpinned them, the CPI was in a poor state of health. It had been in this condition for some time and although it had finally achieved unity on its political strategy at the 16 November meeting – for the first time that year – recovery remained doubtful. The reasons for this were both objective and subjective. During McLoughlin's time in jail objective conditions had deteriorated, making it virtually impossible for the CPI to grow. The revolution had been defeated and the carnival of reaction predicted by James Connolly was in full swing. In the Free State, the new government, boosted by its easy victory over the IRA, had also inflicted a series of defeats on the organised working class. Disputes involving postal workers, Dockers and farm labourers in Waterford,[18] to name but three, had all been won by the Free State, demoralizing socialists and rolling back the tide of class militancy that rose between 1919 and 1922.

The reactionary nature of the Free State regime was fully developed and forged during these struggles with the Irish workers. In fact these struggles were crucial to the future character of this government and the party which had formed it, Cumann na nGaedheal. The days of wage increases, of general strikes, of workplace occupations, of soviets being established in IRA-controlled areas, were coming to an end. The Free State was now a formidable battering ram that would be used to smash the interests of the working class over the coming period, which was to be one of continued economic downturn.

In addition to these harsh objective conditions there were the weaknesses within the Irish communist movement. At the 1922 Comintern Congress, held in Moscow between November-December and attended by four CPI members, the main discussions centred on the need for united fronts between communists and social democratic workers in this an era of temporary reaction.[19] Leading Russian communist Bukharin criticized the CPI for its failures here and its lack of involvement in the class struggles of Irish workers.[20] Congress went on to strongly reaffirm that communists in imperialist colonies should be involved in both their various national independence struggles and in the class struggles of the proletariat.[21] The overwhelming defeat of the IRA, and the intense nature of the CPI involvement in the Civil War, however, necessitated a re-think for Moscow in relation to the first part of this directive, as applied to Ireland. Again, this was articulated by Bukharin, who argued that the CPI should conserve its forces by withdrawing from the collapsed republican struggle altogether until the fighting was over.[22] Ultimately, it led to the formation of a policy for Irish communists different to that prescribed for communists in other colonial states.

The issue was discussed in full shortly after the close of the Congress by the Praesidium of the Executive Committee of the Communist International (ECCI), and a 9-point resolution drafted. The main points of this were that the CPI was to devote most of its future energies towards class struggles, and offer only 'moral support' to the IRA.[23] The organization, already in two minds on this very question, as well as riven with destructive personal vendettas and jealousies, became further divided and weakened as it tried to apply this new directive. One notable casualty was Connolly. Although formerly the most vocal supporter of communist involvement in the Civil War, Connolly returned from Moscow with a revised attitude. In January 1923, he submitted a long article to the *Workers' Republic* in which he advocated a communist break from the IRA and new orientation towards the Labour party, in line with the Moscow strategy of united fronts. Connolly also advised republicans to call a ceasefire, set up a new 'workers' republican' party, and enter the Dail.[24] He later claimed that this advice constituted 'moral support' of the republican struggle and was the correct interpretation of the Comintern directive.[25]

The CPI did not view it in that fashion, however. Instead Connolly's new position was seen as an unacceptable *volte-face*, and evidence that he had been 'bought off' by the Free State.[26] As a result of this, and a series of personality disputes he evidently had with many other members,[27] Connolly was dumped off the party executive and editorial board of the party journal.[28] The CPI attempted something of a break from republicanism, but this seems to have been only temporary; the replacement policy of united fronts with social democracy proved to be unworkable in Ireland given the gulf, made unbridgeable during the Civil War, which existed between the CPI and an Irish Labour party that was supportive of the Free State. The end of the

Civil War fighting in May 1923 paved the way for a degree of communist re-involvement with the republicans and August of that year saw some CPI members play a part in the organizing of the Sinn Fein general election campaign.[29]

Party fortunes, though, did not improve. Personal squabbles and infighting made the situation worse. A section of the party, headed by Connolly, objected to the new leadership and, in contrast to the views he had advocated in January, appeared during the election campaign to be arguing for a policy of unconditional support for republican candidates, now that the Civil War was over. This was in contrast to the more conditional backing envisaged by the new leaders. Connolly's faction refused to obey party directives and undermined the leadership to the point where some resigned.[30] Moscow intervened. CPGB leader Arthur MacManus was soon sent to Ireland to investigate. As a result, he restructured the party executive, pending a report on its future and Moscow deliberation thereof. This restructuring led to Connolly's re-emergence as leader, but did little to restore CPI fortunes and left it, in the view of British Intelligence, still 'almost certain to fail'.[31] It was into this situation that McLoughlin had walked following his release from prison.

Back in Britain, McManus drafted a report, endorsed by the CPBG Political Bureau, which recommended the CPI's dissolution.[32] In truth, McManus was a long-standing critic of the CPI, and had expressed real doubts over the party's capabilities after his previous visit to Ireland in September 1922.[33] The reason he was now going further and recommending dissolution was that by this stage he was in contact with Jim Larkin, who had recently returned to Ireland following his imprisonment in the USA. McManus wished Larkin to take over the leadership of the Irish communist movement, but knew that with Larkin leading a separate body, the Irish Worker League, (IWL), the CPI would need to be killed off first. During his brief visit to Ireland, McManus also met secretly with Larkin and discussed the situation with him again the following week in London.[34] With Larkin agreeing to head the communist movement the fate of the CPI was sealed. The report recommending dissolution was posted to Moscow, where the final decision would now be made.

The CPI had long regarded the CPGB as centrist and a hindrance rather than a help to its struggle against British imperialism and Irish capitalism. When it learned of this report, reaction was swift. A special party meeting was called on 1 December. Feeling that the party was now more unified and had a greater chance of success, McLoughlin and Connolly moved and seconded a resolution that condemned the 'exceedingly misleading, inaccurate and insulting' report penned by McManus. According to the resolution, there had been a swing to the left amongst sections of the working class. The party's fortunes would soon improve as a result. Another factor to be considered was the 'intense agitational work' carried out by imprisoned CPI members like McLoughlin. This too would lead to an influx of members. The CPI stated that it would send a detailed report to Moscow on these positive developments, all of which, it claimed, had been completely ignored by McManus 'in a truly unmarxian manner'. The resolution concluded by expressing confidence that once Moscow became aware of the true situation, it would realize the need to maintain the CPI as its section in Ireland.[35]

This spirited appeal by the CPI for a stay of execution fell on deaf ears. Instead, the Comintern decided to follow to the letter the advice given to it by the CPGB. The CPI was instructed to dissolve by January 1924, and was replaced by Larkin's IWL as the Comintern's Irish section. One final meeting of the CPI was held to formally comply with the directive. This took place on 26 January 1924. At the meeting, all party letters and documents were taken and destroyed by McLoughlin, Connolly and Thomas O'Connor, another executive member. This included correspondence between the party and the Cleeves creamery soviet. CPI leaders apparently feared that the Minister for Justice, Kevin O'Higgins, was about to open up an investigation into the matter, raising the prospect of them being prosecuted in the courts.[36] After a lifetime of just 27 months, coinciding with one of the most turbulent periods in modern Irish history, Ireland's first vanguard party of the working class was no more.

McLoughlin and Larkinism

Coincidental with the wind up of the CPI was the collapse of Irish communist attempts to revive the James Connolly Labour College. With the CPI in its death throes, this attempt had been made in order to keep a communist structure alive in Ireland and a focus for the political activities of communist party members. A committee was formed, of which McLoughlin became secretary, and circulars were sent out to sympathizers advertising a re-launch conference.[37] But the communist efforts were to be thwarted. The James Connolly Labour College, although an empty and moribund shell since its November 1920 destruction by the Black and Tans, was still officially controlled by the Labour leadership. And whilst it had no intention of reviving the body itself, Labour was not above using dog-in-a-manger tactics in order to trump its communist opponents.[38]

For most Irish communists, the failure to revive the James Connolly

Labour College marked a temporary end to their political involvements. Some, like Connolly and Pollock, would re-appear at the head of a new communist project two years later, the Workers' Party of Ireland. Between now and then, the only forum they would have would be the James Connolly workers education club they would establish in October 1924. Very few became active in Larkinite politics. The main reason for this was that it had become obvious, even at this early stage, that Larkin was unlikely to fulfill the hopes invested in him by both Moscow and the CPGB. His new body, the IWL, was 'more a social than political organisation'[39] and never remotely resembled a proper, functioning communist-type political party. Worse still was Larkin's evident inability to work with any person not under his control or organization not of his making.[40] After only a few weeks in Ireland, he had engineered a split in the ITGWU and with it the entire Irish labour movement, mainly on these grounds as opposed to any considerations of political principle. This left him unable to build a credible alternative to the Labour party. The Free State working class was the main victim here. Already reeling under the blows of a combined government/ employer offensive, it now watched as its movement was torn asunder, for no apparent good reason, leaving it more exposed than ever to the economic ill winds that would blow increasingly hard throughout the rest of the decade. The Irish communists looked on grimly. Although publicly supportive of Larkin in his struggle against Liberty Hall, they nonetheless concluded that he had allowed himself to become too 'mixed up in personal squabbles,' and was not fighting on grounds of political principle.[41] Little wonder, then, that most decided to keep their distance from him.

McLoughlin was one of the few exceptions. He decided to throw his lot in with 'Big Jim'. Whatever his failings, Larkin was still a giant of the international labour movement. He had a prestige unequalled in Ireland. It is probable that McLoughlin considered Larkin's reputation and strengths as an agitator and organizer would offset his weaknesses, and provide the basis of a real challenge to the Free State governing party, Cumann na nGaedheal. McLoughlin still believed that when the IRA prisoners were released, the basis for a new socialist movement would exist. Larkinism now represented the only vehicle for such a movement. On 27 January, McLoughlin spoke alongside Larkin at a meeting in College Green, organized by the Larkinite Dublin Trades Council, to mark the death of Lenin six days earlier. At this memorial gathering, a resolution was also passed calling for the release of all Republican prisoners.[42] Around 11,000 were still languishing in jail, even though the Civil War had now been over for nine months. This issue, which McLoughlin had been trying to publicise since his release from jail, but which was ignored by both republican and labour leaders, would become the basis for a popular campaign over the next few months. It was also one in which he would play his part. In April, for example, he was one of the main speakers at a mass rally organised again by Dublin Trades Council, which demanded the emptying of the jails.[43]

In June, a new Larkinite trade union, the Workers' Union of Ireland (WUI), was established. Larkin had eventually been expelled from the ITGWU, so this new development was not unexpected. Larkin himself was not in Ireland when the new union was born, having travelled to Moscow for the Fifth Congress of the Comintern some weeks earlier. In his absence, his brother Peter officially launched the new organization. McLoughlin strongly welcomed the setting up of the WUI. He saw it as the opening of a 'new chapter' in the history of the Irish labour movement, and one that contained 'glorious possibilities and a new hope' for the working class. Showing the continued influence of syndicalism on his outlook, he argued that the establishment of the WUI marked a new beginning for industrial unionism in Ireland, and that it would prove to be superior to 'out of date' and 'pure and simple' craft unionism. The opportunity was there, he concluded, for the building of a 'pure labour' movement, 'cleansed' of reformism and those reformist leaders who 'would sell their mean little souls fifty times a day' in order to hang onto their careers.[44] Shortly after, McLoughlin was elected as branch secretary of the no. 2 branch at Inchicore Railway works.

The WUI was a popular trade union in Dublin, reflecting the esteem in which the working class of the city held Larkin. Around two thirds of the ITGWU in Dublin joined the WUI, a figure of around 16,000 workers, along with 20 of its 300 provincial branches. In Inchicore, 600 men joined the WUI, splitting in the main from the ITGWU. The new union was to have a baptism of fire. Within weeks of it being established, the WUI was involved in several disputes, most notably on the Docks and on the new council house-building scheme in Marino. These disputes were not only with employers, but with other unions as well. One of the most bitter of these conflicts took place at the Inchicore rail plant. For McLoughlin, it would be a fateful dispute and one that marked his final involvement in the Irish revolutionary movement.

The Inchicore Rail Strike

The Inchicore rail strike was declared on Saturday 9 August 1924 and began three days later. There were two aspects to it: a demand for a 3/- per week pay rise by the Millwrights' helpers and running shed workers, and a demarcation dispute between WUI vicemen and fitters who belonged to the Irish General Railway and Engineering Union. (IGR&EU). Both disputes were long standing. The Millwrights' helpers and running shed workers had been in on-off negotiations with the Great Southern and Western Railway (GS&WR) bosses for six months, to no avail. The problem between the vicemen and fitters went back further, to the war years, but had been given fresh impetus by the recent establishment of the WUI and the decision of the GS&WR to negotiate an agreement with the fitters only, redrawing the line of demarcation further in their favour.[45] This was the situation facing McLoughlin when elected branch secretary.

McLoughlin initially counseled against a strike. He felt that, on the demarcation issue, talks between the WUI, GS&WR and IGR&EU should be convened in order to resolve the problem.[46] But there was already bad blood between McLoughlin and the IGR&EU. According to the engineering union leaders, McLoughlin had made speeches in July that 'vilified' their union, prompting them to complain to the Dublin Trades Council.[47] This, added to the more important fact that both the IGR&EU and GS&WR had a clear vested interest in defeating the new and militant WUI, ensured that McLoughlin's appeal fell on deaf ears. Following this rebuttal, a meeting was held of WUI vicemen at Inchicore. There, McLoughlin again urged caution. The issue was complicated, and the WUI did not have in place at Inchicore either the level of organization or the financial resources – it had only £30 in its branch fund – necessary to undertake such action.[48] This, however, was not the mood of the majority. After a burst of 'oratorical fervour' from one of the leading WUI members at Inchicore, James Woodfell, a decision was taken by the WUI vicemen to strike.[49] 'The crusaders of old', McLoughlin later commented ruefully, 'hardly started their pilgrimages so light heartedly'.[50]

Two days later McLoughlin met with the GS&WR bosses and wrung from them the increase for the Millwrights and running shed workers.[51] No solution, however, could be found for the demarcation issue. As a result, a further branch meeting was held and decided that the entire WUI membership at Inchicore should strike in support of the vicemen. At this point, McLoughlin's attitude changed. Although he had initially counseled against strike action, McLoughlin now concluded that, as the fight was on in earnest 'there was nothing else for it but to work as hard as possible for victory'.[52] Picketing was extended to Kingsbridge and North Wall and carters encouraged to withdraw their labour in order to cripple commerce. Despite this escalation, however, trade passing through the railway was only partially disrupted. Efforts were made to gain the support of the ITGWU, and the British-based National Union of Railwaymen (NUR), but these were in vain. Both the NUR, and in particular the ITGWU, were hostile towards the WUI and unlikely in the extreme to back that union in any dispute, far less one that seemed to be directed against another union. McLoughlin argued that the dispute was not between the WUI and IGR&EU. It was, he maintained, a conflict between the WUI and the GS&WR bosses, as it had been they who had set the line of demarcation.[53] His attempts, though, to win backing from the other workers at Inchicore on the basis that it was a capital/labour dispute did not succeed, leaving the WUI isolated and, even at this early stage, unable to place much pressure on the bosses.

The press soon condemned the strike. The *Irish Times*, in particular, was scandalized at what it saw as an attempt by a union of 'unskilled men' to impose its claims 'by methods of public injury' on other unions 'manned by skilled labour' and a 'great company', the GS&WR. It was, indeed, no less than 'industrial Bolshevism', which 'must receive its lesson if the Free State [was] to survive at all'.[54] But whilst such outpourings were entirely predictable – four weeks later the *Irish Times* was egging on Spanish fascism in Morocco[55] – and of little consequence to anybody, within Inchicore itself developments were taking place that did undermine the WUI. As the strike entered its second week, the GS&WR announced its intention to recruit 'auxiliary labour' in order to fill the places of the strikers.[56] With unemployment levels perennially high in the Free State, it was not hard to find desperate men willing to comply. Before long, between two to three hundred scabs – dubbed 'volunteers' by the *Irish Times* – had been recruited,[57] almost all of which were demobbed Free State soldiers.[58]

This must have been a bitter blow to McLoughlin, considering his hopes of bringing such men into the socialist movement. He wrote to the President of the Association of Ex-Officers and Men, National Army, and urged the organization to instruct its members to withdraw from Inchicore.[59] It was to no avail. At a large meeting of the Ex-Officers and Men, a motion was passed by 623 votes to 6 approving of the actions of those who had gone to Inchicore.[60] Neither of the unions, nor any party for that matter, had done anything to alleviate the distress of the ex-soldiers, pointed out Ex-Officers leader Captain Mack. As a result, the organization had resolved 'that their families should not starve when there was legitimate work to be got'.[61] In a bizarre twist, but one in keeping with the whole Inchicore strike itself, Mack pointed out that as the Association now considered itself a trade union, it would soon be seeking affiliation to the ILPTUC.[62] WUI hopes that the other unions at Inchicore would refuse to work with the 'volunteers' were dashed when, one by one, they all declared that the new additions to the

Inchicore workforce would be welcomed. That this was no surprise can be seen by the fact that the ITGWU had actually offered earlier to fill the places of the WUI men itself.[63]

In addition to these problems, the WUI was also hindered by internal weaknesses that were to prove fatal to the strike. According to McLoughlin, all of these related to the Larkin family. In the case of Peter Larkin, McLoughlin later said that he 'did everything in his power to make our position impossible' and that the strike committee constantly complained about his actions. McLoughlin did not offer any details of Larkin's wrongdoings, but the fact that he described the temporary EC of the WUI as consisting solely of Larkin,[64] and that Peter was known to be both a single-minded and confrontational character, suggests that the desire to control everything and everyone was not the preserve of Big Jim within the Larkin family. Secondly, and more seriously, McLoughlin alleged that a lorry bearing the name 'Rapid Transport Company', 'known by every worker in Dublin to be the property of the Larkin family', broke the picket line at Kingsbridge and delivered goods there.[65] It is not known who was behind this action, but for McLoughlin this was a serious blow. Prior to this, most of the carters, even many belonging to the ITGWU, had observed the sanctity of the picket line. From the point when the Larkin lorry broke it, however, such unity proved impossible to maintain. 'Why don't you hold up Larkin's yokes?' was the response now to WUI requests for solidarity action from these same carters.[66]

Big Jim returns

The third and final factor was the return of Jim Larkin from Russia to Dublin on 25 August. Later that evening, he addressed a large rally at the Mansion House. After announcing himself to be one of the world's twenty-five rulers – following his election to the Comintern executive in Moscow – Larkin focused in on matters more mundane. He criticized the strike at Inchicore, saying that it 'never should have taken place' as it involved 'no questions of wages or conditions of employment or fundamental principle of labour'. Larkin concluded with the opinion that an acceptable demarcation line could easily have been set by a 'shop council'.[67]

McLoughlin considered that Larkin's comments concerning his Comintern appointment had 'made him an international laughing stock', but was concerned about this public denunciation of the strike, feeling that it would be seized upon by the bourgeois press and used to weaken the resolve of the men.[68] Larkin's point about how easily a shop's council could have resolved matters also seemed simplistic. On the day he made those comments, McLoughlin had actually approached the GSWR and the leadership of the IGR&EU with a three-point plan designed to end the dispute. This envisaged a conference between the two unions to set an acceptable line of demarcation, an agreement by the bosses that they would ratify the pay deal promised to the Millwrights helpers and running shed workers, and observance of a 'no victimisation' policy, that would allow the strikers to return to work. That same evening, the IGR&EU informed not the WUI but the *Irish Times,* that it was rejecting the proposal.[69]

McLoughlin argued that Jim Larkin exerted a wholly negative influence and that with his return all hopes of gaining an honourable settlement disappeared. Few options were now open to the WUI men. In McLoughlin's opinion, unless they could stop the import of coal into the GS&WR, they were beaten. Larkin, he argued, made no effort to achieve this, but acted instead like a man 'bent on ending the strike at any cost'.[70] 'Gloomy speeches' by Larkin soon followed, demoralizing the strikers, and were accompanied by attempts to cut McLoughlin out of the leadership of the dispute. One example of this involved Larkin 'staging' a breakdown of a car the pair were travelling in, in order to prevent McLoughlin from attending a strike meeting at Inchicore. This occurred after a meeting in Cooley, County Louth, at which Larkin was said to have told those assembled of the 'arrangements' he had made with the USSR government. These were that in the future all emigrants from Ireland would go to Russia rather than the USA, where they would be given large tracts of land by the Soviets. It was an address that shattered McLoughlin's last illusions in Larkin. 'I had heard him tell lies before', McLoughlin later recalled, 'but never anything to equal the Cooley meeting'.[71]

The strike grew increasingly bitter. Carters belonging to John Wallis and Sons, who were contracted to Inchicore, were called out in sympathy action on 29 August. Two days later, however, around 25 of the firm's 80 men scabbed. It was claimed later that a number of these men were beaten up by groups of strikers and warned off from going back to work again. The result was no more scabbing at John Wallis and Sons.[72] At the same time the police, who intervened increasingly in the dispute in order to break picket lines and ferry scabs to work, arrested several strikers.[73] As the dispute dragged into September, with no apparent prospect of success for the WUI, the focus of the strike leaders shifted away from victory and towards ensuring that all the strikers would be allowed to return to work. Aware that the position of the WUI was becoming steadily weaker, the GS&WR had made a number of pronouncements that in the event of the strike ending, some of the 'volunteers' would be retained, with a similar number of WUI men losing their jobs altogether.[74] The figure mooted by the GS&WR was around 100, which of course was a fair percentage of the entire WUI membership in Inchicore.[75] This was unacceptable to McLoughlin, who insisted that any return to work must be on the basis of 'no victimisation'.[76]

Defeat and recrimination

The end of the strike came suddenly, following a series of meetings on 12-13 September. These began when the GS&WR issued yet another public statement offering to take back all of the WUI strikers, bar the 100 or so whose jobs had been forfeited to the scabs.[77] Larkin contacted the GS&WR and arranged for a meeting. McLoughlin attended this meeting and presented a formula for a settlement that upheld the no victimization principle. The meeting terminated on the understanding that the GS&WR would consult McLoughlin's document before giving its answer. Later, however, a telephone call was made to Unity Hall, HQ of the WUI, by whom McLoughlin did not say, informing the union that the men would have to return on the company's terms. These were terms which added the insult of no alteration in the demarcation line to the injury of over 100 job losses.

A mass meeting was held the following morning at Inchicore Picture House. McLoughlin was opposed to the company terms, but unknown to him the WUI leadership had already accepted them. Larkin and the remainder of the EC, along with Jim Woodfell, had met without informing him and had drawn up a proposal that would see the men returning to work on the GS&WR terms. There was a slight sweetener. Those who lost their jobs were to be paid £2 per week by the WUI, pending their eventual re-absorption into the GS&WR workforce, as vacancies presented themselves. At the meeting Larkin dominated the proceedings, apparently justifying his proposals with banalities such as 'the army that cannot retreat, cannot advance', and calling for volunteers to sacrifice themselves to temporary victimization, in order that the strike be ended. McLoughlin opposed the Larkin proposals. He was the only WUI official on the platform that day to do so. He clearly did not trust Larkin and argued that those in favour of returning were acting 'foolishly', as they did not know for sure what the proposals would actually mean. A large number agreed with McLoughlin, but when the vote was taken a majority backed Larkin. The Inchicore rail strike ended on 15 September. On that Monday morning the WUI members, minus the 107 workers who had lost their jobs permanently, assembled outside Kilmainham jail and marched back to work, with McLoughlin at their head.[78]

The WUI had suffered a damaging defeat at Inchicore. In its aftermath, a mood of bitter recrimination set in. Two factors were at work here. From the outside, Larkin began a campaign of vilification against the Inchicore strike leaders, and McLoughlin in particular. They were blamed for beginning the strike in the first place and accused of betraying it in the end. At the same time, within Inchicore itself, resentment also grew, but was directed against Larkin. For many, it seemed that Larkin's assurances that the sacked men would be maintained financially by the WUI were, as McLoughlin put it, 'mendacious', and that the unlucky 107 had simply been cut adrift by the union.[79]

This mood reached a peak at a specially convened meeting at Inchicore Picture House on 4 October. McLoughlin and his supporters in Inchicore called the meeting as a means of drawing Larkin into the open, ensuring that his accusations could be dealt with fully. Larkin took up the challenge and arrived at Inchicore Picture House backed up by the rest of his EC, with the intention of securing McLoughlin's removal as branch secretary. But Larkin had been absent from Inchicore since the end of the strike and was unaware of the hostility that had developed there against him. As the meeting, attended by 200 members, unfolded, it became clear that he had little support. Proceedings became stormy, and ended in uproar when Larkin stormed off the platform, accusing McLoughlin of planning to have him shot.[80] Order was restored, however, and the business of the meeting continued without Larkin. Motions of confidence were passed in the strike committee, and in McLoughlin as secretary.[81] Despite this show of support from the Inchicore men, McLoughlin decided to resign from the WUI. He was upset at the treatment of the 107 men who had lost their jobs, and felt that they had been 'betrayed' by Larkin. For McLoughlin, the WUI was finished, and he no longer felt he could be part of it. The following day, he handed over all of the branch books and accounts to a group of auditors elected at the meeting. Shortly after this, McLoughlin left Dublin for England.[82]

After McLoughlin's departure, Jim Larkin mounted a campaign of character assassination against him. He was accused of running away with union funds, with the figure ranging from £200 to £1000 'according to strength of imagination, credulity or stupidity'.[83] This was despite the fact that no financial discrepancies appeared in the branch books and that McLoughlin, who kept receipts for all cash transactions, could account for every penny of branch expenditure. It was also despite the fact that McLoughlin had only been able to leave Ireland because his brother Danny had scraped together some money for him.[84] When McLoughlin learned, through friends in Dublin and British communists, of the allegations that were being made against him, he offered to return to Ireland and meet Larkin in a court of law, where the matter could be dealt with. Larkin chose not to take up this offer. McLoughlin's summation of Larkin highlights the bitterness that the entire business had created:

> The workers were disgusted and disillusioned. They fought like heroes. They had stood loyally and manfully together for principle and they had been tricked by one of the most unscrupulous men that ever disgraced this country by his presence.[85]

McLoughlin's trenchant conclusion was:

> The day Larkin and his brutal and underhand tactics are banished from the arena of working class struggle, that day the workers will have made a huge step towards emancipation.[86]

Exile and Retirement

McLoughlin was not to return to Ireland following this departure. It might be thought that this was as a result of the Inchicore events which, coming on top of the other disappointments and traumas he had suffered, perhaps acted as the last straw. There is evidence to suggest that this may well have been the case. Roddy Connolly, for example, seems to have felt that McLoughlin left because he had become 'totally disgusted' with the political situation in Ireland.[87]

According to McLoughlin, however, this was not the reason he left Ireland permanently in 1924. Rather, it seems that McLoughlin throughout this period was suffering ongoing harassment from the Free State forces. This, of course, was nothing new. Since 1916, he had been no stranger to either the police van or the prison cell. But it was not just McLoughlin himself who was being persecuted. His sisters and brothers, including those who had no involvement in politics, were also being 'hounded, victimized and raided' as punishment for his activities. With both his parents now dead, he felt that there was little left for him in Ireland and, in order to 'give [his] family a chance', he decided to leave.[88] The carnival of reaction had claimed another victim. McLoughlin's involvement in Irish revolutionary politics was over.

McLoughlin settled for a while in the north east of England following his move from Ireland. He was based in Hartlepool, and continued for a period with some form of socialist activity, coupled with the delivery of lectures on Ireland. It would seem that he linked up here with some of his old SLP comrades, in particular Bill Burnup, who had been an activist in the party's Hartlepool branch.

In May 1926, the General Strike occurred in Britain. It was probably the most impressive display of working-class power and solidarity in British labour history, but one which was brought to an abrupt end after eight days by the TUC and Labour Party leadership. The period following this defeat was one of reaction that affected every section of the working class and 'immeasurably advanced the transformation of the workers' movement into a tame, disciplined trade union and electoral interest'.[89] It also coincided with the end of Sean McLoughlin's involvement in revolutionary politics. He was living in Hartlepool at the time of the strike and was arrested under the Emergency Powers legislation. On 14 June McLoughlin appeared at Hartlepool Magistrates Court. There he pleaded not guilty to charges that on 3 and 9 June he had attempted 'to cause disaffection amongst the civilian population'.[90]

Although the General Strike was over at this point, the miners, for whom it had been called, remained on strike until November 1926. Hartlepool was linked by rail to the South Durham coalfields, and many of the town's inhabitants worked at the pits. It is possible, therefore, that McLoughlin was actively supporting local striking miners and addressing propaganda meetings on their behalf. For the authorities, however, the precise nature of McLoughlin's activity seemed irrelevant; the presiding judge made it clear that he was to be tried on his past record, details of which had been supplied to him courtesy of the Irish Free State. McLoughlin's dossier was then read out in court as part of the proceedings. 'At times like these, we must be careful', the judge informed McLoughlin, and he was sent to Durham jail for a month. McLoughlin said later that this 'ended his career', and, in a reference to his poor health, that he was 'physically unable' to do any more.[91]

Revolution is, as Leon Trotsky once pointed out, a 'mighty devourer of human energy, both individual and collective'.[92] It can be unforgiving in its demands, both physical and mental, and can exhaust the last sinew of strength, and drop of vitality from even the most hardy and dedicated participant. May 1926 marked the 10th Anniversary of the Easter Rising. During those ten years McLoughlin had devoted his life to the struggle for a socialist Irish Republic, and had been involved, from beginning to end, in many of the events of the Irish Revolution. He had not enjoyed success, unlike those in Cumann na nGaedheal, and could have had no real hope that it might come in the foreseeable future, unlike those who had joined de Valera's new party, Fianna Fail. Instead, McLoughlin represented that section of the revolutionary movement that suffered defeat after defeat, before being crushed altogether. Now in exile, and with his health fluctuating unpredictably, he perhaps felt that he had no option but to leave the past behind, and build for himself a new life free of the intolerable demands of the old.

Epilogue[93]

In Middlesbrough, in August 1927, McLoughlin married Blanche Burnup, who was the sister of Bill. McLoughlin's address at the time of the wedding was given as 47 Alphonsus Street, which was also the address of local Labour Party town councillor and Blastfurnacemen's trade union activist Thomas Meehan. Meehan was one of the most prominent Labour movement activists in Middlesbrough. However, although intriguing, details of the nature of McLoughlin's association with Meehan unfortunately remain unknown. McLoughlin and his wife moved to Sheffield the following year, soon after the birth of their first child, Jack. McLoughlin found employment in the local council's engineering office and eventually became chief clerk. But if McLoughlin's life as a revolutionary activist was now over, his interest and involvement in politics was not. Jack recalls as a young boy in the 1930s being taken to meetings addressed by his father in the local ILP hall. It is not known what these meetings actually related to, or if McLoughlin actually joined the ILP. He did, though, have friends and contacts within that party and the Labour party itself in Sheffield. One such friend was Joe Curtis, who later became Mayor of Sheffield. McLoughlin was also involved in organizing local activities in support of some of the hunger marches that took place in the early 1930s.

One afternoon during these years, CH Burden, formerly of the SLP in Dewsbury, noticed a familiar figure chalking up a notice of a meeting due to begin at Batley market place. It was Sean McLoughlin. Burden hadn't seen McLoughlin since he parted company with the SLP over ten years earlier. Thinking back to the spectacular mass meetings he had conducted during those days, Burden decided to attend. The experience was dispiriting. Burden recalled that McLoughlin looked a 'tired and worn out old man', and that his 'mild labour speech' was both devoid of the fire and brimstone of the past and received with little enthusiasm by the sparse crowd in attendance. The collection raised only a few bob. McLoughlin, accompanied by another man unknown to Burden, then packed away the tressels and platform, which were stored behind Batley town hall, and left. Burden never saw him again.[94]

By the mid 1930s, this spell of limited activity was over. It seems that after the birth of his second child, daughter June in 1935, McLoughlin faded from political involvement. He did, though, retain an interest in politics and wrote many speeches for labour and left wing activists in the city. Many of these, like Joe Curtis, went on to enjoy fruitful careers within the Labour movement and local government. McLoughlin's other interests included reading. He was a great and constant devourer of knowledge and as such an intellectual in the real sense of the word. Music was another passion. Like his old communist colleague Roddy Connolly, McLoughlin was a huge fan of classical music and throughout the rest of his life regularly attended concerts at the town hall in Sheffield.

After the outbreak of the Second World War in 1939, McLoughlin, through his work in the council engineering office, became involved in the ARP and Civil Defence. He eventually became O/C training and operations, rescue and decontamination, Civil Defence, and ran camps at both Great Ayton and Cramlington, Northumbria. In 1943, however, McLoughlin suffered a serious accident. He was giving a demonstration on mustard gas when one of the canisters exploded in his face. But for the fact that a decontamination unit was close at hand, he would have died. As it was, he was badly burned and had considerable internal damage. McLoughlin spent many months in hospital, before being allowed home. For some in his family, it was an accident from which he never fully recovered.

In 1947, McLoughlin applied for a Military Pension.[95] De Valera's government had introduced legislation in 1934 extending the entitlement to those who had fought in the Civil War, as well as the Rising and Tan War. Most socialists and many republicans, however, had refrained from applying, feeling that the struggle of which they had been part had still not succeeded, and that de Valera was trying to buy them off. McLoughlin's decision to apply for a pension 13 years later seems to have been as a result of his poor health and a fear that his family would face financial hardship in the event of his death. His application was rejected initially, on the grounds that he was time-barred.[96] New legislation was passed later that year, however, which opened a window for fresh applications. Even so, it was not until 1952 that McLoughlin eventually received his military service certificate, enabling him to get the pension. His rank, however, was incorrectly established as that of D, ignoring his promotion during Easter Week, his leading position in the immediate post-Rising, re-organisation period, and his post as an IRA commandant during the Civil War.[97]

McLoughlin duly contested this award and attempted to have his true rank recognized. His case was pressed by various members of his family, including his younger brother Christy, who was both a member of the

ITGWU and Fianna Fail. The key figure in the campaign, however, was his niece Margaret, daughter of Danny. Margaret McLoughlin worked in the WUI head office as a secretary, and was also the secretary of the Jim Larkin branch of the Labour Party in Dublin.[98] She was a strong admirer of her uncle, and appears to have had more than a touch of his spirit about her. As she made clear at an Old IRA meeting in Dublin in 1954, she 'resented' the fact that whilst many of the participants in the Irish revolution had become ignored or marginalized figures, there were plenty of others who had achieved power or were seeking power, 'at [their] expense'.[99] Margaret also enlisted the help of Jim Larkin Jr, leader of the WUI and a key strategist within the Irish Labour movement throughout the 1950s-60s. Young Jim spoke on McLoughlin's behalf and had several meetings with leading figures in the Irish political establishment. These included successive Defence Ministers, General Sean MacEoin and Oscar Traynor. It was all to no avail, however, and there was no change made to McLoughlin's rank.

McLoughlin's frustration over the matter was evident in two letters he sent to the Department of Defence in July 1952. In the first letter, he pointed out the role he had played during the Rising and the fact that his promotion to the rank of commanding officer had been ratified by Connolly, Pearse, Clarke and MacDiarmada. McLoughlin also commented that Oscar Traynor had been amongst the men he had sectioned off as part of his 'death or glory' squad, adding in reference to the Defence Minister's apparent bout of amnesia concerning his rank, 'I could jog his memory still further if necessary'. In the conclusion of his letter, McLoughlin also made it clear that he felt his communist past was being used against him. He noted how his association with 'various movements...particularly in regard to Russia' was being portrayed 'as something to be ashamed of'. McLoughlin, however, was adamant that he had nothing to be ashamed of and would 'apologise for no action' taken by him during the struggle for Irish freedom.[100]

A reply from the Department of Defence, which 'regretted' that no alteration could be made to McLoughlin's rank[101] added fuel to his anger. He immediately wrote back, describing the reply as 'pure humbug' and 'exactly the kind of treatment' that he had expected from that department. McLoughlin then informed the department that he no longer wished his pension claim to be processed and that he felt 'terribly ashamed' of the whole business. The remainder of his letter showed just how deeply he had been affected by the matter:

> I have always been proud of my association with the events of "Easter Week" and after and I bitterly regret I ever was foolish enough to

submit my efforts for financial assessment, and to have it treated as if I were a beggarman by people who rose to power and position on the efforts of people like myself, is the last straw.[102]

McLoughlin's health deteriorated during the 1950s. A letter from Danny in 1955 shows that his family was concerned about his life at that point, following what was obviously a very serious relapse.[103] This came just months after a previous bad bout of illness.[104] In addition, McLoughlin suffered from depression and had a nervous breakdown during these years. The treatment he received included electroconvulsive therapy, a common procedure then, but seen by many medical experts today as a dangerous and even counter-productive method of dealing with mental health problems.[105] Amongst its other consequences, this decline in McLoughlin's health compelled him to finally accept the disputed pension award from the Irish state. He wrote to the Department of Defence in March 1958 and pointed out that whilst he was 'very proud' of his military record and had been justifiably 'stubborn' on the matter previously, he was now 'an old man in very poor health'. The small pension on offer, a sum of £1 and five shillings per week, would, McLoughlin believed, be a 'godsend' to him in these circumstances.[106] The Department of Defence acceded to his request and, eleven years after receiving his initial inquiry, began to pay McLoughlin his military pension, backdating the payments to 1952.

Towards the end of his life, McLoughlin seemed to have become disillusioned about Ireland, seeing little connection between the 32 county socialist vision that had motivated him, and the type of state that emerged in the decades after 1922. Neither did he appear to hold its chief architect, Eamon de Valera, in very high regard, commenting on one occasion that he could not understand how de Valera had become such a prominent figure, considering 'that he had only been a captain in 1916'.[107] Towards the end of his life, McLoughlin did, though, have something of a reconciliation with the Catholic Church. He had not brought his children up in that faith, but lived out his own last years as a practicing adherent and regular Mass attender.

On Friday 12 February 1960, McLoughlin collapsed at home and was rushed to the Sheffield Royal Infirmary. He died in the early hours of the following morning. The cause of his death was later ascertained as heart failure and hypertension.[108] It seems that he had been unaware that he was suffering from high blood pressure until it was too late. In accordance with his wishes, he was cremated four days later at the City Road crematorium. Jack later scattered his ashes over the hills of Howth. It was a death that went unnoticed in Ireland, illustrating that long before his untimely passing, Sean McLoughlin, leading figure in some of the most significant and tumultuous events in modern Irish history, had indeed become Sean McLoughlin, Ireland's forgotten revolutionary.

Notes

1   Sean McLoughlin Private Papers.
2   UCDA, Communist Party Ireland, report, 6-11-23, P7a/87/100, Mulcahy papers.
3   Eunan O'Hailpin, *Defending Ireland*, (Oxford: 1999) p. 58.
4   UCDA, Communist Party Ireland, report from 101A to Minister for Defence, 30-10-23, P7a/87/75.
5   NA, Communist Party Ireland, report, 16-11-23, S5074A.
6   UCDA, Report from 1923 Sinn Fein Ard Fheis, in de Valera papers, P150/582/87-88.
7   *Workers' Republic*, 3-11-1923.
8   *Workers' Republic*, 10-11-1923.
9   UCDA, Communist Party of Ireland report, 12-11-23, Mulcahy Papers, P7a/87/133.
10 *Irish Press*, 25-11-1966.
11 MA, Dublin Command General Survey for period 15-1-24, S/12352 in Box CW/ops/8.
12 Dorothy McArdle, *the Irish Republic*, (London: 1968), p. 790.
13 UCDA, Communist Party Ireland, report, 12-11-23 Mulcahy Papers, P7a/87/133. See also Communist Party Ireland, report, 6-11-23, P7a/87/100, and CPI report from 101A to Minster of Defence, 30-10-23, P7a/87/75, for more on McLoughlin's views regarding this matter.
14 UCDA, Communist Party Ireland Report, 12-11-23, P7a/87/133, Mulcahy Papers.
15 UCDA, Communist Party Ireland report, 6-11-23, P7a/87/100, Mulcahy papers.
16 NA, Communist Party Ireland report, 16-11-23, S5074A.
17 MA, Dublin Command, General Survey 15-12-23, S12352 in Box CW/ops/8. See also reports for 3-12-23 and 31-12-23 in same file for further examples of communist contact with IRA.
18 For more on these disputes see: The *Irish Independent* 11-9-1922 – 30-9-1922, Mike Milotte, *Communism in Modern Ireland* (Dublin: 1984), pp71-72, and Emmet O'Connor, 'Agrarian Unrest and the Labour Movement in County Waterford 1917-23,' *Saothar 6*, (1980).

19 See *Workers' Republic,* 24-2-1923. For more discussion on the adoption of the United Front tactic see Agnew/ McDermott, *The Comintern: International Communism from Lenin to Stalin,* (Basingstoke: 1996), pp. 27-40. See also, RGASPI, Report of Comrade Zinoviev on the further tactics of the Communist International, from Proceedings of Fourth Comintern Congress, 491/1/23-43.

20 Mike Milotte, 'Communist Politics in Ireland, 1916-1945', PhD thesis, QUB, (1977) pp. 119-20 and Emmet O'Connor, 'Communists, Russia and the IRA 1920-3, *the Historical Journal,* 46, 1, (2003) p. 128.

21 As Fernando Claudin points out in *the Communist Movement from Comintern to Cominform,* (London: 1975), pp. 266-7, the 1922 Congress, in light of the experience gained since the 1920 Congress, took a sharper line on the question of the precise nature of communist relations with bourgeois nationalist revolutionaries. But there was no departure from the view that these communists should be actively involved in their various anti-imperialist struggles. The resolution passed at the Congress on the colonial question highlighted the two main tasks facing the communists in colonial states. It described a communist refusal to take part in the anti-imperialist struggle as 'opportunism of the worst kind', but also viewed as 'not less harmful' the argument that communists should ignore involvement in class struggle on the grounds that such activity might upset 'national unity'. For the Colonial question debate in full see, RGASPI, Fourth World Congress of the Communist International, Theses on the Eastern Question, 491/1/223-46/54.

22 Mike Milotte, 'Communist Politics in Ireland, 1916-45', p. 120.

23 RGASPI, Resolution of the Praesidium of the EC on the Irish Question, 13-12-22, 495/89/11-6/7.

24 Roddy Connolly, 'Past and Future policy', *Workers' Republic,* 6-1-1923, 13-1-1923, 20-1-1923.

25 Connolly sent copies of 'Past and Future Policy' to the Comintern in Moscow, complete with annotations, in which he made it clear that this is why he offered the republicans such advice, RGASPI, Past and Future Policy, 495/89/25-13.

26 *Workers' Republic,* 3-2-1923.

27 RGASPI, ABF White and JJ O'Leary to Comintern, 28-2-1923, 495/89/22-35.

28 RGASPI, Report of 1st annual congress of the CPI, 23-1-23, 495/89/21-5.

29 See letters by Connolly (*Irish Press,* 29-1-48, *Irish People,* 14-2-48), and Pollock, (*Irish People,* 14-2-48), in reply to Sean McEntee's red scare

tactics during the 1948 general election.
30 RGASPI, CPI Report to October 1 1923 from April 1923, 495/89/22-74/77.
31 BNA, Report on the revolutionary organizations in the United Kingdom, CAB 24/162/cp473, 29-11-23.
32 RGASPI, Bob Stewart to Comrades Kolarov and Bukharin, 495/89/23-79.
33 RGASPI, Untitled report (from CPGB) 495/89/13-82-84.
34 RGASPI, Minutes of CPGB Politbureau, 3-10-23, 10-10-23, 495/100/104.
35 RGASPI, CPI to executive committee Comintern, 1-12-23, 495/89/22-81/82.
36 UCDA, Communist Party of Ireland, report by 101A, 26-1-24, Mulcahy Papers, P7b/140/206.
37 NLI, Sean McLoughlin to Hanna Sheehy Skeffington, 3-1-24, Accession no 5203, Hanna Sheehy-Skeffington papers.
38 See: *The Irish Worker*, 12-1-1924, and 19-1-1924.
39 Emmet Larkin, *Jim Larkin, Irish Labour Leader*, (London: 1965), p. 170.
40 See Emmet O'Connor, *Jim Larkin*, (Cork: 2003), pp. 115-117.
41 RGASPI, CPI report to October 1 from April 1923, 495/89/22-76.
42 *Irish Worker*, 2-2-1924.
43 *Irish Worker*, 12-4-1924.
44 Sean McLoughlin, 'Clearing the Decks' *Irish Worker*, 12-7-1924.
45 *Irish Times*, 16-8-1924.
46 NLI, Sean McLoughlin 'How Inchicore was lost', in William O'Brien papers, 15,670, p. 2.
47 See letters from Thomas Balfe, secretary IGR&EU to PT Daly, secretary to Dublin Trades Council, *Irish Worker*, 27-9-1924. The IGR&EU had been an affiliate to the Trades Council, but was expelled following the Inchicore strike.
48 Sean McLoughlin, 'How Inchicore was lost', p. 2.
49 Ibid.
50 Ibid.
51 *Irish Times*, 16-8-1924.
52 Sean McLoughlin, 'How Inchicore was lost', p. 4.
53 *Irish Times*, 16-8-1924
54 *Irish Times*, 18-8-1924.
55 *Irish Times* 11-9-1924. This editorial came eight days after one that praised the aims of fascism as 'excellent'.

56 *Irish Times*, 19-8-1924.
57 *Irish Times*, 20-8-1924.
58 *Irish Times*, 21-8-1924.
59 Ibid.
60 *Irish Times*, 22-8-1924.
61 Ibid.
62 Ibid.
63 *Irish Times*, 18-8-1924.
64 Sean McLoughlin, 'How Inchicore was lost', p. 3.
65 Sean McLoughlin, 'How Inchicore was lost' pp. 5-6.
66 Ibid.
67 *Irish Times*, 26-8-1924.
68 Sean McLoughlin, 'How Inchicore was lost', p. 6.
69 *Irish Times*, 26-8-1924.
70 Sean McLoughlin, 'How Inchicore was lost', p. 7.
71 Sean McLoughlin, 'How Inchicore was lost', p. 7.
72 *Irish Times*, 30-8-1924, 2-9-1924.
73 *Irish Times*, 26-8-1924.
74 See for example, *Irish Times*, 5-9-1924.
75 *Irish Times*, 8-9-1924.
76 Sean McLoughlin, 'How Inchicore was lost', p. 7.
77 *Irish Times*, 15-9-1924.
78 Sean McLoughlin, 'How Inchicore was lost' p. 9.
79 Sean McLoughlin, 'How Inchicore was lost', pp. 9-10.
80 Ibid., p. 10 and *Voice of Labour*, 11-10-1924.
81 Sean McLoughlin, 'How Inchicore was lost', p. 10.
82 Sean McLoughlin, 'How Inchicore was lost', p. 11.
83 Sean McLoughlin, 'How Inchicore was lost', p. 1.
84 I am obliged to the Shiel family for this information.
85 Sean McLoughlin, 'How Inchicore was lost, p. 10.
86 Sean McLoughlin, 'How Inchicore was lost, p. 14.
87 Interview with Ross Connolly (Roddy Connolly's son), 9-4-2002.
88 Sean McLoughlin, Private Papers.
89 Ralph Miliband, *Parliamentary Socialism*, (London: 1971), p. 148.
90 I am obliged to Stuart Pacitto of Teeside Archives for this information.
91 Sean McLoughlin, Private Papers
92 Leon Trotsky, *Revolution Betrayed, What is the Soviet Union and where is it going?*, (New York: 1972), p. 88.
93 I am obliged to the McLoughlin family for much of the following

information.
94　Peter Brearey interview with CH Burden, 1975.
95　Sean Nolan (solicitor for Sean McLoughlin) to Department of Defence, 22-7-1947.
96　Department of Defence to Sean Nolan, 7-8-1947.
97　Sean McLoughlin's Military Service Certificate, courtesy of McLoughlin family.
98　The *Irish Independent* 8-9-54 and *Sunday Independent* 16-1-55 carries reports and photographs of Margaret McLoughlin representing the Labour party at various debates in Dublin.
99　May (Margaret) McLoughlin to Sean McLoughlin, 21-10-54, Sean McLoughlin private papers.
100　Sean McLoughlin to Department of Defence, 11-7-1952.
101　Department of Defence to Sean McLoughlin, 17-7-1952.
102　Sean McLoughlin to Department of Defence, 21-7-1952.
103　Danny McLoughlin to Sean McLoughlin, 29-7-55, Sean McLoughlin private papers.
104　Christy McLoughlin to Sean McLoughlin, 17-1-55, Sean McLoughlin private papers.
105　Radical politician and psychiatric specialist, Dr Noel Browne, who was always deeply opposed to ECT, gives a harrowing account of the procedure in his autobiography *Against the Tide*, (Dublin: 1986), pp. 243-44.
106　Sean McLoughlin to Department of Defence, 6-3-1958.
107　Sean McLoughlin made this comment to his son Jack. Of course de Valera was a commandant in 1916, but the remark nonetheless offers an insight into McLoughlin's views on him. It should also be noted here that McLoughlin very rarely spoke about his political involvements, and never in any detail, to his family. His children were aware that he had been involved in the 1916 Rising, and had been promoted to a high rank during it, but were unaware of the actual significance of his involvement. They had virtually no knowledge of his subsequent activity during the 1917-24 period.
108　Sean McLoughlin death certificate, courtesy of Births, Deaths and Marriages Registrar, Sheffield.

Conclusion

Sean McLoughlin's death passed by unnoticed in Ireland. There was neither a mention of his passing in any newspaper nor representation from any Irish political organization at his cremation. This omission may seem strange, given the significance of McLoughlin's activities, particularly during the Easter Rising, but there are possible explanations for it. Perhaps it was simply the consequence of McLoughlin being gone so long from Ireland. Perhaps it was the case that by 1960 he had been so long Ireland's forgotten revolutionary, that it was inevitable his death would cause no ripples in the small pond of Irish political life. Maybe it was simply that the passage of time had seen him fade from the memories of those who had once known him.

But rather than dwell on why McLoughlin's actual passing was such a non-event in the eyes of Ireland's great and good, a more apposite, if related, enquiry should be why had he become such a forgotten figure in the first place? McLoughlin, after all, was an important participant in the Irish revolution. Throughout the period 1916-23, he combined intense levels of activism with a capacity for innovative thinking, designed to map out a route to victory for the Irish struggle. Why was it that someone who possessed these qualities became the forgotten man of Irish history, whilst others, including some who arguably contributed less to the struggle for Irish freedom, became celebrated figures? The question is an important one because, as will be seen below, in attempting to engage with it, we will also raise a lot of other important questions about the character of the Irish State as it developed in its different phases in the post-1922 period.

Before tackling that, however, it is necessary first to summarise and evaluate McLoughlin's contribution to the Irish Revolution. His 1916 story was one of the most significant of Easter Week. Setting off with Sean Heuston on Easter Monday morning, McLoughlin could scarcely have believed that by the end of the week he would be the Commandant-General of the army of the Irish Republic. The timing of his rise to prominence, towards the end of the fighting, reveals much about his character. Men far older and more experienced than McLoughlin were reduced to panic or paralysis by the conditions created as the Rising entered its final hours. In contrast, and by the general consensus of the many eye-witnesses who have passed comment on his 1916 performance, McLoughlin displayed considerable leadership qualities and an ability to think logically and strategically, and act decisively and quickly – a *coup d'oeil infaillible* as Clausewitz might have termed it – in the most disorientating of circumstances. McLoughlin's subsequent promotion to the head of military command was testament to this and shows that he, and not Eamon de Valera, was the highest-ranking survivor of 1916.

These same qualities were again to the fore in the post 1916 years, when McLoughlin was both an energetic and efficient Volunteer organizer. His activism during that period is important, because it offers an insight into how the Volunteer movement re-built itself following the trauma of 1916. It shows the actual methods of organization, and the links between centre and localities, adding detail to the body of work that has already been compiled on this question. Important too was McLoughlin's capacity for inventive thinking, which manifested itself throughout this period. His plans for resisting conscription, which involved breaking the Volunteers up into smaller more mobile units capable of engaging in hit-and-run tactics, were detailed and displayed a willingness to devote time and mental energy to the solution of the serious problems he felt faced the movement. The plans are significant because they represented a break from the type of orthodox military planning that characterized 1916, and were amongst the early attempts by the Irish Volunteers to formulate a strategy based on the principles of guerrilla warfare. That strategy, of course, would eventually become the strategy of the Volunteers during the 1919-21 period.

McLoughlin's combination of activism and reflection can be seen most clearly following his move towards communism. Consequently, it is as an activist within the communist movement that McLoughlin is of most value to those seeking to understand the nature and course of the Irish Revolution, the political, economic and social processes that underlay it, and the developments that took place in its aftermath. The Irish Revolution has been characterized as a purely conservative revolution. English, Garvin, Hart and Patterson are just four of a long list of historians who have asserted this view. The activities of communists like McLoughlin, however, suggest that this is an assumption in need of major qualification. It is surely more accurate to see the Irish Revolution as springing from various, and at times conflicting, sources, some proletarian, others bourgeois. True, it was led by bourgeois and petty bourgeois elements and ultimately served sectional interests within those classes. This, though, does not alter the fact that there was a proletarian aspect to it also. The levels of strike activity and agrarian disturbance, and the existence of soviets, show this to be the case. There are of course many historians who, when faced with the evidence of this activity, argue that it was provoked mainly by economic factors, and as such, distinct from those generating the national struggle.[1] However, it is extremely doubtful if there has ever been a revolutionary movement of the working class devoid of an economic source or given sustenance, at least to a degree, by economic factors. This arbitrary separation of politics from economics is not the method of the impartial inquirer, but appears to be more the application of a formal analysis which by its very nature ignores the relationship that exists between economics and politics, between economic struggles and political struggles. In Ireland significant economic discontent arguably had the potential to be transformed into political opposition and was evidence of a social strand within the overall revolutionary situation.

The activity of the communists helps to illustrate the social aspects of the revolution. It introduces a Marxist subjective factor into the overall objective situation, helping to highlight its class component. This is particularly so in the post-Treaty situation, when the fledgling CPI made its most strenuous attempts to influence the course of the Irish Revolution. Sean McLoughlin and most Irish communists worked within the IRA, partly because they saw it as a revolutionary anti-imperialist force, partly because they considered its proletarian base to be a fertile recruiting ground for party development. Had it been able to recruit sufficiently, perhaps the party would have intervened more regularly and directly in these struggles of the working class. This growth did not occur, but the communists did recognize the significance of the rising class militancy and the need to harness it in a revolutionary fashion. The party did intervene to the best of its ability in various working-class struggles before the Civil War began. Included here were two strikes in Dublin,[2] the unemployed workers' movement (which it led)[3] and, as we have seen, one of the soviets set up at Cleeve's creamery combine in May 1922. The party also had an influence within both the unpurchased tenants' movement,[4] which was dominated by small tenant farmers affected by the war and post-war slow-down in land redistribution, and the Kilkenny Workers' Council, whose chairman was a member of the CPI.[5]

After the outbreak of the Civil War, the party focused its attentions on that conflict, seeing in it a historic opportunity for developing communist strength in Ireland. But it did not ignore the working-class militancy that was still in evidence. The CPI recognised the class nature of the Treatyite forces, and insisted that only by counterposing working-class militancy to it, through the issuing of a social programme, could both the grievances of the workers be addressed and the anti-Treaty, anti-imperialist campaign of the IRA succeed. Only by harnessing the workers, urban and rural, to the anti-Treaty struggle could the Free State and British imperialism be toppled. In short, the communists recognized the social strand within the Irish revolution and, considering it to be its most significant component, sought to make it the basis of the entire anti-Treaty movement, warning that it was the only way the revolution could succeed. This shows that there was logic behind the argument the party leadership made, that involvement in the Civil War was also involvement in the class war.

McLoughlin was central to this strategy. His military record was more significant than that of any other Irish communist. Indeed, it was more significant than that of most Republicans. As a result, he had a great deal of authority and respect within the Republican movement. Because of this, he was seen as a huge asset by the CPI in its efforts to develop the proletarian strand of the revolutionary struggle. As seen, McLoughlin devoted much energy to this end during the Civil War, and had some success. As an IRA commandant and leader of IRA prisoners, McLoughlin not only carried out his military duties, but also took the opportunity to introduce socialist ideas, and the socialist conception of the nature of the revolution they were involved in, to those he had influence over. From his perspective, the results were encouraging. Certainly, when he left prison in October 1923, it was with the belief that when the jails were emptied the Irish communist movement would be boosted by an influx of new members.

Also worthy of mention here is McLoughlin's communist activity in Britain. This was important for two reasons. First his attempt to link the two revolutionary struggles, Irish and British, together. This was designed to illustrate to British socialists and advanced workers the significance of the Irish revolution and to help them re-evaluate the struggle in Ireland as central to their own fight for revolutionary change. It also highlighted for Irish immigrant workers in Britain the class nature of the revolutionary struggle in Ireland, and the need for them to get involved in the British socialist movement in order to help and protect the revolutionary movement back home. Second was McLoughlin's insistence that socialism could triumph in Ireland before Britain. Whilst of the view that Irish socialism would need the support of British socialism to endure, McLoughlin argued that such a revolutionary transformation would happen in Ireland first. This was a view clearly influenced by the events of October 1917, which contradicted the belief that socialist revolution could happen only in advanced capitalist states. Through his attachment to the SLP, McLoughlin was able to apply this thinking to Ireland and become one of the early pioneers of the concept within both the British and Irish socialist movements.

The Irish communists did not succeed. Instead of the 32 County workers' republic, Ireland was partitioned and dominated by Britain, politically and economically. Ultimately, the CPI arrived onto the political stage just as the revolution was being rolled back, and far too late to have the impact it hoped for. Neither was it aided by the fact that, for the most part, it had a very young and inexperienced leadership that toiled badly in the extremely tough objective situation created after December 1921. The party clearly needed help and guidance from the wider international communist movement. In contrast to the CPGB, whose contribution to both the CPI and the Irish revolution was weak, Moscow did try to provide such assistance. This was seen most clearly when it sent Mikhail Borodin to Britain in the summer of 1922. His subsequent arrest and deportation, however, helped scupper what was probably the best opportunity that had existed for the development of Irish communism.

It is easy to write off the efforts of communists like Sean McLoughlin during the Civil War. In fact, most historians, even those dealing specifically with the development of socialist politics in this period, do not even consider the party worthy of such a cursory dismissal. Instead, they prefer to ignore them almost entirely, and completely so as an active force within the Irish Revolution.[6] Yet the communists were important. The CPI, its serious organizational and political weaknesses and inconsistencies notwithstanding, was probably the only political party that understood to any degree, and attempted to deal with, the economic and political consequences of British imperialism in Ireland. It was certainly the only party of that period that attempted to both keep alive and implement the teachings of James Connolly. Unlike the Irish Labour Party, which closed its eyes to it and wished it away, the CPI believed that the national question was part of the Irish political landscape and could not be ignored. Whilst Labour saw the national question as a problem to be solved by other agencies, the communists regarded it as a reality that had to be faced, and could only be resolved, by the Irish working class. Similarly, in relation to the economy, and in reply to those nationalists like Michael Collins who believed that British military withdrawal from the 26 counties equated to economic withdrawal[7] and a chance for a strong Irish economy to develop, the communists argued that the economic power of British capitalism in Ireland remained undiminished by the Treaty.

As we have seen, there was a substantial degree of contact between the communists and republicans during the Civil War. The communists did attempt to illustrate to republicans the class nature of the struggle they were involved in and did point out to them their likely fate if they continued to ignore this. McLoughlin's articles in the *Workers' Republic* of July and August 1922 are clear evidence of this, and show that he was to the fore in pursuing this policy. This did have an ideological impact within the IRA, evidenced with the flowering of a distinctly socialist tendency later in the decade.[8] The view that the Treaty was the result of collaboration between British imperialism and the Irish capitalist class and the consequence of a republican struggle fought without reference to social issues, producing in its wake a puppet state of British imperialism, became common currency within, and even beyond, that IRA faction later in the decade. But it has its roots in early 1920s communist, not republican, discourse. Similarly, the view of late 1920s IRA socialists that Republicans were defeated during the Civil War because they failed to adopt the social programme that might have fired the workers into the anti-Treaty struggle and toppled the British-backed Free State, had been put forward earlier by the CPI and very forcefully by McLoughlin during the Civil War. It exposes as questionable the assertions by commentators such as Howe, who argue that this type of socialist analysis, and 'the notion that Ireland was a victim of informal imperialism or neo-colonialism' only developed in the 1930s 'long after the keys of Dublin Castle were handed over'.[9]

One of the most important aspects of any discussion involving the communist contribution to the Irish Revolution is that the communists, although they made many mistakes and ultimately failed, were nonetheless correct in some of their predictions concerning future Irish social, economic and political development; aspects of the communist perspective and analysis of 1921-23 were borne out in a fashion unforeseen by every other political tendency. As will be seen, this was particularly so with the manner in which the Irish Free State developed from that point onwards.

Conversely, it is here that the arguments of the revisionist historians are open to the greatest challenge. Few of those who dominate Irish historiography offer a convincing analysis of, or explanation for, the character of the Treatyite administration headed by Cumann na nGaedheal, or the policies it pursued during its ten years of power. The nature of the relationship between Cumann na nGaedheal and the British state is often overlooked. For example, Tom Garvin, who devoted a whole work to the establishment of the Free State, did not investigate the influence of the British, both in its creation and development, politically and economically. Consequently, the question of Free State dependency on British imperialism is completely ignored. Garvin blamed the 'parsimony' of the Free State government on the financial costs of the Civil War,[10] an assertion that begs two questions: why, if the government was so cash strapped, did it insist on two tax cuts in the mid-1920s? And why was it that the administration which replaced it in 1932 was willing and able to devote more to social and welfare spending? Other analysts such as Henry Patterson and Richard English have also described Cumann na nGaedheal as a conservative government,[11] which supported the large farming classes.[12] Both are correct, but again neither offered much by way of analysis or explanation. The proposition that there might be a link between British imperialism, the Treaty and the reactionary nature of Cumann na nGaedheal was not explored. Yet the question is important, not only because it increases our understanding of the factors that underpinned the development of the Free State, but it also allows us to gain more of an understanding as to why Sean McLoughlin was forced out of Ireland in the first place, and why his name was forgotten in that first decade of Irish self-rule

But before turning to this important question, it is necessary to look at some of the other factors behind the marginalisation and defeat of McLoughlin and the Irish communists. Undoubtedly one such factor was the combined attitude and actions of the CPGB, Moscow and Larkin. Given the link between McLoughlin's marginalisation and subsequent consignment to oblivion, any discussion about why he became such a forgotten figure would be incomplete without mention of this.

The CPGB were significant here. Relations between the British and Irish communist parties were always fractious; the CPGB regarded the CPI as small, factionalised and ineffective, whilst the Irish communists looked on their British counterparts as centrist and of little use by way of direct involvement in the revolutionary struggle in Ireland. The return of Larkin to Ireland in 1923 was seen by the CPGB as an opportunity to start afresh the task of building a serious and healthy communist movement in Ireland. As a result, connivance commenced between the CPGB, Larkin and Moscow resulting in the disbandment of a party that Irish communists had spent five years attempting to establish and build.

The consequence of all of this was the placing of Larkin at the head of the Irish communist movement. Whilst there can be no doubt that Larkin was a courageous and self-sacrificing leader of the Irish working class during the 1907-13 period, what equally cannot be gainsaid is that as a communist leader in the 1920s he was deeply ineffectual. That this was always likely to be the case became evident as soon as he returned to Ireland. Within weeks of arriving back in Dublin, Larkin engineered a split in the ITGWU and with it the Irish labour movement as a whole. As a revolutionary socialist Larkin had deep political objections to the pro-Free State stance of the Labour movement leaders. Crucially, however, he did not fight against them on these grounds. Larkin's offer to resign from the ITGWU one week after his return to Ireland was as a result of his objections to the move by the leadership that replaced him to limit the powers of his general secretaryship;[13] Larkin wanted the type of full control he had enjoyed in the pre-1914 period. The resignation offer was withdrawn at the same meeting, but a cleavage had been opened, not on the high ground of political principle but rather the more base terrain of egoism. The subsequent conflict between Larkin and the ITGWU leaders reflected this and was one characterized by jealousy and showers of invective from all sides. The result was confusion where there should have been clarity in the minds of workers and, consequently, a failure to build a serious alternative to reformism.

A similar performance was served up by Larkin during the Inchicore rail strike. As with his dispute involving the ITGWU, Larkin had grounds for criticizing the strike at Inchicore. It could be argued that there had been inadequate preparation for it and that as it stood, and appeared to the returning Larkin, the strike was unwinnable. As such, its continuation had the potential to demoralize rather than embolden or inspire those militant workers who had joined the newly formed union. However, just as in his war with the ITGWU, this type of concern did not seem to motivate Larkin's intervention. Instead, it appeared to be egoism that informed his actions. Larkin was unhappy that the WUI had been launched in his absence and clearly felt threatened by the new and militant leadership that stood at its head. Upon return to Ireland, he set about taking control of the new body and was prepared to fish in the muddiest waters to do so. This included undermining those who were leading the strike at Inchicore and engaging in character assassination against them.

The great tragedy concerning Jim Larkin's leadership of the Irish communist movement is that it came at a time when there was a window of opportunity for the development of a radical alternative to the conservatism of Cumann na nGaedheal. Labour ostensibly filled the role of opposition to the Free State party, but in reality, as can be seen most clearly from a speech Johnson gave in March 1923, Irish social democracy was deeply loyal to the Treaty settlement.[14] As such, Labour did not appear to many as a viable or credible alternative to the Free State government.

With Sinn Fein dangling on the hook of abstentionism, and the IRA still in the embryonic stages of a review of its own years of inactivity, the field seemed clear for the development of a socialist alternative to the Free State. Economic slump, perhaps, ruled out the emergence of a mass movement, but the basis of a socialist challenge to Cumann na nGaedheal could have been created during the 1924-26 period. Larkin, however, wasted the opportunities that came his way. In 1925, he sabotaged the efforts of Comintern representative and CPGB leading figure Bob Stewart to found a genuine Marxist party in Ireland[15], preferring the existing situation, where he could sit unchallenged in Moscow as representative of the IWL – a party that now didn't exist – and use the prestige of his position there to build up his union. This sabotage finally compelled the Irish communists to set up a new party in opposition to Larkin – the Workers Party of Ireland – in March 1926.[16] Once more, however, when faced with the choice, Moscow decided to back Larkin. As in 1924, the Comintern eventually instructed the communists to dissolve their organization and give their support to Larkin.[17] 1926, the year that the short-lived Workers' Party was formed, was also the year that the price for years of missed opportunities by the left was finally paid, when de Valera set up Fianna Fail. Although neither socialist nor republican de Valera's new party employed rhetoric that appeared to make concessions in both these directions. He twinned the national and social questions, albeit in a non-republican, non-socialist fashion, finally plugging the gap which had lain vacant for a radical alternative to Cumann na nGaedheal since 1923. And in the years to come he would prove for socialists to be a foe far more durable and resilient than the Free Staters ever were.

The connivance of the CPGB, Larkin and Moscow and the eventual impact of Larkinism 1924-style was clearly a contributory factor to the defeat and marginalisation of the Irish communist movement and activists such as McLoughlin. For McLoughlin, the dissolution of this party was a huge blow. He clearly had high hopes of building a socialist alternative to both the brutality of the Free State, and the weak opportunism of its petty-bourgeois republican opponents. In breaking completely from the IRA, and attempting to place the CPI in direct and open opposition to it, McLoughlin had reached a turning point in his revolutionary career but one that he approached with great optimism. All the more devastating for him, therefore, must have been the outcome of the connivance between the CPGB, Larkin and the ECCI. After that, all that was left was the Larkin vehicle itself. And ejection from that particular ramshackle in October 1924 finally brought the curtain down on McLoughlin's involvement in Irish revolutionary politics.

Clearly, there is evidence to suggest that it was this split from Larkin that led to McLoughlin's departure from Ireland, and was the real reason he did so. It can be argued that, for a variety of reasons, McLoughlin now had nowhere to go politically, making emigration a more attractive prospect. But this is perhaps assuming too much; political defeat, even the shattering type that clearly befell McLoughlin between 1922-24, does not automatically or necessarily lead to the emigrant boat. Other factors have to be considered too. Moreover, it is also the case that in the same month McLoughlin left Ireland, October 1924, a new organization was set up by Irish communists titled the James Connolly Workers' Club.[18] This body included in its ranks ex-CPI leaders such as Roddy Connolly, and although confining its activities to lectures and socialist education classes, it did nonetheless act as a forum for communist politics, as well as a nucleus for the new party to be set up in March 1926. This is not to dispute the negative impact of the CPGB/Moscow/Larkin axis on McLoughlin. It was a powerful contributory factor to his political defeat and marginalisation. As such, it can be seen as one reason why McLoughlin was consigned to oblivion. But it was not the only factor, or even the main one. McLoughlin himself said that he was hounded out of Ireland by the Free State, not by Larkin. And so it is to the nature of the Free State that we must now turn our attentions, because in addition to being the reason why McLoughlin was run out of the country, it also provides a context for understanding why he became Ireland's forgotten revolutionary.

Although the term 'neo-colony' and the development of neo-colonialist and dependency theory is associated with African political leaders such as Kwame Nkrumah[19] and political thinkers such as Andre Gunder Frank, both of whom first formulated their theories during the 1950s-60s, it is clear that the Irish communist analysis of the Irish Free State was a forerunner of that tradition.[20] As we have seen, historians like Howe have argued that this type of thinking only began to develop in Ireland from the 1930s onwards but there is much evidence to contradict this; as early as 1922, McLoughlin was pointing out that the Irish Free State was the 'puppet state' of British imperialism, where a colonial bureaucracy was 'controlled and manipulated' from London, and upheld the rights of 'private property and exploitation'.[21]

This analysis anticipated later neo-colonial theory and was very much in line with its basic tenets. It was also one that is worthy of interrogation, because if neo-colonialism can be seen as the 'survival of the colonial system in spite of formal recognition of political independence in emerging countries, which became the victims of an indirect and subtle form of domination by political, economic, social, military or technical [forces]',[22] then it is arguable that the Free State was a neo-colony. Endorsed by the British government, and armed and supported by it during the Civil War, the subsequent political and economic development of the Free State was also influenced strongly by imperial considerations.

Economically, the Free State was bound to British capitalism. Over 90 per cent of exports were sold to Britain, with 78 per cent of imports travelling in the opposite direction.[23] Of these exports, 76 per cent were agricultural, maintaining Ireland's role as a British feeding ground, whilst the imports largely took the form of finished industrial goods. That Ireland was locked into an unequal relationship with British capitalism can be seen by the fact that between January-July 1924, imports to the Free State were valued at £38,544,743, whilst exports were only £25,930,437, a shortfall of 33 per cent.[24] Only 13 per cent of the Free State workforce was involved in industrial manufacturing,[25] the motor force of capitalist economic and political development. Huge currency reserves remained outside Ireland and in Britain,[26] helping contribute to the lack of investment in native Irish industry. In 1925, the Free State followed Britain back on to the Gold Standard, highlighting the fact that economic sovereignty remained in London. Two years later a currency act was passed, establishing an Irish currency fully backed by British Sterling securities. As Haughton indicated, this effectively ended any possibility of an independent Irish monetary policy and helped to maintain between the Bank of England and the Irish economy, an exploitative relationship not dissimilar to those forced on underdeveloped Third World economies by the World Bank in the 1980s.[27]

Overseeing this process was Cumann na nGaedheal. Neo-colonialism requires the installation of an agent class, a comprador bourgeoisie incapable of promoting native industrial or political development and profiting directly from the maintenance of a subservient relationship with the imperial power. There is evidence to suggest that the interests served by Cumann na nGaedheal, were very much those of such an agent class. In order to defend the Treaty settlement and establish the rule of the classes that stood to benefit – the upper sections of the Irish bourgeoisie – Cumann na nGaedheal was compelled to repress the struggles of the Irish workers, as well as the IRA. It did so enthusiastically, forging fully in this process its own class nature and outlook. This narrowed further its bases of support amongst the working class and petty-bourgeoisie within the Free State and pushed it closer to imperialism as a means of survival. Willing to remain locked into a relationship that could promise only indefinite underdevelopment, collaboration with imperialism became for the Free State party its 'guiding principle, as far as possible'.[28]

This was evident in both its economic and diplomatic relations with the British. Economically, the 26 County State was maintained as a de-industrialised pastureland, acting as an adjunct to British agriculture.

Tariffs, which might have boosted native industrial development, were largely rejected on the grounds that they would affect agricultural exports to Britain. The only industries that did develop were those linked to agriculture, such as biscuit making, brewing and distilling. This of course had its effect on the working class. In order to keep taxes low for this neo-colonial bourgeoisie – and there were two such tax reductions in 1925 and 1927 – social spending was pared to the bone. In 1924, total outlay on Blind and OAP pensions was £3,180,783; by 1927 it was down to £2,543,342.[29] Between 1922-32 only 25,540 state aided houses were built, a mere 8,376 of which were constructed by local authorities.[30] This was far short of the 67,000 or so that the Sinn Fein Convention of 1917 had deemed as 'urgently needed' for urban areas alone in Ireland at that point in time, or the much higher figure, itself now superseded, that Michael Collins in 1922 admitted would now be necessary.[31] The same period saw the wages of agricultural workers drop by 20 per cent.[32] Official white guard organizations such as the Special Infantry Corps were deployed to break up strikes and brutalize workers.[33] Unemployment stayed perennially high: around the 80,000 mark. Cumann na nGaedheal decided that the best way to deal with this latter problem was to cut off whole sectors of the unemployed from what existed of a benefits system. Thus in December 1924 uncovenanted payments to the unemployed were stopped. Commenting on this, Free State industry minister McGilligan stated, 'there are certain limited funds at our disposal. People may have to die in this country and die through starvation.'[34] This was the quintessential Cumann na nGaedheal attitude towards Irish workers, but arguably one determined by the fact that the Irish economy was shaped to meet the needs of British imperialism.

On the political front, too, continued deference to British imperialism was the order of the day. This was seen most clearly during the Boundary Commission crisis of 1925, which resulted in the British partition of Ireland becoming a permanent, rather than temporary arrangement. This was clearly at odds with the stepping stone theory forwarded by those who had justified their support of the Treaty on the grounds that it marked advancement towards a republic, and was something of a humiliation for the Free State at the hands of the British state. Despite this, however, a Bill endorsing the new arrangement was soon passed in the Free State parliament.

By the mid 1920s, the neo-colonial reaction had triumphed in Ireland and showed signs of becoming even stronger. The increased power within the Free State administration of Kevin O'Higgins, dominant in the government from 1924 onwards, opened up the prospect of a closer relationship with imperialism. As his letters show, O'Higgins had talks with Churchill,

Birkenhead and Carson with the aim of returning the whole of Ireland to full Crown colony status.[35] His 1927 assassination at the hands of the IRA prevented O'Higgins from developing this policy, but that he was pursuing it in the first instance shows just how far the neo-colonial counter-revolution had gone.

It is important to bear in mind, however, that although the Free State appeared to be a neo-colony ruled over by a comprador elite, it was not presented as such by those who headed and supported it. Instead, Cumann na nGaedheal took great pains to cloak itself in nationalist garb, and tried to claim for itself the vanguard position in the march of the Irish nation. To do this successfully, it had to portray its opponents in a particular fashion, not dissimilar to that used by the Thermidorians against the Jacobins in the French revolution. Just as the Jacobins were crushed, not as Jacobins but as terrorists, so republicans and socialists opposed to the Free State were crushed, not as republicans or socialists, but as wreckers and incendiarists. Hanley has shown how the Treatyite regime at various points portrayed its enemies as pro-British, criminal and unconcerned and uninterested about the economic and social conditions of Irish workers.[36] This was in contrast to the Free State national army, which was portrayed as having shouldered the burden of the fighting before and during the 1919-21 period.[37]

This explains the motivation of the Free State government in building a monument to Arthur Griffith and Michael Collins in August 1923, one year after their deaths. The clear intention of the Cumann na nGaedheal regime was to place Griffith and Collins in the pantheon of national heroes and martyrs, in order that it could bask in their reflected glory. True, the construct, a Cenotaph on Leinster lawn, was at a cost of just £833,[38] a miserable and shoddy façade. But it was what it represented, and was supposed to achieve, that is important. The Cenotaph was designed to gain for the Free State the blessing of the millennial struggle for Irish freedom, and those who had led it from Brian Boru to Padraig Pearse; an attempt to legitimize the particular conception of the Irish revolution, as held by the Free State, and stamp out of sight any conflicting view or conception; a Cumann na nGaedheal declaration to the world that this is what 700 years of struggle had been about. No other view could be tolerated.

In this scenario, it is easy to see why McLoughlin was run out of the country. There did not appear to be any compromise between his conception of the Free State and that of Cumann na nGaedheal. Cumann na nGaedheal saw the Free State as enshrining Irish independence; McLoughlin saw it as the puppet state of British imperialism. Cumann na nGaedheal promoted itself as the national party, the inheritor of the mantle passed down through the ages by those who had struggled for Irish freedom, McLoughlin saw it as an imperialist clique controlled and manipulated from London. For Cumann na nGaedheal, the Free State marked the beginning of the process of nation building, for McLoughlin it was an impediment to such a development. In sum, McLoughlin did not consider Cumann na nGaedheal to be a nationalist revolutionary party that had fought for Irish freedom, before being forced into an honourable compromise by the British, but an active, conscious, counter-revolutionary administration, supportive of imperialism and willing to do its bidding.

McLoughlin's was a clear critique, and not garbled or obtuse. It was a critique that went to the heart of the Treatyite settlement, as opposed to one that skirted around its periphery, like de Valera's Document no. 2. It was a critique that threatened the Cumann na nGaedheal strategy – the pursuit of which included events such as the holding of an 'Independence Day' celebration in December 1924[39] – of attempting to pass off the Free State as genuinely independent. It was a critique that was unacceptable to the Free State. In contrast to the British, who did not even attempt to legitimize their rule in Ireland during the previous period, Cumann na nGaedheal, the 'national' government, required acceptance and legitimacy. The Civil War fighting may have ended in May 1923, but the march of reaction continued and grew more powerful as the decade wore on.

This provides a possible context for understanding why McLoughlin – regarded by the Free State as more of a threat than any other Irish communist – and his family were victimized and why he left Ireland and was denied his place in history. It shows why the Free State would continue this harassment even after McLoughlin had been forced out, as seen with the role it played in his conviction in Hartlepool in June 1926. Larkin might have caused him political frustration but it was Cumann na nGaedheal who ran Sean McLoughlin out of Ireland and built in their image a state that, by its very nature, was required to bury everything he and those like him had stood for and fought for.

De Valera's Fianna Fail finally took office in 1932. It would enjoy political power throughout most of the following four decades, seeing off in its early days a fascist challenge from the 'democrats' of 1922 who, following a second electoral defeat in 1933, had threatened to use force in order to regain power.[40] Fianna Fail would go on to shape much of the character of the modern Irish Free State and later Republic. De Valera's long period of dominance can be used to introduce two propositions: first that there was a section of the Irish bourgeoisie willing to lead a successful struggle against colonialism and the neo-colonial Treaty settlement and that those like McLoughlin who stood in the Connolly tradition were wrong in their assertions that only the working class, through socialism, could solve the national question; and second that the responsibility for the continued marginalisation of McLoughlin and his ideas cannot be laid simply at the door of Cumann na nGaedheal. Both are worthy of further examination.

In relation to the first proposition, it is arguable that during the Treaty and Civil War period, de Valera was more a representative of the petty-bourgeoisie than the more powerful bourgeois class itself. By the late 1930s, he had certainly become the spokesperson and promoter of the Irish capitalist class as a whole, but this was a bourgeoisie that had changed to a degree, both in its composition and outlook, since 1922. The bourgeois class, as it existed in that earlier period, was instead represented by what would become Cumann na nGaedheal and was, without doubt, overwhelmingly pro-Treaty. The petty-bourgeoisie was divided over the Treaty. The poor performance, though, of its anti-Treaty section in the Civil War, which de Valera was part of, when it was exposed as incapable of defeating imperialism and an imperialist settlement, does little to weaken the viewpoint that only the Irish working class was capable of leading this struggle to success.

The objective situation de Valera faced in the years following his election victory in 1932 was very different. The global power of British imperialism was weaker in the mid-to-late 1930s than it had been 15 years earlier. In 1922 the British ruling class was willing to wage war on Ireland if such as the Constitution was not altered and the electoral pact between Collins and de Valera not scrapped. By the mid and late 1930s it had many more pressing challenges to deal with. These included the problems posed by deep economic slump; the urgent need to re-equip what was an antiquated military machine; the understanding that it had been eclipsed totally by Nazi Germany as the major capitalist power in Europe and was dwarfed by the USA on a more global scale; and the continued existence of the USSR, led by unpredictable intriguer Stalin.

In these changed conditions de Valera, and the indigenous, Irish capitalist class he represented, had more room to operate and gain concessions than had Cosgrave fifteen years earlier. The objective situation in 1922-23 was very different. Had de Valera come to power then or soon after, there is every likelihood that his Free State would have been as much a neo-colony as that presided over by Cosgrave. The notion that de Valera, his forces crushed in the Civil War, could have begun to unpick the economic and political threads of the Treaty settlement during these years simply omits from analysis the very real power of British imperialism in the 1920s and the subordinate position of the Irish Free State in relation to it.

Socialists such as Connolly and those who followed, including McLoughlin, could not have foreseen the constellation of forces, the factors that would combine to weaken British imperialism in the mid and late 1930s or the space this would provide sections of the Irish bourgeoisie for economic and political advancement. Their analysis was formed in a different time and was borne out by the unfolding of events throughout the 1920s. The 1930s did produce changes. Even so, however, these were of such a limited character that they arguably do little to refute the central arguments of the Irish socialists. This is because during the years of Fianna Fail rule, when these changes occurred, British imperialism, its decline in power notwithstanding, was still strong enough to prevent de Valera from achieving much of what he nominally aspired to. For example, de Valera, his successes in removing the most obvious imperial trappings of the Free State notwithstanding, was unable to move the British on partition. True, having little to offer either protestant or catholic workers, and aware that the incorporation of 800,000 protestants into the Free State would dilute its catholic nationalist character, he expended minimum energy in this direction. The point is, however, that Ireland remained partitioned because Britain decided so; de Valera's views on the matter were irrelevant. Ultimately, de Valera, like Cosgrave before him, found that he could reconcile the interests of the Irish bourgeoisie with the continued existence of partition and imperial control in the north. The relationship he forged with imperialism was far less subservient than that of Cosgrave, but was still shaped to a large extent by British interests.

This process was mirrored economically. De Valera dreamed of an industrialized, independent, self-sufficient 26 County State, in contrast to the pastureland presided over by Cumann na nGaedheal. He condemned the Treatyite regime for keeping Ireland as a 'British outgarden'[41] and convinced the Irish bourgeoisie as a whole, including eventually the neo-colonialist element, that greater independence from Britain was its best option and a feasible one at that. Under his control, the Fianna Fail government established such bodies as the Industrial Credit Organisation, in order to stimulate native capitalist development, and erected tariffs in order to protect them from British and European competition. De Valera also scrapped the payment of land annuities to the British exchequer. Fianna Fail's industrialization policy paid some dividends: between 1932 and 1939, 51,000 industrial jobs were created.[42]

In many other important respects, however, the Free State economy continued to be dominated by British capitalism. The banking system, for example, established by Britain and long a target for Fianna Fail propaganda, which accused it of siphoning Irish money into British securities, was not dismantled.[43] Thus one of the most important features of the neo-colonial economic framework survived, Fianna Fail rhetoric notwithstanding. The Bank of England also continued to set the value of the Irish pound on the international markets, keeping it within the sphere of Sterling control.[44] Also, throughout this period, Irish exports were as reliant on the British market as they had been under Cumann na nGaedheal. Indeed, it was the logic of this dependency that compelled de Valera to seek an end to the economic war – begun after his withholding of land annuity payments in 1932 – a move which, as Mike Cronin has pointed out, marked the Free State's return once more to the 'Informal Empire' of British capitalism.[45] In short, failure to achieve political independence for Ireland had been matched by failure to break from British economic control.

This is not to deny that notable economic and political developments took place in the Irish Free State during de Valera's tenure. Neither is it to dispute that de Valera did aspire towards complete independence from Britain. In the last analysis, however, de Valera in power would find, just as he had in the different conditions of 1922, that the forces he represented were no match for the British state. Instead, the truncated Irish State would continue to be dominated by Britain, economically and politically.

Like Cumann na nGaedheal, Fianna Fail attempted to hide this reality. Like Cosgrave before him, but with far greater success, de Valera too appropriated 700 years of struggle and presented Fianna Fail as its modern day standard bearers. The building up of a self-sufficient, industrial 26 counties – the north would come in later, it was said – was now seen as the aim of the Irish Revolution. Unlike the Treatyites, de Valera even felt able to invoke the memory of James Connolly, and soon had him conscripted into Fianna Fail's ranks. Of course, this was not Connolly as he had been, not Connolly the Marxist, Connolly the working-class leader, Connolly the implacable opponent of British imperialism and Irish capitalism. Instead it was a sanitized Connolly, a Connolly shorn of his socialism, Connolly the national hero, the patriot, a martyr for Ireland, the same Ireland that de Valera was trying to develop, and a victim in the same struggle that de Valera was leading to victory. Hospitals and railway stations in his name eventually followed. The Easter Rising, fought for the most material of aims by Connolly, was commemorated in 1935 by de Valera with the erection of a statue of an Irish mythical figure in his dying agony; valour was to be combined with suffering, bravery with death, reducing 1916 to a blood sacrifice, instead of the revolution that it had been, with real, tangible objectives, most of which had yet to be fulfilled.

That Connolly's son had been imprisoned by de Valera's government for his part in the tram strike that began in March 1935, and was released just days before these Easter celebrations – even Fianna Fail recognized the embarrassing irony of the situation – shows perhaps a different side of de Valera's Ireland.[46] And all the while the emigrant boats were filled to overflowing. Irish capitalist development proved to be a chimera, but one whose pursuit was painful from a working-class perspective. The 1950s, a decade which saw the 1921-51 rate of population decline doubled,[47] marked the final disappearance of this illusion. This was in contrast to the dole queues, which shot up by over 50 per cent in the two years between April 1951 and April 1953.[48] McLoughlin's vision for Ireland had as little in common with this as that of the previous regime. The revolution he had fought in was not the one celebrated by Fianna Fail every Easter. The class interests he opposed when breaking completely from the IRA in jail in 1923 were very much those upheld by Fianna Fail from 1932 onwards. The leaders he condemned for their combination of military incompetence and reactionary political ideas were the very ones who would shape the Irish State and its ideology for 35 of the next 41 years. This again provides a possible context for understanding why McLoughlin would remain in obscurity.

Despite this, however, McLoughlin's name would occasionally surface. A fine article written by Proinsias MacAonghusa in 1966, as the Irish State marked the 50th anniversary of the Easter Rising, pointed out McLoughlin's significance to that event, and noted that he had also been involved in the Civil War and left-wing politics in Britain. But even MacAonghusa, his clear enthusiasm notwithstanding, was in the dark about McLoughlin's later life, commenting that although he had heard McLoughlin had died some years earlier, he was unable to confirm this.[49] A few letters followed in the next couple of weeks, one from a Fianna comrade of McLoughlin, who remembered him,[50] and another from a reader who had heard the story of McLoughlin in the GPO in the 1916, but 'put it down to rumour, etc'.[51] Just like the statue of Cuchullain in the GPO, it seemed that McLoughlin had become part of the mythology associated with the Rising. By this stage he had been dead six years, but buried much longer. This situation is one that continued in the post 1966 period, notwithstanding the phenomenal developments that would take place in Irish historiography from that point on.

In some respects, however, McLoughlin was fortunate that he became Ireland's forgotten revolutionary; at least this prevented him from being conscripted posthumously, like so many other dead revolutionaries, to serve causes and interests that he opposed in life. Instead, he can be seen as an activist who was motivated by high humanitarian ideals and an important figure in a movement whose men and women may now be long forgotten, but who in Ireland tried against insurmountable odds to build a society based on equality and one where all forms of oppression – national, social, political and economic – would be abolished. Today, McLoughlin's life and ideas can be seen not just as a means of gaining a better and more nuanced understanding of one of the most important periods in modern Irish history, but act also as an inspiration to those around the world who continue to struggle against this oppression wherever it is to be found.

Notes

1. For example, Richard English, *Radicals and the Republic: Socialist Republicanism in the Irish Free State 1925-1937*, (Oxford: 1994), pp. 42-43.
2. These two strikes involved gasworkers and capmakers. See the *Workers' Republic*, 8-10-21, 15-10-21, 29-10-21, 19-11-21, 26-11-21 and RGASPI, Report of CPI to ECCI, October 1921 – October 1922, 495/89/16/40/131.
3. Ibid., RGASPI, 495/89/16/40-53, and 495/89/16/40/133-34.
4. RGASPI, Mikhail Borodin interviews delegates from Irish Party, 15-7-22, 495/89/13/6-11.
5. This was Douglas Bligh. For his favourable comments on the CPI see the journal of the Kilkenny Workers' Council, the *Torch*, 26-11-21. Bligh died in August 1923. For a brief obituary, in which he was described by the CPI as one of their 'ablest and most enthusiastic members', see the *Workers' Republic*, 18-8-23.
6. Two such examples are English, *Radicals and the Republic*, and Henry Patterson, *The Politics of Illusion*, (London: 1989). In both accounts the *Workers' Republic* newspaper is given a brief mention, but the actual activities of the CPI are omitted entirely, as is any mention of its leading figures.
7. Michael Collins, *Path to Freedom*, (Cork: 1996), p. 94.
8. Emmet O'Connor introduces this proposition in 'Communists, Russia and the IRA 1920-3' *Historical Journal*, 46, 1 (2003) p. 131. Important too, as will be seen below, was the contribution of the Irish Marxists to Marxist theory as a whole in the field of neo-colonial and dependency theory.
9. Stephen Howe, *Ireland and Empire*, (Oxford: 2000), p. 64.
10. Tom Garvin, *1922: the Birth of Irish Democracy*, (Dublin: 1996), p. 164.

11 Patterson, *Politics of Illusion*, p. 23.
12 English, *Radicals and the Republic*, p. 96. To this list we can also add Stephen Howe. His *Ireland and Empire* is, however, even less satisfactory; the chapter that deals with the economic question (8) omits entirely ten years of Cumann na nGaedheal rule and its economic and political consequences.
13 ITGWU *Annual Report 1923*, p. 7.
14 This was a speech Johnson gave during a Civil War debate on military estimates. He described the anti-treaty campaign as directed 'against the social fabric...against the very idea of society' and committed Labour to the support of any measures 'at any cost and at any sacrifice' to protect the Free State, and a hundredfold increase in military spending if necessary. Dail Debates, Volume 2, Col 2279-2281, 9-3-23.
15 See Bob Stewart, *Breaking the Fetters*, (London: 1967) pp. 147-54, and Mike Milotte, *Communism in Modern Ireland*, (Dublin: 1984) pp. 77-81.
16 For more on the establishment of this party see, Public Records Office Northern Ireland, D/24 79/1/9, Charlotte Despard diaries, 9-2-26, 28-2-26, 5-3-26, 10-3-26, 11-3-26, 14-3-26, 17-3-26, 20-3-26, and RGASPI, McLay to ECCI, Report on formation and activities of the party, 30-10-26, 495/89/34/8-10.
17 The WPI was ordered to disband following a meeting of the ECCI presidium on 5-1-1927, RGASPI, 495/89/38/1, 495/89/38/4-6 and *Workers' Republic*, (WPI), 2-4-1927.
18 *Irish Worker*, 4-10-1924, 11-10-1924. and PRONI, Charlotte Despard Diaries.
19 Kwame Nkrumah was the prime minister of Ghana. For his analysis of neo-colonialism, see Nkrumah, *Neo Colonialism, the Highest Stage of Imperialism*, (London: 1965). Andre Gunder Frank has written extensively on dependency theory. For one early example see, Frank, 'The development of underdevelopment' in *Monthly Review*, New York, September 1966. (Later reprinted in Rhodes ed, *Imperialism and Underdevelopment: a Reader*, (London: 1970).
20 Again, the Irish Marxists of the early 1920s were developing a line of thought that had first been promoted by James Connolly many years earlier. In his article 'Nationalism and Socialism' (*Shan Van Vocht 8-1-1897*) Connolly argued that 'if you remove the English army tomorrow and hoist the green flag over Dublin Castle, unless you set about the organization of the socialist republic your efforts will be in vain. England will still rule you. She would rule you through her capitalists,

through her landlords, through her financiers, through the whole array of commercial and individualist institutions she has planted in this country.' With this analysis, Connolly deserves to be seen as the first neo-colonial and dependency theorist. The manner in which the Irish communists in the early 1920s developed and applied this type of thinking to an actual concrete situation marks them as out too as highly important figures in the progress of this strand of Marxist thinking. For more discussion on this see Charlie McGuire 'Irish Marxism and the Development of the Theory of Neo-Colonialism' in *Eire-Ireland*, Vol 41, (2), Fall/Winter 2006

21 Sean McLoughlin, 'Social Programme an absolute necessity' in *Workers' Republic*, 19-8-1922.

22 Michael Barratt Brown, *Economics of Imperialism*, (London: 1978) p. 256. The comment came from the official declaration made at the Third All-African Peoples Conference in Cairo, in 1961.

23 Mike Cronin, 'Golden Dreams, Harsh Realities: Economics and Informal Empire in the Irish Free State', in Cronin/Regan (Eds) *Ireland: the Politics of Independence, 1922-49*, (Basingstoke: 2000), p. 151.

24 *Irish Times*, 27-9-24.

25 Terence Brown, *Ireland, a Social and Cultural History*, (London: 1985), p. 104.

26 D.R. O'Connor Lysaght, 'British Imperialism in Ireland', in Purdie/Morgan (eds) *Ireland, Divided Nation, Divided Class*, (London: 1980), p. 24.

27 J. Haughton, 'Historical background' in O'Hagan (Ed), *The Economy of Ireland: Peformance, Policy and Perspective of a Small European Country*, (Dublin: 1995), p. 29.

28 Rumpf/Hepburn, *Nationalism and Socialism in Twentieth Century Ireland*, (Liverpool: 1977), p. 74.

29 Department of Industry and Commerce Statistical Abstract 1931, p. 102.

30 Ibid., 1933, p. 92.

31 Michael Collins, *The Path to Freedom*, p. 113.

32 Joseph Lee *Ireland 1912-85*, (Cambridge: 1989), p. 115.

33 See Emmet O'Connor, 'Agrarian unrest and the Labour Movement in County Waterford', *Saothar 6*, (1980).

34 Arthur Mitchell, *Labour in Irish Politics*, (Dublin: 1974), p.197.

35 John Regan, *The Irish Counter Revolution, 1921-36*, (Dublin: 2000), pp. 266-7.

36 Brian Hanley, 'The Rhetoric of Republican Legitimacy' in McGarry

(Ed) *Republicanism in Modern Ireland,* (Dublin: 2003), pp. 168-70.
37 Ibid.
38 Anne Dolan, *Commemorating the Irish Civil War,* (Cambridge: 2003), p. 10. This was in contrast to both the £25,000 spent on the care of British military graves and the £50,000 allotted to the creation of a World War One memorial at Islandbridge. For more on this see: Dolan, Commemoration: 'shows and stunts are all that is the thing now' in Augusteijn (Ed) *The Irish Revolution, 1913-23,* (Houndsmills: 2002), p. 187.
39 David Fitzpatrick, 'Commemoration in the Irish Free State, a chronicle of embarrassment' in Ian McBride (ed*), History and Memory in Modern Ireland,* (Cambridge: 2000), p. 198.
40 This of course was the Blueshirt movement, which was headed by leading Cumann na nGaedheal figures and had as its aim a dictatorship similar to that which had crushed the left in fascist Italy and Germany.
41 Kieran Allen, *Fianna Fail and Irish Labour,* (Dublin: 1996), p. 19.
42 Cronin, 'Golden Dreams and Harsh Realities', p. 156.
43 Ibid., p. 158.
44 Ibid.
45 Ibid., p. 161.
46 Roddy Connolly was arrested on 27 March 1935 and charged with membership of an illegal organization. No evidence was produced to substantiate the charge. He was eventually released on 16 April, five days before the statue of Cuchullain was unveiled in the GPO. See: NA, Military Tribunal File S7560, and also *Irish Press,* 28-3-1935, 17-4-1935.
47 Kennedy et al, *Economic development of Ireland in the 20th Century,* (London: 1988), p. 60.
48 Unemployment in the Irish Republic rose from 54,900 in April 1951 to 84,000 in April 1953, The Trend of Unemployment, 1950-2, (report gives unemployment figures to August 1953) p. 27.
49 Proinsias MacAonghusa, 'the leader history has forgotten', in the 50th Anniversary Easter Rising supplement, *Irish Independent,* April-May 1966.
50 Sean Hynes letter, *Evening Herald,* 24-5-1966.
51 Letter from 'interested, Ballymun,' *Evening Herald,* 17-5-1966.

Four texts by
SEAN McLOUGHLIN

Sinn Fein and the Irish Workers

The eyes of many people are being turned upon Ireland, and all are wondering what is going to happen next. To those of us who are awaiting or helping to hurry on the Social revolution, the situation is fraught with many possibilities. We see in the struggle for Freedom in Ireland something that gives us hope and courage, and we are hoping that a spark from the flames of revolt may blow across the Channel, a spark that may blow into a flame as strong and as unquenchable as that in Ireland; and yet there are many who are not convinced that the struggle in Ireland will be of benefit to those who are bearing the brunt of the fight – the Irish working class. But to those of us who know Ireland and her people that knowledge makes us more sanguine as to the outcome of the struggle against Imperialism. Yet while we may be confident that the workers of Ireland will be alive to their own interest, it behoves us to watch carefully and endeavour by every means at our disposal to guide the fight for National Freedom into a fight for Social Freedom. The whole movement working for Ireland's independence today is working under the flag of "Sinn Fein", and in order to thoroughly understand the situation it is necessary to examine, to some extent, what "Sinn Fein" really is. It is not, as many people seem to imagine, a fight waged on behalf of the working class, nor is it yet wholly a bourgeois movement. In its earlier days, prior to the "Easter rising" in 1916, it was for the most part an unknown movement, with a purely bourgeois outlook, and with no economic programme that would be acceptable even to a mild Socialist. It did not even recommend itself to many of the Irish Revolutionaries, who did not care for the "golden link to the Crown", and who were not to be reconciled to British Imperialism with a bribe of an "Irish Parliament". Yet the whole movement survived in a humble way, until it came into power some time after the "Easter" revolt. It is not our purpose to go over all the events that have brought the movement into its present position, but today it stands out against the whole force of the British Empire, backed by the majority of the people of Ireland, who are determined that it shall achieve its purpose and establish an Irish Republic. So far, no Revolutionary Socialist can disagree. But it is right at this point that the differences begin to appear. Who is going to rule in the Irish Republic? That will be the rock on which "Sinn Fein" will be wrecked. It is idle for anyone to pretend that Ireland will be any exception to the law of evolution. Many people are consoling themselves today, in Ireland and out of it, with the idea that they have entered the "promised land". With the taking over of the country by an Irish Government they will receive a rude shock. There is very little deep thinking required to realise the truth that "the working class and the employing class have nothing in common", and it will come no easier to an Irish worker to toil for an Irish capitalist under a Republic than it did under a Monarchy. Yet all these things can be avoided if in [the] process of revolution the Irish workers (or that class conscious section of them) are able to accomplish the same task as the Russians, who did not allow their revolution to stop at the point marked by the exploiters, but carried it on to the point where the working class assumed control. To that end we must set ourselves, to point out to Irish workers at home and abroad that we have a bigger task than the establishing of a Republic. We as revolutionaries are prepared to assist "Sinn Fein" in order to clear the way for the real struggle. We can see quite clearly the force of Marx's teaching pointed out in "Revolution and Counter-Revolution"[1] "The working class itself never is independent, never is of an exclusively proletarian character until all the different factions of the middle class have conquered political power, and remodelled the State according to their wants. It is then that the inevitable conflict between the employer and the employed becomes imminent, and cannot be adjourned any longer; that the working class can no longer be put off with delusive hopes and promises never to be realised; that the great problem of the century, the abolition of the proletariat, is at last brought forward fairly and in its proper light." We can assist in the revolution and act in it for the benefit of our own class. We will be bitterly opposed in our attempt. The fight to overthrow British power in Ireland may not be half as bitterly contested as the fight between the Irish working class and the Irish middle class for the control of the country. This is inevitable. The "Meath Land War"[2] of last summer and the 1913 strike in Dublin show quite clearly what will happen. Many people in Ireland look at the class war as unthinkable when applied to their country, but it will appear and must appear, before the Irish working class can come to their own. Ireland may not have big capitalists, she may even eliminate big landowners, and may find comfort in that fact; but while the present form of society exists she will have what constitutes the biggest antagonists to working class freedom, small shopkeepers and manufacturers, and they along with the farmers, form a big element in Irish life. True to their class traditions, they will not fall into line. They will resist, and no persuasion will move them except superior force. Let the Irish workers bear these things in mind. Let each and every individual amongst us, no matter what his ideas may be, assist by every means in his power the coming fight, help to overthrow the power of the British ruling class in Ireland, and at the same time see to it that the fight will be transformed into a struggle not only for the freedom if Ireland, but the freedom of the working class of Britain and Ireland. It is for the workers of Great Britain to see to it that they are ready to act when the moment arrives. They need not expect help from leaders. They must be prepared to act for themselves. The Irish working class have a history behind them. They have the memory of Connolly and Larkin to inspire them. They are not depending on leaders, for they cannot have men of that type with them always, and the sorry opportunists who have stepped into the shoes of Connolly and Larkin would be swept aside in a crisis. That crisis may be nearer than we think, and it will be a pitiful thing if, when the opportunity arises, we should fail to grasp it. Let us be ready to echo with Freiligrath[3]—

"When the last of crowns like glass shall break
On the scene our sorrows have haunted.
And the people the last dread 'guilty' shall speak,
By your side ye shall find me undaunted.
On Rhine or on 'Liffey', in word and in deed,
You shall witness, true to his vow,
On the wrecks of thrones, in the midst of the freed
The rebel who greets you now!"

From *The Socialist (Official Organ of the Socialist Labour Party)* February 26th, 1920.

Notes

1. A reference to a series of articles by F. Engels. The words quoted are from the article of October 25th, 1851. The whole text is available on http://www.marxists.org/archive/marx/works/1852/germany/index.htm
2. Following a lockout the Irish Transport and General Workers' Union called a strike which spread from Kildare to Meath and beyond; 2,500 workers were involved by July 1920.
3. The original text has Freilgaath, but this reference is to the sometime German radical Ferdinand Freiligrath (1810 - 1876).

The Song Of John Bull

Rule Britannia! Britons rule the waves!
The Imperialist slogan rings over the world.
Who cares for suffering, for millions enslaved,
For famine, disease, or premature graves,
When by murder and plunder our empire its saves.
And our flag over all is unfurled?

We have vanquished the Boers on African plains,
With rifle and cannon and good British pluck;
The Irish, the Zulus, the Indians and Danes,
For daring to live and ignoring our claims,
We have waded knee-deep in the blood of their slain,
And the world at our frown it has shook.

We are still carrying on our heaven blest work,
That our land may be prosperous and free.
With Bible and gun we will never shirk
The complete civilising of Christian and Turk.
Where Freedom exists, there danger will lurk;
So all must bow down before me.

But the workers in anger have risen at last,
And struck at these tyrants so well
That their empire of sin reels at the blast.
The cant and cowardice of John Bull is unmasked.
Oh! Free men rejoice as you see him swept past
By the red tide of war into hell.

From *The Socialist (Official Organ of the Socialist Labour Party)*
January 6th, 1921.

How the Republicans may Win

The Republicans have only one object, a purely sentimental one, as far as the masses are concerned—the establishing of a Republic, separated completely from Britain. This is supported by Communists and advanced Labour elements, in so far as it is a revolutionary step, in helping to smash British imperialism, but the masses are not swayed by these questions of high politics. They are moved by economic pressures, and will not respond to sentimental appeals, no matter how impassioned they may be. And the masses are correct. In the first place they are tired of war. In the second, they see that, no matter who wins, they will still be slaves grinding out their lives for wages and ruled with a rod of iron by bosses and landlords, and they cannot summon up enthusiasm enough to enable them to fight on behalf of wage-slavery.

The Republicans need support. They are in their present position because they dallied and vacillated, while the Free State was concentrating its forces and preparing for the fight. The Republicans trusted everyone—but the workers, and every section betrayed them. De Valera was in the clouds. He trusted to his power of persuasion, and they failed him as was inevitable. He and his gallant friends are now fighting for their lives. How can they win? There is only one way. If they refuse to go the only road to victory they will go down to history as a band of noble idealists, but utterly hopeless as revolutionaries.

The way is clear. Victory lies with the side that can attract to itself the masses, the workers of the towns and cities and the landless peasants. The Irish Labour Party alone can never beat the Free State—the British Government will see to that. The Labour Party alone cannot beat the Free State plus the British Government, but the Labour Party, supported by the Communist Party, backing the Republicans and appealing to the people with a proper social programme, will be absolutely invincible. The programme will be based upon the present needs of the masses, comprising confiscation of the land, the big estates and ranches to become the property of the landless peasants; social ownership of creameries, etc.; confiscation of all heavy industries, banks, etc.; repudiation of all debts, and the controlling and running of industry; land and housing to be in the hands of councils elected by the workers and peasants.

Republicans here is your chance; with the workers behind you the Free State relapses into the black hell from whence it came.

Representatives of Irish Labour, here is your chance to fulfil your pledges and be true to your class.

War against Imperialism and Capitalism, the land for the peasants, the factories for the workers, and a full, free life for all who toil.

If the Republicans fail to grasp their opportunity and the Labour Party has not the courage to act, all may rest assured the struggle is not lost. Everyday the people will see with clearer eyes, and inevitably the future is with them, and led by a determined and vigorous Communist Party, the workers and peasants will march unaided over the corpse of the Free State to the Workers' Republic.

The war between the Republicans and the Free Staters has entered upon its most desperate stage. After the fall of the Four Courts, after the evacuation of O'Connell Street by the Republican forces, the hirelings of Capitalism and Imperialist Britain, in their newspapers, set up a howl of joy—"The 'rebels' are defeated." "Glorious victory of the Artillery Field-Marshal Griffiths.*" But the howls of triumph were short-lived, as the Republicans have merely transferred the seat of war from Dublin to the south of Ireland. And so the struggle begins anew.

As the struggle progresses it becomes more and more evident that the Free State is merely a puppet State, controlled and manipulated from London. The Army, though nominally controlled by the Free State Government, is dependent upon the British War Office for its military supplies, and the organisation of the various departments in the Free State has been conducted on practically the same lines as obtained under the former rulers. The whole of the police force in Dublin, and with it all the detective branches and secret service groups, have been incorporated into the Free State, and in addition a special spy department has been established at Oriel House**, under the control, ironically enough, of a man who was responsible for the illegal importation of arms for the rebel forces when the struggles against the "Black and Tans"*** was raging. This spy department bears all the familiar imprints of its predecessors. Raids, searches, arrests, etc., are conducted in a vindictive spirit that exceeds even the procedure of the old detective and police raids. There is no respect shown to anybody. Terrorism and militarism are the watchwords of the new order. And over all rules the sacred spirit of private property and private execution.

The Free State government is, nakedly and unashamed, a purely bourgeois and capitalist Government, hostile to Labour, and carrying its hostility into action. Even the pink Labour Party is hated by this reactionary clique. And it is this crowd of place-hunters, renegades, and tools that has arrayed an army and launched it against the Republicans—an army composed, for the most part, of half starved proletarians—men who hate the Free State, yet are compelled by unemployment and misery to take up arms on behalf of reaction.

On the other side are the Republicans, badly armed and ill-equipped, fighting on behalf of an ideal; and yet fighting bravely and resolutely. They hold part of the south of Ireland, and are defending their position with the utmost determination. These Republicans have the support of every honest and clear-thinking man in Ireland, and are supported by the Irish Communists, because of their determined stand against British Imperialism in its fight against world revolution. Nevertheless, it is realised by most Communists today that the Republicans are faced with a tremendous task, and one which they will be compelled to meet by something more than guns and munitions.

With the exception of groups here and there, a big percentage of the Irish are apathetic to the struggle; that is particularly true of the landless peasants and the workers in the cities and big towns. In the war that is progressing only one side has a definite programme, and that side is the Free State. They declare for capitalism, and, as a result, all of the shopkeepers, large landholders, factory owners, and capitalists, in short, everyone interested in the exploitation of Labour are backing the Free State.

From: *The Workers Republic, (Official Organ of the Communist Party of Ireland)* July 29th, 1922.

--

* Free State forces used artillery supplied by the British Army to overcome anti-Treaty IRA forces at the Four Courts, overall there were 300 dead or wounded in the Dublin conflicts of June-July 1922.

** Oriel House Westland Row hosted plain clothes security forces, notorious for rough justice, torture and executions.

*** Black and Tans: British security forces clothed in black police and khaki army uniforms.

Social Programme for Republicans

AN ABSOLUTE NECESSITY

Since the beginning of the present struggle against the forces of the Free State the Irish Republican Army in the field has been able to withstand all the attacks of its enemies, and at the present moment occupies a favourable position from a military point of view. The positions held are being strengthened, supplies are good, and most important of all, the morale of the Army is splendid. Yet these things while being fine achievements do not necessarily spell victory for the Republican forces.

In order to carry the war to a successful issue, it is essential that the Republican authorities seize every opportunity of any nature, that will assist the gallant troops in the field. To be successful in a revolutionary struggle, something more than military prowess and skill must be taken into account. It is the duty of those responsible for maintaining the fight for the Republic to inquire into ways and means that will ensure a speedy and successful termination to the present struggle.

FREE STATE METHODS

First of all it will do no harm to analyse the methods adopted by the Free State, and to examine the forces behind it. When the Free State Provisional Government struck at the Republicans entrenched in the Four Courts, they were of the opinion that a swift and sudden blow, if successfully struck, would put all organised opposition to their plans definitely and for ever out of the way. Their plan failed because of the loyalty of the sections of the IRA outside Dublin. Foiled in their attempt to crush the Republican opposition at one blow, they soon realised that they were faced with a long and protracted struggle, and immediately began to mobilise all the forces possible. They carried on propaganda on an extensive scale, claiming that they were hard-headed practical men, whose sole aim was the regeneration of Ireland, all *they* wanted was peace, prosperity, and trade, and above all law and order. When the reactionary and anti-Irish elements realised what the nature of the new Government was, they immediately rallied to its support. Capitalists, large landowners, ranchers, shopkeepers, etc., praised the wisdom of Collins and Griffiths#, and firms like Guinness urged their men to join the Free State Army. When Collins found he had rallied sufficient support he immediately hurled his armies against the forces of the Republic, and proclaimed to the world that his only reason for doing this was, that the Republican were wild men, visionaries, dreamers, and looters who were out to destroy his schemes for Irish property. The reactionary press opened in full blast on behalf of the Free State, and the lie factories worked overtime. Yet in spite of all this, the Free State would have failed in their offensive, were it not that economic forces operated to aid them. Large numbers of men from the towns and the countryside flocked to the recruiting stations, in response to frantic newspaper appeals for men. These men did not respond because they believed in the Free State or because they were hostile to the Republic, but solely because unemployment, misery, and hunger drove them, and here was a way of escape from their misery. It will be objected—"But these men could have joined up with the Republicans." The truth is they never had the chance. The Free State Government was strong in Dublin, it was centralised, it had the power, money and influence of Imperial Britain. While the Republicans were falling back in the South and organising their forces, the way was left clear for the Free State to consolidate its position and capture the waverers.

WORKERS APATHETIC

In spite of the amount of propaganda carried on it is generally admitted that the mass of the workers and peasants are apathetic to the Free State, and in some cases even hostile. This does not mean that these people are sympathetic to the Republicans. On the contrary, the same spirit is manifested against both sides. The only party that derives any support from these sections (the workers and peasants) is the Labour Party. But it is a party unable to use this support, partly because of disunity in its ranks, and partly through cowardice. It is thus a vacillating party swinging to whatever side seems strongest and most likely to win.

ASSISTANCE OF WORKERS AND PEASANT NECESSARY

No party in Ireland today can win without the active assistance and co-operation of the workers and peasants, who, holding economic power can strangle any Government or party which fails to deal with them correctly. To win this war, it is of the most vital importance that workers and peasants be won over by the Republicans, and to do this the Republican Executive must draw up a programme that will meet the most pressing needs of the labouring masses. No party in the world today can exist without formulating its programme in a clear and lucid manner. The Free State Provisional Government has outlined its programme and policy, both harmonising with the Policy and programme pursued by the Imperial Government of Great Britain, government by the few for the many, exploitation of the poor and weak, and aggrandisement for the powerful and rich, the bayonet and the prison cell for those who disagree. This programme will not attract the masses. It remains for the Republicans by outlining just and equitable proposals, and an honest and fearless economic policy, to capture the people, and so win the present struggle.

IDEALISM NOT ENOUGH

At the present moment the people are asked to support a Republic without being told what *kind* of a Republic they are to get. The people are tired of war, they have suffered for many years for an ideal. That ideal is gradually receding into the shadow. The worn-out, impoverished and struggling masses need the substance more than the shadow. Idealists may die, and do, for principles, but People cannot die en masse for dreams. The Irish people have gone a long way on the road. Let the Republicans show that they are not mere dreamers and visionaries, but men who can translate dreams into realities, and visions into tangible good for the benefit of those in Ireland who have borne the brunt of the struggle against a foreign imperialism.

INTERNATIONAL WORKERS SUPPORTS

In addition to securing the support of the masses of the Irish people a just and fair economic programme, carried through by the Republicans for the benefit of the Irish masses, will be bound to attract the sympathy and support of the oppressed elements in every corner of the world. International support is of the highest importance to the Republicans, in these days when the oppressed elements in every country are tending more and more to international solidarity as a means to assist them in their common struggle against the plundering imperialistic Empires and exploiters of the entire world.

The fate of Ireland is now in the hands of the Republicans. If they fail, the responsibility will lie with them if they have not used the opportunities that presented themselves.

From: *The Workers Republic, (Official Organ of the Communist Party of Ireland)* August 19th, 1922.

#Michael Collins was killed three days after this article was published, on August 22nd, 1922; he was an ally of Arthur Griffith who had been largely responsible for forcing through the Treaty establishing the Free State; Griffith died of natural causes on August 12th, 1922.

Bibliography

Interviews

Ross Connolly, 9 April 2002, Dublin
Jack McLoughlin, 16-5-2004, Sheffield

Tape Recordings
Peter Brearey interview with former SLP member, C.H.Burden, Dewsbury, 1975, copy of tape in author's possession, courtesy of Raymond Challinor
Roddy Connolly speech to Ireland-USSR Friendship Society, 1974, copy of tape in author's possession, courtesy of Mike Milotte

Private papers
Charlotte Despard papers, PRONI
Cowan/McGowan papers, UCDA
Eamon de Valera papers, UCDA
Charles Diamond papers, NLI
Desmond Fitzgerald papers, UCDA
Sighle Humphries papers, UCDA
Rosamond Jacob diaries, NLI
Tom Johnson papers, NLI
James Klugmann papers, MULHA
Sean McLoughlin papers, (in the possession of Jack McLoughlin, Sheffield)
Sean McEntee papers, UCDA
Richard Mulcahy papers, UCDA
William O'Brien papers, NLI
Ernie O'Malley papers/notebooks, UCDA
Desmond Ryan papers, UCDA
Hanna Sheehy Skeffington papers, NLI

Public Records: **Ireland**
Irish Labour History Archives
Irish Citizen Army minutes book, 1919-1920

James Hardiman Library, National University Ireland Galway
British Colonial Office papers, CO 904, 1913-20

Military Archives
Civil War papers

National Archives
Statements to the Bureau of Military History, 1913-1921
Dick Balfe
Sean Beaumont
Joseph Connolly
Nora Connolly O'Brien
Ina Connolly Heron
Garry Holohan
Jim Larkin Junior
Frank McGrath
Mary McLoughlin
Sean McLoughlin
Liam Manahan
Eamon Martin
Seamus Reader
Seamus Robinson
Michael Staines

Department of Taoiseach files
DT, S5074A, S5074B, S5864A, S5864B, S7560

General Prison Board file, 1919/2051

Sinn Fein papers, file 1094

Dáil Éireann papers, file DE2

National Library Ireland
Irish National Aid and Volunteer Dependent's fund papers
Heuston's Fort, unpublished Easter Rising memoir of Patrick J. Stephenson

England

British Library of Political and Economic Science
Communist International Congresses, 1919-35, microfiche
ECCI Plenums, 1919-35, microfiche
Socialist Labour Party of Great Britain records, 1920-21

British National Archives, Kew
Cabinet Office papers, CAB 24, 1916-24,

Manchester University Labour History Archives
Communist Party Great Britain Political Bureau minutes, 1922-24

Russia

Russian State Social and Political Archives, Moscow
Fond 495, ECCI, records of the Communist Party Ireland

Published Reports
American Commission on Conditions in Ireland, Interim Report, London, 1921
Dáil Éireann Debates, Vols. 1-2, 91-93, 110-125
ECCI, *Bulletin of the Fourth Comintern Congress*, 1922
Independent Labour Party (Britain), Annual Report 1920
ILPTUC Annual Conference reports, 1916-24
ITGWU, *Attempt to Smash the ITGWU*, 1924

Newspapers

Camillian Post, 1948 (Order of St Camillus, copy in author's possession)
Communist, 1920-21 (CPGB)
Communist International, 1919-24 (ECCI)
Dublin Evening Mail, 1919-1922
Dublin Evening Herald, 1919-1922
Forward, 1917-1923 (Glasgow ILP)
Free State, 1922
Freeman's Journal, 1921-22
Glasgow Evening Times, 1920-21
Glasgow Observer, 1918-1923
Irish Independent
Irish Opinion, 1917-1918 (ILPTUC)

Irish Press
Irish Times
Irish Worker, 1914; 1923-1924
Liberty, 1966 (ITGWU)
Limerick Leader, 1921-23
Limerick Chronicle, 1922-1923
Shan Van Vocht, 1897
Socialist, 1917-1924 (SLP)
Sunday Independent, 1966
Tipperary Star, 1918-20
Torch, 1921, (Kilkenny Workers' Council)
Voice of Labour, 1918-1919; 1921-1927 (ILPTUC)
Watchword, 1919-1920 (ILPTUC)
Worker, 1915
Workers' Republic, 1915-1916; 1921-1923 (SPI/CPI);

Articles, Books, pamphlets
Adams, RJQ., *Bonar Law*, (Stanford University Press: 1999)
Allen, K., *Is Ireland a Neo-Colony?* (London: Bookmarks, 1990).
    The Politics of James Connolly, (London: Pluto, 1990).
    Fianna Fail and Irish Labour, (London: Pluto, 1997).
Anderson, W.K., *James Connolly and the Irish Left*, (Dublin: Irish Academic Press, 1994).
Augusteijn, J., *From Public Defiance to Guerrilla Warfare*, (Dublin: Irish Academic Press, 1996)
Barratt Brown, M., *Economics of Imperialism*, (London: Penguin, 1974).
Bew, P., Gibbon, P., Patterson, H., *Northern Ireland 1921-1994: Political Forces and Social Classes*, (London: Serif, 1995).
Barton., B., Foy, M., *The Easter Rising*, (Basingstoke: Sutton, 1999)
Bew, P., Hazelkorn, E., and Patterson, H., *the Dynamics of Irish Politics*, (London: Lawrence and Wishart, 1989).
Boyce, D.G., *Englishmen and Irish Troubles: British Public Opinion and the making of Irish Policy*, (London: Cape, 1972).
Braunthal, J., *History of the International, Vol 2, 1914-1943*, (London: Nelson, 1967).
Brennan, J.J., 'Mendicity Institution Area', in *Capuchin Annual* (1966).
Breznikov, A., 'Strategy and Tactics of the Comintern in the National and Colonial Question', in Ulyanovsky, R.A., (ed) *The Comintern and the East*, (Moscow: Progress, 1979).
Briscoe, R., *For the Life of Me*, (London: Longmans, 1959).

Brown, T., *Ireland: a Social and Cultural History 1922-1985*, (London: Fontana, 1985).
Browne, N., *Against the Tide*, (Dublin: Gill and MacMillan, 1986).
Caballero, M., *Latin America and the Comintern, 1919-1943*, (Cambridge University Press, 1986).
Cahill, L., *Forgotten Revolution: Limerick Soviet 1919*, (Dublin: O'Brien, 1990)
Carr, E.H., *the Bolshevik Revolution, Vol. 3*, (London: MacMillan, 1953).
Caulfield, M., *the Easter Rebellion*, (Dublin: Gill and MacMillan, 1995).
Challinor, R., *the Origins of British Bolshevism*, (London: Croom Helm, 1977).
Claudin, F., *the Communist Movement from Comintern to Cominform*, (London: Penguin, 1975).
____ *Eurocommunism and Socialism*, (London: New Left Books, 1977).
Clydebank District Library, *the Singer Strike of 1911*, (Clydebank: 1988).
Coffey, T., *Agony at Easter*, (London: Harrap, 1970).
Collins, M., *Path to Freedom*, (Cork: Mercier, 1996).
Connolly, J., *Socialism Made Easy*, Chicago: Kerr, 1908).
____ *The Irish Revolution*, (Dublin: James Connolly Publishing Company, 1923).
____ *Labour in Irish History*, (Dublin: ITGWU, 1933).
____ *Labour, Nationality and Religion*, (Dublin: New Books, 1969).
____ *The Connolly/Walker Controversy on Socialist Unity in Ireland*, (Cork Workers' Club, 1974).
____ *Ireland Upon the Dissecting Table*, (Cork Workers' Club, 1983).
____ *the Connolly/De Leon Controversy*, (Cork Workers' Club, 1986).
____ *Collected Works, Vols. One and Two*, (Dublin: New Books, 1987-1988).
Connolly, Roddy, 'Past and Future Policy', *Workers' Republic*, 6-1-1923—20-1-1923.
____ *Republican Struggle in Ireland*, (Dublin: Irish Communist Organisation reprint, 1966).
____ 'A Glimpse of Collins', Michael Collins Foundation supplement, *Irish Independent*, 20-8-1966.
____ and MacAlpine, E., (as Thomas Darragh) 'Revolutionary Ireland and Communism', *Communist International*, June-July 1920.
Coogan, T.P., *Michael Collins*, (London: Hutchinson, 1990)
____ *the IRA*, (London: Harper Collins, 2000)
CPI, *Outline History*, (Dublin: CPI, 1975).
Cronin, M., 'Golden Dreams and Harsh Realities: Economics and

Informal Empire in the Irish Free State' in Cronin, M., and Regan, J., (eds) *Ireland: the Politics of Independence, 1922-1949*, (Basingstoke: MacMillan, 2000).

____ and Regan, J., Introduction in Cronin/Regan (eds), *Ireland: the Politics of Independence, 1922-1949.*

Deasy, L., *Brother against Brother,* (Cork: Mercier, 1999).

Degras, J., *Soviet Documents on Foreign Policy, 1925-1932,* (Oxford: Royal Institute of International Affairs, 1956).

De Rosa, P., *Rebels,* (London: Ballantine, 1991).

Dolan, A., 'Shows and Stunts Are All That Is The Thing Now' in Augusteijn (ed) *The Irish Revolution, 1913-23,* (Houndsmills: Palgrave, 2002).

_____*Commemorating the Irish Civil War,* (Cambridge: CUP, 2003).

Dooley, T., 'IRA Veterans and Land Division in Independent Ireland 1923-48', in McGarry, F., (ed) *Republicanism in Modern Ireland,* (Dublin: UCD Press, 2003).

Land for the People: the Land Question in Independent Ireland, (Dublin: UCD Press, 2004).

Dunphy, R., *The Making of Fianna Fail Power in Ireland, 1923-48,* (Oxford University Press, 1995).

Dwyer, T.R., *Michael Collins and the Treaty,* (Cork: Mercier, 1991).

____ *Big Fellow, Long Fellow: A Joint biography of Collins and De Valera,* (Dublin: Gill and MacMillan, 1998).

R., and Louis, W., (eds) *Churchill,* (Oxford: Clarendon, 1996).

English, R., *Radicals and the Republic: Socialist Republicanism in the Irish Free State, 1925-1937,* (Oxford University Press, 1994).

Farrell, M., *Arming the Protestants: The Formation of the USC and RUC, 1920-27,* (London: Pluto, 1983).

Fitzpatrick, D., *Harry Boland's Irish Revolution, 1887-1923,* (Cork University Press, 1999).

_____ 'Commemoration in the Irish Free State, a Chronicle of Embarrassment' in Ian McBride (ed*), History and Memory in Modern Ireland,* (Cambridge: CUP, 2000).

Foley, Conor, *Legion of the Rearguard,* (London: Pluto, 1992).

Forester, M., *Michael Collins, the Lost Leader,* (Dublin: Gill and MacMillan, 1989).

Fox, Ralph, *Marx, Engels and Lenin on the Irish Question,* (London, nd).

Fox, R.M., *History of the Irish Citizen Army,* (Dublin: James Duffy, 1943).

Frank, A.G. 'Development of Underdevelopment', in Rhodes, R., (ed) *Imperialism and Underdevelopment, a Reader,* (New York: Monthly Review

Press, 1970).

―― *Critique and Anti-Critique: Essays in Dependence and Reformism,* (London: MacMillan, 1984).

Gallacher, W., *Last Memoirs,* (London: Lawrence and Wishart, 1966).

Gaughan, J.A., *Thomas Johnson, 1872-1963,* (Dublin: Kingdom, 1980).

Good, J., *Enchanted By Dreams,* (Dingle: Brandon, 1996).

Greaves, C.D., *Life and Times of James Connolly,* (London: Lawrence and Wishart, 1986).

―― *Liam Mellows and the Irish Revolution,* (London: Lawrence and Wishart, 1971).

―― *ITGWU: the formative years, 1909-1923,* (Dublin: Gill and MacMillan, 1982).

Haithcox, J.P., *Communism and Nationalism in India: MN Roy and Comintern Policy,* (Princeton University Press, 1971).

Hally, Colonel P.J., 'The Easter 1916 Rising in Dublin—The Military Aspects' *Irish Sword,* Volume VII, No 29, (1966).

Hanley, B., *The IRA 1926-1936,* (Dublin: Four Courts, 2002).

―― The Irish Citizen Army after 1916', *Saothar,* 28, 2003.

―― The Rhetoric of Republican Legitimacy' in McGarry (Ed) *Republicanism in Modern Ireland,* (Dublin: UCD, 2003).

Harman, C., *the Lost Revolution: Germany 1918-23,* (London: Bookmarks, 1997).

Hart, P., 'Definition: Defining the Irish Revolution' in Augusteijn, (ed), *the Irish Revolution 1913-1923,* (Houndmills: Palgrave, 2002).

Haughton, J., 'The Historical Background' in O'Hagan, (ed), *the Economy of Ireland,* (Dublin: Gill and MacMillan, 1995).

Haywood, H., *Black Bolshevik: Autobiography of an Afro-American Communist,* (Chicago: Liberator Press, 1978).

Hegarty, P., *Peadar O'Donnell,* (Cork: Mercier, 1999).

Henderson, F., *Frank Henderson's Easter Rising,* (Cork: Mercier, 1998).

Heuston, J.M., 'Headquarters Battalion-Army of the Irish Republic, Easter Week 1916', *Nationalist,* (Carlow: 1966).

Hoar, A., *In Green and Red: the lives of Frank Ryan,* (Kerry: Brandon, 2004).

Hopkinson, *Green Against Green: the Irish Civil War,* (Dublin: Gill and MacMillan, 1988).

Howe, S., *Ireland and Empire,* (Oxford: Oxford Univ. Press, 2000).

Howell, *A Lost Left,* (University of Chicago, 1986).

Hyland, J.L., *James Connolly,* (Dundalk: Dundealgan Press, 1997).

Johnson, T., *Future of Labour in Ireland,* (Dublin: ITUCLP, 1916).

Johnston, A., Larragy J., McWilliams, E., *Connolly: a Marxist analysis,* (Dublin: Irish Workers' Group, 1990).
Kendall, W., *the Revolutionary Movement in Britain, 1900-21,* (London: Weidenfield and Nicholson, 1969).
Kennedy, K., Giblin, T., McHugh, D., *Economic Development of Ireland in the 20th Century,* (London: Routledge, 1988).
Kostick, C., *Revolution in Ireland,* (London: Pluto, 1997).
____ and Collins, L, *The Easter Rising 1916,* (Dublin: O'Brien 2000)
Kotsonouris, M., *Retreat from Revolution: the Dail Courts, 1920-24,* (Dublin: Irish Academic Press, 1994).
Labour Party, *Labour's Constructive Programme,* (Dublin: Labour Party, 1936).
____ *Planning For the Crisis,* (Dublin: Labour Party, 1940).
Laffan, M., *Resurrection of Ireland: the Sinn Fein party, 1916-23,* (Cambridge University Press, 1999).
Larkin, E., *James Larkin: Labour leader 1876-1947,* (London: Routledge and Kegan Paul, 1965).
Lee, J., *Ireland 1912-85,* (Cambridge: Cambridge Univ. Press, 1989).
Lenin, V.I., *Collected Works, Volume 31,* (London: Lawrence and Wishart, 1966).
____ , *Imperialism: the Highest Stage of Capitalism,* (Moscow: Progress, 1982).
____ *Left Wing Communism: An Infantile Disorder,* (Peking: 1971).
____ *Speeches at the Congresses of the Communist International,*(Moscow: Progress, 1972.)
Levenson, S., *James Connolly,* (London: Martin Brian and O'Keefe, 1977).
Lyons, F.S.L., *Ireland Since the Famine,* (London: Fontana, 1973).
MacArdle, D., *The Irish Republic,* (London: Corgi, 1968).
McDermott, K., and Agnew, J., *the Comintern: International Communism from Lenin to Stalin,* (Basingstoke: MacMillan, 1996).
McGarry, F., *Frank Ryan,* (Dundalk: Dundealgan, 2002).
McGuire, C., *Roddy Connolly and the Struggle for Socialism in Ireland,* (Cork: CUP, 2008).
____ 'Irish Marxism and the Development of the Theory of Neo-Colonialism' in *Eire-Ireland,* Vol 41, (2), (Fall/Winter 2006)
McInerney, M., *Peadar O'Donnell: Irish Social Rebel,* (Dublin: O'Brien, 1974).
____ 'Roddy Connolly, Sixty Years of Political Activity', *Irish Times,* 27-8-1976.
MacIntyre, S., *Little Moscows: Communism and Militancy in Interwar*

Britain, (London: Croom Helm, 1980)

McLoughlin, B., and O'Connor, E., 'Sources on Ireland and the Communist International 1920-43', *Saothar*, 21, 1996.

McLoughlin, S., 'Sinn Fein and the Irish Worker', *The Socialist*, 26-2-1920.

____ 'Standing Up for Ireland', *The Socialist*, 25-3-1920.

____ 'Britain and the Struggle in Ireland', *The Socialist*, 27-5-1920.

____ 'The Orange Fraud in Ulster', *The Socialist*, 8-7-1920.

____ 'Drifting', *The Socialist*, 3-3-1921.

____ 'Counter-Revolution in Europe', *The Socialist*, 24-3-1921.

____ 'How the Republicans May Win', *The Workers Republic*, 29-7-1922.

____ 'Social Programme for Republicans an Absolute Necessity,' *Workers Republic*, 19-8-1922.

____ 'Heritage of Easter Week', *Irish Worker*, 19-4-1924.

____ 'Memories of the Easter Rising', *Camillian Post*, spring 1948.

McManus, A., 'James Connolly: Socialist and Revolutionary', *The Socialist*, 17-4-1919.

Marx, K. and Engels, F., *On Ireland*, (London: Lawrence and Wishart, 1971).

____, and Engels, F., *Selected Works in Three Volumes, vol.1*, (Moscow: Progress, 1977).

Miliband, R., *Parliamentary Socialism*, (London: Merlin, 1973).

Milotte, M., *Communism in Modern Ireland: The Pursuit of the Workers' Republic Since 1916*, (Dublin: Gill and MacMillan, 1984).

Milton, N., *John MacLean*, (London: Pluto, 1973).

Mitchell, A., *Labour in Irish Politics, 1890-1930*, (Dublin: Irish University Press, 1974).

____ *Revolutionary Government in Ireland: Dáil Éireann 1919-22*, (Dublin: Gill and MacMillan, 1995).

Murphy, J.T., *Preparing For Power*, (London: Cape, 1934).

____ *New Horizons*, (London: John Lane, 1941).

Nevin, D., *James Connolly: A Full Life* (Dublin: Gill and Macmillan, 2005).

Nkrumah, K., *Neo-Colonialism: the Last Stage of Imperialism*, (London: Nelson, 1972).

O'Connor, E., 'Agrarian Unrest and the Labour Movement in County Waterford, 1917-23,' *Saothar*, 6, 1980.

____ *Syndicalism in Ireland, 1917-23*,(Cork University Press, 1988).

____ *James Larkin*,(Cork University Press, 2002).

____ 'Communists, Russia and the IRA, 1920-23', *Historical Journal*, 46, 1, (2003).

____ *Reds and the Green: Ireland, Russia and the Communist Internationals*

1919-43, (University College Dublin Press, 2004).

O'Connor Lysaght, D.R., 'British Imperialism in Ireland' in Purdie, B., and Morgan, A., (eds) *Ireland: Divided Nation, Divided Class.*

____ 'Rakes Progress of a Syndicalist: the Political Career of William O'Brien, Labour leader' in *Saothar,* 9, 1983.

____ *Communists and the Irish Revolution,* (Dublin: Litereire, 1993).

O'Donnell, P., *The Gates Flew Open,* (London: Cape, 1932).

____ *There Will Be Another Day,* (Dublin: Dolmen, 1963).

Ó Drisceoil, D., *Peadar O'Donnell,* (Cork University Press, 2001).

Ó Hailpín, E., *Defending Ireland: the Irish State and its Enemies Since 1922* (Oxford University Press, 1999).

O'Malley, E., *The Singing Flame,* (Dublin: Anvil, 1978).

O'Neill, Colonel Eoghan 'The Battle of Dublin 1916: A Military Evaluation of Easter Week' in *An Cosantoir,* Volume XXVI, No 5, (1966)

Patterson, H., *The Politics of Illusion,* (London: Hutchinson and Radius, 1989).

Pimley, A., 'the Working Class Movement and the Irish Revolution' in Boyce, D.G.(ed) *Revolution in Ireland, 1879-1923,* (Basingstoke: MacMillan, 1988).

Ransom, B., *Connolly's Marxism,* (London: Pluto, 1980)

Regan, J., *The Irish Counter-Revolution, 1921-36,* (Dublin: Gill and MacMillan, 2001).

Riddel, J., (ed) *The Comintern in Lenin's time: Founding the Communist International, Proceedings and Documents, Vol 1,* (New York: Pathfinder, 1987).

Rumpf, E., and Hepburn, A., *Nationalism and Socialism in Twentieth Century Ireland,* (Liverpool University Press, 1977).

Sigerson, S., (Kathleen Coyle*),* *Sinn Fein and Socialism,* (Cork Workers' Club, n.d.).

Ryan, D., *The Rising, the Complete Story of Easter Week,* (Dublin: Golden Eagle, 1949

Stewart, R., *Breaking the Fetters,* (London: Lawrence and Wishart, 1967).

Strauss, E., *Irish Nationalism and British Democracy,* (London: Methuen, 1951)

Thompson, W., *The Good Old Cause: British Communism, 1920-91,* (London: Pluto, 1992).

Townshend, C., *The Easter Rebellion,* (London: Penguin, 2005)

Trotsky, L., *The Third International After Lenin,* (New York: Pathfinder, 1970).

____ *The Revolution Betrayed: What is the Soviet Union and Where is it*

Going? (New York: Pathfinder, 1973).
Two Participants, 'Inside the GPO', in Roger McHugh (ed), *Dublin 1916*, (London: Arlington, 1976)
Walker, B., *Ulster Politics: The Formative Years, 1868-1886*, Belfast: Ulster Historical Foundation, 1989).
Weiner, M., 'The Comintern in East Asia, 1919-39' in McDermott/Agnew, *The Comintern: International Communism from Lenin to Stalin.*
Yeates, P., *Lockout: Dublin 1913*, (Dublin: Palgrave MacMillan, 2001)
Young, J.D., 'John MacLean, Socialism and the Easter Rising' in *Saothar*,16, 1991.
Younger, C., *Ireland's Civil War*, (London: Fontana, 1968)

Theses:
Campbell, F., 'Land and Politics in Connacht 1898-1909', University of Bristol, PhD (1997)
Milotte, M., 'Communist Politics in Ireland, 1916-1945', PhD thesis, (Queens University Belfast, 1977)
Vernon, H.R., 'the Socialist Labour Party and the Working Class Movement on the Clyde, 1906-1923', M.Phil thesis (University of Leeds, 1967).

Index

Aiken, Frank, 106
Asquith, Herbert, 56

Balfe, Dick, 17, 25
Barrett, Dick, 98
Barton, Johnny, 36
Beaslai, Piarais, 24
Bell, Tom, 51, 78
Biggar, John, 56
Birkenhead, Lord, 152
Boland, Harry, 32, 44
Borodin, Mikhail, 93, 94, 144
Boru, Brian, 152
Breen, Dan, 47, 105
Brennan, Major-General, 101
Brennan, J.J., 27
Breslin, Pat, 116
Brugha, Cathal, 87
Bruton, Henry, 17, 36, 48
Bukharin, Nikolai, 118
Burden, C.H., 83, 86-88, 131
Burns, Bella, 43
Burnup, Bill, 129, 131
Byrne, James, 14

Carpenter, Walter, 54
Carr, E.G., 54
Carson, Edward, 152
Churchill, Winston, 56, 92, 151
Clarke, Tom, 14, 16, 32, 34, 35, 133
Clark, Tom (S.L.P.), 52, 57
Clunie, James, 88
Clyde Workers Committee, 51, 54-55, 57, 61
Colbert, Con, 13, 36
Collins, Michael, 42-48, 52, 69, 91, 92, 144, 150, 152, 154, 169
Communist International (Comintern), 53-54, 57, 58-59, 65, 67, 75, 78, 85, 92, 93, 97, 103, 108, 122, 125, 136, 148; Second Comintern Congress, 1920, 68-69; Third Comintern Congress, 1921, 88, 90,; Fourth Comintern Congress, 1922, 117-118
Communist Groups (CGs), 68
Communist Party of Germany (KPD), 79
Communist Party of Great Britain (CPGB), 78, 80, 83, 85, 88, 89, 93, 94, 100, 107, 109, 119, 120, 121, 137, 144, 146, 148, 149
Communist Party of Ireland (CPI), formation, 90; and the Civil War, 91-94, 101, 106, 115-116; demise of, 117-120; contribution to Irish Revolution, 135, 142, 143-149
Connolly, James, 9, 13-18, 23-27, 29-32, 34, 36, 37, 41, 43, 44, 50, 51, 53, 56, 64, 89, 117, 120, 133, 144, 154-156, 164
Connolly, Roddy, 44, 52-55, 68, 69, 90, 92-94, 101, 103, 116-121, 129, 132, 149, 156
Cook, A.J., 83
Cosgrave, W.T., 154-156
Cuchullain, 157
Cumann na nGaedheal, class nature of, 121, 145-148, 150-156
Curtis, Joe, 131, 132
Curtis, Lionel, 90
Daly, Ned, 26, 28, 30, 33, 35, 36

Deasy, Liam, 100, 102-104
Derrig, Tom, 100
de Courcy, Bob, 98
de Leon, Daniel, 50
de Valera, Eamon, 44, 48, 92, 95, 116, 130, 132, 134, 141, 148, 153-157, 166
Donohoe, Sergeant (R.I.C.), 48
Drew, William, 56, 57
Dublin Metropolitan Police (DMP), 14

Emmet, Robert, 48
Executive Committee Communist International (ECCI), 118, 148, 159

Farrell, Elizabeth, 35
Fianna Fail, 130, 132; ecomomic and political programme of, 148, 153, 155-157
Fitzgerald, Desmond, 30
Fitzpatrick, Mick, 106
Fitzpatrick, Sean, 106
Frank, Andre Gunder, 149

Gaelic League, 9, 13, 19, 45
Gallacher, Willie, 51, 55
Good, Joe, 35
Great Southern and Western Railway (GS&WR), and Inchicore rail strike, 123-127
Griffith, Arthur, 13, 60, 91, 152, 167, 169

Hart, Finlay, 83
Haskins, Rory, 4
Hennessy, Patrick, 98
Heuston, Sean, 12, 16-19, 23-25, 36, 140
Hoare, Samuel, 97
Hobson, Bulmer, 19
Hoey, Daniel, 48
Holohan, Garry, 13, 14, 43, 44
Holohan, Patrick, 13
Hughes, Governor, 98
Hunt, D.I., 45
Hynes, Sean, 17, 36, 37
Inchicore rail strike, 1924, 122-129

Independent Labour Party, Belfast (ILP), 109
Independent Labour Party, British (ILP), 43, 57, 58, 61, 83
Irish Citizen Army (ICA), 14, 18, 22, 32, 53, 59, 67
Irish Communist Labour Party (ICLP), 65, 67-69
Irish General Railway and Engineering Union (IGR&EU), 123-124, 126
Irish Labour Party Glasgow (IrLP G), 55-57
Irish Republican Army (IRA), 9, 34, 42, 63; communist attitude towards, 60, 68-70, 92, 115-117, 118, 121; relations with communists during Civil War, 93-106
Irish Republican Brotherhood (IRB) 13-18, 42-43
Irish Trade Union Congress and Labour Party/Irish Labour Party and Trade Union Congress (ITUCLP/ILPTUC), 43, 55, 66, 124
Irish Transport and General Workers Union (ITGWU), 12, 14, 20, 43, 49, 59, 63, 65, 67, 93, 121-125, 132, 146-147
Irish Volunteers, 9, 15-18, 49, 60, 94, 141; and the Easter Rising, 23-27, 31-34; and the post-Rising reorganisation, 42-47
Irish Workers' League (IWL), 119-121, 148
Industrial Workers of the World (IWW), 57, 73

Jessop, Mary, 42
Johnson, Tom, 43, 49, 147

Keane, J.J., 15
Kilroy, Michael, 106
Kirkwood, Davie, 83

Lacey, Denis, 47
Larkin, Delia, 66
Larkin, Jim, 13-15, 50, 66, 68, 119-122,

125-129, 133, 146-149, 153, 164.
Larkin, Jim (Junior), 133
Larkin, Peter, 122, 125
Leahy, James, 45, 46
Lehane, Con, 105
Lehane, Sean, 106
Lenin, Vladimir Ilyich, 68, 69, 78, 90, 121
Lloyd George, David, 63, 91, 92
Lowe, General, 35
Luxemburg, Rosa, 79
Lynch, Liam, 94, 104, 106
Lynn, Alexander, 99

MacAlpine, Eamon, 68, 69
MacAonghusa, Prionsias, 157
MacDiarmada, Sean, 17, 19, 30-35, 133
MacDonagh, Thomas, 28
MacDonald, Ramsay, 57, 58
MacEoin, Sean, 133
McGilligan, Patrick, 151
MacLean, John, 51, 53
MacNeill, Eoin, 19, 23
Mack, Captain, 124
Maher, Patrick 'Wedger', 44
Maloney, Con, 47
Manahan, Liam, 46, 47, 96-99, 103, 104
Markievicz, Constance, 13, 18
Martin, Eamon, 13, 28
Marx, Karl, 62, 65, 91, 163
McAuley, James, 55
McCullough, Denis, 43
McGarry, Sean, 48
McGowan, Seamus, 106
McGrath, Frank, 44
McKelvey, Joe, 92, 98, 100
McLoughlin, (nee Burnup), Blanche, 131
McLoughlin, (nee Shea), Christina, 12, 28
McLoughlin, Christina, 12
McLoughlin, Christopher, 12, 132
McLoughlin, Daniel (Danny), 12, 13, 16, 42, 89, 128, 133, 134
McLoughlin (nee Barr), Isa, 54, 89
McLoughlin, Jack, 131, 134

McLoughlin, Margaret, 133
McLoughlin, Mary, 12, 28, 99
McLoughlin, Patrick (Ruggie), 12, 14, 49
McLoughlin, Patrick (Junior), 12, 115
McLoughlin, Sean, birth, 12; early life, 12-13; early involvements in nationalist politics, 13-19; and the Easter Rising, 24-36; promotion to rank of Commandant during Rising, 32; imprisonment in 1916, 36-37; and the reorganisation of the Irish Volunteers, 43-49; imprisonment in 1919, 48; influenced by socialist politics, 49-52; joins SPI, 49; elected President of SPI, 54; 1920 speaking tour in Scotland, 54-66; marriage to Isabella Barr, 54; analysis of British and Irish Revolutions, 58-63; attitude to Orangeism, 64-65; Elected chairman of ICLP, 65; joins SLP, 77; propagandist abilities, 80-85, Expelled from SLP, 85-87; death of Isabella and Terence McLoughlin, 89; analysis of 1921 Treaty, 91-92; returns to Ireland in July 1922, 93; Civil War activity, 94-97; arrest and imprisonment 1922, 97; death sentence passed, 98; and the Limerick prison republican prisoners peace proposals, 100-105; moved to Mountjoy jail, 105; leaves IRA, 106; and new communist strategy, 115-117; and dissolution of the CPI, 120; involvement with Larkin, 120-122; and Inchicore Rail Strike, 122-129; leaves Ireland for England, 129; imprisonment in 1926, 129; marriage to Blanche Burnup 131; applies for military pension, 132-134; death, 134; contribution to Easter Rising, 140-41; contribution to Irish and British socialist movements, 141-43
McLoughlin, Terence Sean MacSwiney, 69, 89
McMahon, Cornelius, 98

McManus, Arthur, 50, 52, 53, 78, 119, 120
McManus, General, 98, 101
Meehan, Thomas, 131
Mellows, Barney, 13
Mellows, Frederick, 13
Mellows, Liam, 13, 92, 98, 100
Mendicity Institute, and the Easter Rising, 24-28
Mulcahy, General, 102
Mullings, Frank, 48
Murnane, Liam, 17
Murphy, William Martin, 14, 60

National Union of Railwaymen (NUR), 123-124
Nolan, James, 14
Nkrumah, Kwame, 149

O'Brien, William, 43, 65
O'Connor, Emmet, 10, 43
O'Connor, Lord Justice, 99
O'Connor, Rory, 92, 98
O'Connor, Thomas, 120
O'Donnell, Hugh, 97
O'Donnell, Peadar, 92, 105
O'Donovan Rossa, Jeremiah, 16, 17
O'Duffy, Eoin, 96
O'Higgins, Kevin, 120, 151, 152
O'Kelly, Sean T., 93
O'Leary, Michael, 53
O'Malley, Ernie, 100, 101, 115
O'Rahilly, The, 30, 31, 33
O'Shannon, Cathal, 54, 65
O'Sullivan, Gearoid, 99

Pankhurst, Sylvia, 68
Paul, Willie, 50-52, 78
Pearse, Padraig, 14, 17, 23, 26, 29-34, 36, 56, 133, 152
Pearse, Willie, 36
Plunkett, Joseph, 32, 35, 42
Pollock, George, 93, 100, 121

Redmond, John, 16
Robinson, Joe, 101

Robinson, Seamus, 34, 94, 101
Rutledge, P.J., 106
Ryan, Patrick, 13

Sheehan, (British Soldier), 45
Shinwell, Manny, 57
Sinn Fein, 115-117, 119, 147, 151, 162-163; founded, 13; and the Irish War of Independence, 43, 46, 48-49, 55, 57; class character of, 59-60, 63, 67
Socialist Labour Party of Great Britain (SLP), 50-52, 54, 56-57, 66, 69, 76-78, 80, 83-89, 129, 131, 143
Socialist Party of Ireland (SPI), 49, 52-54, 59, 60, 65, 90
Snowden, Ethel, 57, 58
Snowden, Philip, 57
Stack, Austin, 93, 105, 115
Staines, Liam, 13
Staines, Michael, 13
Stalin, Joseph, 154
Stewart, Bob, 148
Swifte, Justice, 48

Thiers, Adolphe, 91
Traynor, Oscar, 133
Trotsky, Leon, 51, 130

Von Clausewitz, Carl, 141

Workers Party of Ireland (WPI) (1926), 121, 148, 159
Workers Union of Ireland (WUI), 131, 147; formation, 122; and Inchicore rail strike, 1924, 122-128

www.ingramcontent.com/pod-product-compliance
Lightning Source LLC
Chambersburg PA
CBHW051434290426
44109CB00016B/1552